P9-CKP-049

828 "I" Street

Sacramento, CA   95814

1/10

Bloom's Modern Critical Views

Bloom's Modern Critical Views

JOHN STEINBECK
New Edition

Edited and with an introduction by
Harold Bloom
Sterling Professor of the Humanities
Yale University

BLOOM'S
LITERARY CRITICISM
An imprint of Infobase Publishing

Bloom's Modern Critical Views: John Steinbeck, New Edition

Copyright © 2008 by Infobase Publishing

Introduction © 2008 by Harold Bloom

All rights reserved. No part of this publication may be reproduced or utilized in any form or by any means, electronic or mechanical, including photocopying, recording, or by any information storage or retrieval systems, without permission in writing from the publisher. For more information contact:

Bloom's Literary Criticism
An imprint of Infobase Publishing
132 West 31st Street
New York, NY 10001

Library of Congress Cataloging-in-Publication Data
John Steinbeck / edited and with an introduction by Harold Bloom. — New ed.
     p. cm. — (Bloom's modern critical views)
  Includes bibliographical references and index.
  ISBN 978-0-7910-9787-8
  1. Steinbeck, John, 1902–1968—Criticism and interpretation. I. Bloom, Harold. II. Title. III. Series.

  PS3537.T3234Z71546 2008
  813'.52—dc22

                                    2007038676

Bloom's Literary Criticism books are available at special discounts when purchased in bulk quantities for businesses, associations, institutions, or sales promotions. Please call our Special Sales Department in New York at (212) 967-8800 or (800) 322-8755.

You can find Bloom's Literary Criticism on the World Wide Web at
http://www.chelseahouse.com

Contributing Editor: Amy Sickels

Cover designed by Takeshi Takahashi

Cover photo AP Images

Printed in the United States of America

Bang EJB 10 9 8 7 6 5 4 3 2 1

This book is printed on acid-free paper.

All links and Web addresses were checked and verified to be correct at the time of publication. Because of the dynamic nature of the Web, some addresses and links may have changed since publication and may no longer be valid.

Contents

Contents

Editor's Note

My Introduction addresses itself to Steinbeck's aesthetic limitations, even in his best book *The Grapes of Wrath*.

Steinbeck's anxiety of influence in regard to Hemingway is the undersong of Edward Waldron's contrast between *The Pearl* and *The Old Man and the Sea*.

Of Mice and Men is generously evaluated by Lewis Owens, while Howard Levant is equally indulgent toward *The Red Pony*.

Ma Joad, admirable matriarch in *The Grapes of Wrath*, is studied by Nellie Y. McKay, after which the biographer Jay Parini conveys something of Steinbeck's marital agonies before his saving remarriage.

The influence of *Moby-Dick* upon *East of Eden* helped sink Steinbeck's flawed novel, and is chronicled here by Robert DeMott.

Ecological Steinbeck is surveyed by the Gladsteins and by Marilyn McEntyre.

David Wyatt sensitively explores the varied imagery of light and lightness in Steinbeck, after which Morris Dickstein analyzes Steinbeck's eminence as our fictive chronicler of the Great American Depression.

HAROLD BLOOM

Introduction

It is almost forty years since John Steinbeck died, and while his popularity as a novelist still endures, his critical reputation has suffered a considerable decline. His honors were many and varied, and included the Nobel Prize and the United States Medal of Freedom. His best novels came early in his career; *In Dubious Battle* (1936); *Of Mice and Men* (1937); *The Grapes of Wrath* (1939). Nothing after that, including *East of Eden* (1952), bears rereading. It would be good to record that rereading his three major novels is a valuable experience, from an aesthetic as well as an historic perspective.

Of Mice and Men, an economical work, really a novella, retains considerable power, marred by an intense sentimentality. But *In Dubious Battle* is now quite certainly a period piece, and is of more interest to social historians than to literary critics. *The Grapes of Wrath*, still Steinbeck's most popular and famous novel, is a very problematical work, and very difficult to judge. As story, or rather, chronicle, it lacks invention, and its characters are not persuasive representations of human inwardness. The book's wavering strength is located elsewhere, in a curious American transformation of biblical substance and style that worked splendidly in Whitman and Hemingway, but seems to work only fitfully in Steinbeck.

Steinbeck suffers from too close a comparison with Hemingway, his authentic precursor though born only three years before his follower. I think that Steinbeck's aesthetic problem *was* Hemingway, whose shadow always hovered too near. Consider the opening of *The Grapes of Wrath:*

To the red country and part of the gray country of Oklahoma, the last rains came gently, and they did not cut the scarred earth. The plows crossed and recrossed the rivulet marks. The last rains lifted the corn quickly and scattered weed colonies and grass along the sides of the roads so that the gray country and the dark red country began to disappear under a green cover. In the last part of May the sky grew pale and the clouds that had hung in high puffs for so long in the spring were dissipated. The sun flared down on the growing corn day after day until a line of brown spread along the edge of each green bayonet. The clouds appeared, and went away, and in a while they did not try any more. The weeds grew darker green to protect themselves, and they did not spread any more. The surface of the earth crusted, a thin hard crust, and as the sky became pale, so the earth became pale, pink in the red country and white in the gray country.

In the water-cut gullies the earth dusted down in dry little streams. Gophers and ant lions started small avalanches. And as the sharp sun struck day after day, the leaves of the young corn became less stiff and erect; they bent in a curve at first, and then, as the central ribs of strength grew weak, each leaf tilted downward. Then it was June, and the sun shone more fiercely. The brown lines on the corn leaves widened and moved in on the central ribs. The weeks frayed and edged back toward their roots. The air was thin and the sky more pale; and every day the earth paled.

This is not so much biblical style as mediated by Ernest Hemingway, as it is Hemingway assimilated to Steinbeck's sense of biblical style. The monosyllabic diction is hardly the mode of the King James Version, but certainly is Hemingway's. I give, very nearly at random, passages from *The Sun Also Rises*:

We passed through a town and stopped in front of the posada, and the driver took on several packages. Then we started on again, and outside the town the road commenced to mount. We were going through farming country with rocky hills that sloped down into the fields. The grain-fields went up the hillsides. Now as we went higher there was a wind blowing the grain. The road was white and dusty, and the dust rose under the wheels and hung in the air behind us. The road climbed up into the hills and left the rich grain-fields below. Now there were only patches of grain on the bare hillsides and on each side of the water-courses.

We turned sharply out to the side of the road to give room to pass to a long string of six mules, following one after the other, hauling a high-hooded wagon loaded with freight. The wagon and the mules were covered with dust. Close behind was another string of mules and another wagon. This was loaded with lumber, and the arriero driving the mules leaned back and put on the thick wooden brakes as we passed. Up here the country was quite barren and the hills were rocky and hard-baked clay furrowed by the rain.

The bus climbed steadily up the road. The country was barren and rocks stuck up through the clay. There was no grass beside the road. Looking back we could see the country spread out below. Far back the fields were squares of green and brown on the hillsides. Making the horizon were the brown mountains. They were strangely shaped. As we climbed higher the horizon kept changing. As the bus ground slowly up the road we could see other mountains coming up in the south. Then the road came over the crest, flattened out, and went into a forest. It was a forest of cork oaks, and the sun came through the trees in patches, and there were cattle grazing back in the trees. We went through the forest and the road came out and turned along a rise of land, and out ahead of us was a rolling green plain, with dark mountains beyond it. These were not like the brown, heat-baked mountains we had left behind. These were wooded and there were clouds coming down from them. The green plain stretched off. It was cut by fences and the white of the road showed through the trunks of a double line of trees that crossed the plain toward the north. As we came to the edge of the rise we saw the red roofs and white houses of Burguete ahead strung out on the plain, and away off on the shoulder of the first dark mountain was the gray metal-sheathed roof of the monastery of Roncesvalles.

Hemingway's Basque landscapes are described with an apparent literalness and in what seems at first a curiously dry tone, almost flat in its evident lack of significant emotion. But a closer reading suggests that the style here is itself a metaphor for a passion and nostalgia that is both defensive and meticulous. The contrast between rich soil and barren ground, between wooded hills and heat-baked mountains, is a figure for the lost potency of Jake Barnes, but also for a larger sense of the lost possibilities of life. Steinbeck, following after Hemingway, cannot learn the lesson. He gives us a vision of the Oklahoma Dust Bowl, and it is effective enough, but it is merely a landscape where a process of entropy has been enacted. It has a social and an economic meaning, but as a vision of loss lacks spiritual and personal intensity. Steinbeck is more overtly biblical than Hemingway, but too obviously so. We feel that the Bible's sense of meaning in landscape has returned from the dead in Hemingway's own colors, but hardly in Steinbeck's.

If Steinbeck is not an original or even an adequate stylist, if he lacks skill in plot, and power in the mimesis of character, what then remains in his work, except its fairly constant popularity with an immense number of liberal middlebrows, both in his own country and abroad? Certainly, he aspired beyond his aesthetic means. If the literary Sublime, or contest for the highest place, involves persuading the reader to yield up easier pleasures for more difficult pleasures, and it does, then Steinbeck modestly should have avoided Emerson's American Sublime, but he did not. Desiring it both ways, he fell into bathos in everything he wrote, even in *Of Mice and Men* and *The Grapes of Wrath*.

Yet Steinbeck had many of the legitimate impulses of the Sublime writer, and of his precursors Whitman and Hemingway in particular. Like them, he studied the nostalgias, the aboriginal sources that were never available for Americans, and like them he retained a profound hope for the American as natural man and natural woman. Unlike Whitman and Hemingway and the origin of this American tradition, Emerson, Steinbeck had no capacity for the nuances of literary irony. He had read Emerson's essay "The Over-Soul" as his precursors had, but Steinbeck literalized it. Emerson, canniest where he is most the Idealist, barbs his doctrine of "that Unity, that Over-soul, within which every man's particular being is contained and made one with all other." In Emerson, that does not involve the sacrifice of particular being, and is hardly a program for social action:

> We live in succession, in division, in parts, in particles. Meantime within man is the soul of the whole. . . .
> The soul knows only the soul; all else is idle weeds for her wearing.

There have always been Emersonians on the Left, like Whitman and Steinbeck, and Emersonians on the Right, like Henry James and Wallace Stevens. Emerson himself, rather gingerly planted on the moderate Left, evaded all positions. Social action is also an affair of succession, division, parts, particles; if "the soul knows only the soul," then the soul cannot know doctrines, or even human suffering. Steinbeck, socially generous, a writer on the left, structured the doctrine of *The Grapes of Wrath* on Jim Casy's literalization of Emerson's vision: "Maybe all men got one big soul and everybody's a part of it." Casy, invented by Steinbeck with a rough eloquence that would have moved Emerson, speaks his orator's epitaph just before he is martyred: "They figger I'm a leader 'cause I talk too much." He is a leader, an Okie Moses, and he dies a fitting death for the visionary of an Exodus.

I remain uneasy about my own experience of rereading *The Grapes of Wrath*. Steinbeck is not one of the inescapable American novelists of our century; he cannot be judged in close relation to Cather, Dreiser, and Faulkner, Hemingway and Fitzgerald, Nathanael West, Ralph Ellison, and Thomas Pynchon. Yet there are no canonical standards worthy of human respect that could exclude *The Grapes of Wrath* from a serious reader's esteem. Compassionate narrative that addresses itself so directly to the great social questions of its era is simply too substantial a human achievement to be dismissed. Whether a human strength, however generously worked through, is also an aesthetic value, in a literary narrative, is one of those larger issues that literary criticism scarcely knows how to decide. One might desire *The Grapes of Wrath* to be composed differently, whether as plot or as characterization, but wisdom compels one to be grateful for the novel's continued existence.

EDWARD E. WALDRON

The Pearl *and* The Old Man and the Sea: *A Comparative Analysis*

Within five years, two major modern American writers produced novels of interesting similarities. Both works are simplistic in style and both deal with the struggle of simple people against staggering forces of man and nature. John Steinbeck's *The Pearl* (1947) and Ernest Hemingway's *The Old Man and the Sea* (1952) also share similarities in their publication history and, more importantly, in critical reaction to them. Warren French, in his initial study of Steinbeck's works, finds *The Pearl* "defective," and Philip Young, revising his earlier praise of *The Old Man and the Sea*, accuses Hemingway of "thinking more of his own lines than of Santiago's. . . ."[1] Yet the works survive and remain popular, although Hemingway's novel, perhaps because it was specifically cited in his Nobel Prize, does seem to attract more attention. For all their problems and faults, however, these two short parables contain within them much that is the essence of their authors, in theme as well as in style.[2] A close examination of *The Pearl* and *The Old Man and the Sea* [hereafter referred to as *OMAS*] reveals some intriguing parallels between the two works and offers evidence that each should be accepted fully within the canon of its author.

The fact that both novels originally appeared in print in popular magazines has probably added greatly to their difficulty in attaining full critical acceptance. French refers to the publication of *The Pearl* (as "The

From the *Steinbeck Quarterly*, 13 (Summer-Fall 1980), pp. 98–106. Reprinted in *Steinbeck's Literary Dimension: A Guide to Comparative Studies.* © 1991 by Tetsumaro Hayashi.

Pearl of the World") in the *Woman's Home Companion* (1945) as "an ominous sign,"[3] and, while few critics of *OMAS* cite its publication in *Life* (1952) as cause for concern, one can sense an underlying distrust because of that. The assumption seems to be that anything written for mass consumption in a popular magazine cannot also be good art.

Publication histories aside, there are more important similarities in the two novels. Both of them, though set in the modern world, center on relatively primitive people. Santiago, to be sure, is much more aware of the modern world, especially through his beloved baseball, than are Kino and the people of his village. Still, Santiago fishes as his people always have (he carries no radio, as do some of the other fishermen); and Kino is clearly tied to the ways of his ancestors, in his simple lifestyle and in his recollections of the old songs. Both novels are set in locations that tie men to the sea, and these locations immediately suggest archetypal patterns of the fight for survival. Although Kino's struggles occur on land, the estuary near his hut offers continual evidence that the natural world is a world of the hunter and the hunted. For all the implied criticism of the social and economic oppression of the Gulf Indians in *The Pearl*, neither novel deals with the modern themes of man against machine or man's alienation in a hostile universe. Santiago has Manolin to care for him; Kino has his family. Instead, the novels focus on the beautiful spectacle of man setting himself a goal and doing his utmost to achieve it, even though he fails in the realization of the material reward he anticipates. What Young says about Santiago can also be said of Kino and Juana: ". . . his loss has dignity, itself the victory."[4] These protagonists achieve a stature that is worth all the marlins and pearls in the ocean.

The original sources for both novels are widely known and do not need to be repeated here. What is important for this study concerns the changes each author made in his source story. Hemingway transformed his source's defeated, simpering old man into Santiago, the fisherman who fights the good fight and retains his dignity, shaping defeat into victory. Throughout the novel, the old man chides himself for his weaknesses and draws strength from thoughts of the boy, Manolin, and from his own memories of the lions along the African coast. In essence, Hemingway shapes a rather pathetic tale of "the one that got away" into a paean to human endurance and courage.

Steinbeck made even greater changes in his source. The young unmarried pearl diver is transformed into Kino, a man with a strong wife and a son for whom he can dream great things. Accordingly, the whimsical and lusty "visions" of the original hero of the tale become Kino's mystical visions of improvement for Coyotito—and, by extension, for his people— improvements that would help release them from generations of oppression. Although some critics have attacked the visions Steinbeck gives Kino as being too middle-class American, the intent in these changes, as with the changes in Hemingway's tale, is to create a recognizable, universal point of reference in terms of the struggles involved. Santiago's fight is not so much with the marlin and, later, the sharks, as it is with himself, with his ability to do "what a man can do." Kino's vision is not a vision of riotous living and an attempt to buy salvation for later, visions rooted in the old order; it is, though he never articulates it in this way, a vision of control over his life—democratic freedom that can only be bought for Kino and his people through education and a struggle against the system. These changes clearly serve to bring *OMAS* and *The Pearl* more closely in line with the thematic concerns of their authors.

Before examining the thematic ideas in the novels, we might consider another area of similarity in them, and that is a similarity in style. *OMAS* is often cited as a prime example of Hemingway's "iceberg" theory of writing. It is written in clear, sparse prose. The dialogue is presented, for the most part, in simple sentences, with that stilted syntax Hemingway uses to simulate the Spanish of his speakers. At times, of course, that syntax borders on the ludicrous, but we have long before this learned to accept Hemingway's concept of dialogue for his Spanish-speaking characters. We can forgive Manolin's fear of "the Indians of Cleveland" and "the Tigers of Detroit," though we might question an apparent slip in this formal speaking style when Manolin says to Santiago: "Can I offer you a beer on the Terrace and then we'll take the stuff home."[5]

Steinbeck's prose in *The Pearl* is quite similar; it is very close to the style he created for his stories of the paisanos of California. Like Hemingway, Steinbeck uses a stilted speaking form to capture the sense of a foreign language being rendered in English. Kino and the other Indians speak in the "old language," and that is our pattern for comparison. When the doctor's servant refuses to answer Kino in the language of their people, we hear this bit of garbled English (supposedly a rendering of the Spanish of "the dark ones"): "'A little moment,' he said. 'I go to inform myself.'"[6] Except for the priest, who speaks with the even more formal "thee's" and "thou's" of the church, the other dialogue follows the pattern discussed above.

A more significant area of comparison in the style of the two works is their use of imagery. Both make effective use of circumstances in the natural world as reflections on the human condition. Santiago spies a man-of-war bird circling and knows there must be fish nearby. He watches as the bird makes futile dives after some flying fish which are desperately trying to evade a school of dolphins:

> As he watched the bird dipped again slanting his wings for
> the dive and then swinging them wildly and ineffectually as he
> followed the flying fish. The old man could see the slight bulge

in the water that the big dolphin raised as they followed the
escaping fish.... It is a big school of dolphin, he thought. They
are wide spread and the flying fish have little chance. The bird
has no chance. The flying fish are too big for him and they go
too fast. (pp. 37–38)

In addition to presenting the unrelenting struggle for survival in the natural
world, this passage also suggests a comparison between the bird who has "no
chance" to catch the too-large flying fish and Santiago, who should not be
able to catch the huge fish he does in fact catch. Although Santiago often
thinks to himself that man is not worth much compared to the fishes and
other creatures of the world and occasionally wishes he were the fish below,
the thrust of his endeavors is to show the fish—and himself—"what a man
can do and what a man can endure" (p. 73). That man is part of the natural
world and must face the same tests as other creatures, though his endurance
and his capacity for pain may be greater, is made clear when Santiago
addresses the small bird that comes to rest on his skiff:

"You shouldn't be that tired after a windless night. What are
birds coming to?"
The hawks, he thought, that come out to sea to meet them
... the bird ... could not understand him anyway and ... would
learn about the hawks soon enough.
"Take a good rest, small bird," he said. "Then go in and take
your chance like any man or bird or fish." (pp. 60–61)

At least in the old man's world there is a chance to be taken. For the
natural world presented in *The Pearl*, the imagery is much harsher. After the
doctor leaves Kino's hut following his "curing" of Coyotito, we are confronted
with this scene:

Out in the estuary a tightly woven school of small fishes glittered
and broke water to escape a school of great fishes that drove in
to eat them. And in the houses the people could hear the swish
of the small ones and the bouncing splash of the great ones as
the slaughter went on.... And the night mice crept about on
the ground and the little night hawks hunted them silently. (pp.
43–44)

The parallels here are obvious. Such imagery is an essential part of Steinbeck's
style; it reflects his view of the natural order of the world and its suggested
relation to the human condition. It is against this order that Kino and Juana

throw themselves when Kino decides to go inland to sell his pearl. The "dark thing" which first searches his hut, then attacks him on the beach, and the relentless trackers who pursue the family into the mountains are clearly presented as human counterparts to the savage elements of nature that dictate that life is a struggle for man as well as for fish.

A final area of similarity in style in the two novels concerns the authors' use of refrains or motives as unifying factors. In *OMAS* there are several minor refrains. There are, of course, the almost religious incantation of the name of the mighty DiMaggio and the references to his feats of skill and his endurance of pain. In addition to the DiMaggio references, two other refrains serve to strengthen the old man during his ordeal. Several times during his struggle with the fish his thoughts focus on the boy and the help he would be able to give: "I wish I had the boy. To help me and to see this" (p. 52). Later the refrain is changed to "if the boy was here." Thoughts of Manolin obviously offer Santiago comfort and, perhaps, a vicarious resiliency. A similar purpose is served by the old man's dreams of the lions; the connection is made rather neatly early in the novel, as Hemingway tells us about the nature of Santiago's dreams:

> He no longer dreamed of storms, nor of women, nor of great occurrences.... He only dreamed of places now and of the lions on the beach. They played like young cats in the dusk and he loved them as he loved the boy. He never dreamed about the boy. (pp. 27–28)

While Manolin is a present, observable reminder of youth and strength, Santiago does not dream of him; as the old man drifts farther from the land and the boy, though, his thoughts turn to him, as they had been turning for years to the lions, an obvious symbol for Santiago of his own youth. All three refrains, then, serve the same purpose: to help the old man retain his courage during his long trial at sea. Stylistically, the refrains help give continuity and unity to the novel.

In Steinbeck's novel, the various "songs" also serve to give continuity and unity. Fontenrose says, "*The Pearl* is a morality play set to music," and refers to the combination of songs as a "symphony."[7] The songs are filtered through Kino's awareness. He cannot articulate them, but he associates them with what he senses about him. "The Song of the Family" is, at first, a reflection of the tranquility he feels as he awakens in his hut; the song, a "personal" song now that the old traditions of his people have all but faded, reinforces Kino's sense of being, of belonging. But when Kino goes after the trackers, the Song of the Family becomes "as fierce and sharp and feline as the snarl of a female puma" (p. 111), a variation very much in keeping with the symphonic concept being employed. As a counter theme, the Song of Evil represents the various threats to Kino and his family: the "dark ones" who attack in the night, the trackers, the arid mountain region into which they flee. Even the Song of the Pearl turns evil, becomes "distorted and insane." Of course, any such device can be overworked. One might argue, for example, that wafting phrases of the Song of the Pearl That Might Be through the Song of the Undercurrent is stretching things. As music, such an invention could work admirably; as writing, it asks too much of the reader. On the whole, however, Steinbeck orchestrates the action and emotion of *The Pearl* nicely with Kino's songs.[8] It is a technique that not only adds unity to the novel, but also serves to echo both the simplicity and the struggle of Kino and Juana.

Even in the area of thematic concerns, these two novels reflect similar concepts, although there are also obvious differences. In *OMAS* Santiago operates alone in his struggle against the natural forces of the sea. In *The Pearl* Kino and Juana, although separated at one point in their ideas about the pearl, basically function as a pair, a family. In effect, though, the trials of Santiago and the Indian couple come about for the same reason: they "go out too far," the old man to catch his fish and Kino and Juana to seek a fair price for their pearl. And, just as Santiago must fight the sharks to protect his fish, a hopeless endeavor, Kino and Juana must fight the human sharks—the doctor, the "dark ones," the social system itself—to protect their pearl and their lives.

From the beginning of *OMAS* we see Santiago as a man plagued with "bad luck." He has gone eighty-four days without a catch; his sail is "patched with flour sacks and, furled, it looked like the flag of permanent defeat" (p. 9). The old man wears a shirt that has "been patched so many times that it was like the sail . . ." (p. 20). But, fortified with the good wishes of Manolin and his knowledge of the sea, he sets out alone to face the challenge of "*la mar.*" Once he hooks the marlin he faces two awesome tasks: first, he must land the fish; then he must sail it back into port. After a monumental fight, he succeeds in the first task, but stopping the sharks is simply beyond him. He uses what weapons he can fashion to postpone the complete destruction of his marlin for a while, but finally his beautiful fish is reduced to its skeleton, with only "the great tail of the fish standing up well behind the skiff's stern . . . and the dark mass of the head with the projecting bill . . ." (p. 133) remaining. While the ignorant tourists mistake the marlin's skeleton for that of a shark, Manolin and the others know what the old man has done. His spirit rekindled by Manolin's pride in him and by the boy's declaration that he will sail with the old man again, no matter what his family says, Santiago makes plans to go out once more. That night he dreams about the lions as Manolin watches over him. Like the turtles, Santiago has a heart that cannot be stopped, even by the death which Hemingway suggests is hovering near.

While Steinbeck's ending for *The Pearl* is more ambivalent than Hemingway's ending for *OMAS*, there is a sense of triumph, horribly muted by the death of Coyotito, in the strength that brings Kino and Juana back to their village and allows them to throw the pearl back into the sea. Warren French finds the ending terribly weak, mainly because of the "unresolved problems that have been raised by the action" in the novel. "The conclusion of the novel," he continues, "leaves the impression that Kino is returning to his old life. . . ."[9] But are we to conclude that? Is the Kino at the end of the novel the same Kino who began it? And what of his relationship with Juana? If we read this novel as a positive work and not as a study in the inevitable defeat of the common man by the pressures of society, then clearly we must focus on the change that occurs in the characters of Kino and Juana. Examining those changes through the metaphor of the pearl gives us another view of what the real "pearl of the world" might be.

Early in the novel Steinbeck tells us how a pearl is formed:

An accident could happen to these oysters, a grain of sand could lie in the folds of muscle and irritate the flesh until in self-protection the flesh coated the grain with a layer of smooth cement. But once started, the flesh continued to coat the foreign body until it fell free in some tidal flurry or until the oyster was destroyed. (p. 21)

Kino's timely (and melodramatic) discovery of the great pearl after Coyotito is stung by the scorpion can be read as the accident, the "grain of sand," that starts the process. Until that day, Kino had lived his life as his people had always done; the pattern was as predictable as the tides around which their lives were set. The pearl, however, creates visions for Kino, plans that go against the wishes of the gods. But Kino does not draw back from the attack he knows will come:

. . . to meet the attack, Kino was already making a hard skin for himself against the world. His eyes and his mind probed for danger before it appeared. (p. 38)

The process has begun.

Immediately, the first irritant appears as the doctor, who was too busy to receive Kino earlier in the day, comes out to his hut to see Coyotito. Trapped by his ignorance, Kino must let the doctor work his "magic" on the baby; but when Coyotito gets worse, Kino remembers the white powder, and "his mind was hard and suspicious . . ." (p. 43). At least in terms of modern

American readers, Kino is becoming a more valuable person as he fights himself of the twin tyrannies of ignorance and oppression.

Kino is not alone in this transformation. Juana, a good wife and mother, is a strong woman. While she hears Kino's magnificent visions with awe, she nonetheless is ready to defy him and fling the pearl back to the sea when they are attacked, and it becomes clear that the pearl represents a threat to her family. After the struggle that leaves one man dead and Kino beaten, it is Juana who finds the pearl by the path. Realizing "that the old life was gone forever" (p. 78), she strengthens Kino's will once more so they may fly from the danger around them. Leaving the village, Juana pads behind Kino. Returning from their ordeal in the wilderness with the lifeless Coyotito slung in her shawl, however, she walks by Kino's side: ". . . they were not walking in single file, Kino ahead and Juana behind as usual, but side by side . . . and they seemed to carry two towers of darkness with them" (p. 115).

The vision of their return recalled by the villagers is one of mystery:

> The people say that the two seemed to be removed from human experience; that they had gone through pain and had come out on the other side; that there was almost a magical protection about them. (p. 116)

The change is also made clear in their actions regarding the pearl. Acknowledging Juana's strength and courage, Kino offers to let her throw the pearl back; she, in turn acknowledging his strength and courage, insists that he throw it. "*They* [my italics] saw the little splash in the distance, and *they* stood side by side watching the place for a long time" (pp. 117–18). Kino and Juana have lost their child, their hut, and their boat, but they have gained something more valuable, a "pearl beyond price," in their new-found relationship of mutual respect. This change may be more important, again, to middle-class American readers than to the Gulf Indians about whom the tale is told, but its impact remains.

In these two short novels, then, Steinbeck and Hemingway present portraits of triumph in the face of overwhelming adversity, perhaps the most basic of American themes from William Bradford on. In both works, the writers utilize techniques and ideas central to their larger, more important works. But in *The Pearl* and *The Old Man and the Sea*, John Steinbeck and Ernest Hemingway—both of whom deal so often with outsiders, the renegades, in their explorations of the modern human condition—have presented us with clear statements that the human spirit can endure. As such, the novels become valuable contributions to modern American literature and positive assertions of the value of human existence. The experiences of both

Santiago and the Indian couple demonstrate what Santiago himself observes: "A man can be destroyed but not defeated" (p. 114).

Notes

1. Warren French, *John Steinbeck* (New York: Twayne, 1961), p. 137; Philip Young, "*The Old Man and the Sea*: Vision/Revision," Katherine T. Jobe, ed., *Twentieth Century Interpretations of "The Old Man and the Sea"* (Englewood Cliffs, New Jersey: Prentice-Hall, 1968), p. 26. French's revised study (Boston: Twayne, 1975) does not indicate any change in that attitude; if anything, his criticism of the novel is harsher.

2. The question of whether the two novels are in fact parables has been the subject of some debate, especially concerning *The Pearl*. French asserts that Steinbeck's novel is not a parable "because it is not—as Sheldon Sacks insists a parable should be—more or less complete in itself," while he finds that *OMAS* does meet that criterion (*John Steinbeck*, 1975), p. 129. Joseph Fontenrose, on the other hand, refers to *The Pearl* as a "non-teleological parable," and Young, in his initial appraisal of *OMAS*, refers to it as a "public parable," as opposed to Hemingway's earlier "private" parables (Fontenrose, *John Steinbeck: An Introduction and Interpretation* [New York: Holt, Rinehart & Winston, 1963], p. 114; Young, p. 21).

3. French, 1961, p. 137.

4. Young, p. 22.

5. Ernest Hemingway, *The Old Man and the Sea* (New York: Scribner's, 1951), p. 11. All subsequent references are to this edition.

6. John Steinbeck, *The Pearl* (New York: Bantam, 1947), p. 13. All subsequent references are to this edition.

7. Fontenrose, *John Steinbeck: An Introduction and Interpretation* (New York: Holt, Rinehart & Winston, 1963), pp. 112–13.

8. Steinbeck was obviously very interested in this aspect of his novel. In preparing the screen version of *The Pearl*, he worked with his wife Gwyn to record folk music to fit the various themes used in the novel. See his letter to Elizabeth Otis, May 3, 1945, in *Steinbeck: A Life in Letters*, Elaine Steinbeck and Robert Wallsten, eds. (New York: Penguin Books, 1976), p. 281.

9. French, *John Steinbeck* (Boston: Twayne, 1975), p. 129.

LOUIS OWENS

Of Mice and Men:
The Dream of Commitment

The Eden myth looms large in *Of Mice and Men (1937)*, the play-novella set along the Salinas River "a few miles south of Soledad" (*Of Mice and Men*, p. 1). And, as in all of Steinbeck's California fiction, setting plays a central role in determining the major themes of this work. The fact that the setting for *Of Mice and Men* is a California valley dictates, according to the symbolism of Steinbeck's landscapes, that this story will take place in a fallen world and that the quest for the illusive and illusory American Eden will be of central thematic significance. In no other work does Steinbeck demonstrate greater skill in merging the real setting of his native country with the thematic structure of his novel.

Critics have consistently recognized in Lennie's dream of living "off the fatta the lan'" on a little farm the American dream of a new Eden. Joseph Fontenrose states concisely, "The central image is the earthly paradise. . . . It is a vision of Eden." Peter Lisca takes this perception further, noting that "the world of *Of Mice and Men* is a fallen one, inhabited by sons of Cain, forever exiled from Eden, the little farm of which they dream." There are no Edens in Steinbeck's writing, only illusions of Eden, and in the fallen world of the Salinas Valley—which Steinbeck would later place "east of Eden"—the Promised Land is an illusory and painful dream. In this land populated by "sons of Cain," men condemned to wander in solitude, the

From *John Steinbeck's Re-Vision of America*, pp. 100–106. © 1985 by the University of Georgia Press.

predominant theme is that of loneliness, or what Donald Pizer has called "fear of apartness." Pizer has, in fact, discovered *the* major theme of this novel when he says, "One of the themes of *Of Mice and Men* is that men fear loneliness, that they need someone to be with and to talk to who will offer understanding and companionship."[29]

The setting Steinbeck chose for this story brilliantly underscores the theme of man's isolation and need for commitment. Soledad is a very real, dusty little town on the western edge of the Salinas River midway down the Salinas Valley. Like most of the settings in Steinbeck's fiction, this place exists, it *is*. However, with his acute sensitivity to place names and his knowledge of Spanish, Steinbeck was undoubtedly aware that "Soledad" translates into English as "solitude" or "loneliness." In this country of solitude and loneliness, George and Lennie stand out sharply because they have each other or, as George says, "We got somebody to talk to that gives a damn about us" (p. 15). Cain's question is the question again at the heart of this novel: "Am I my brother's keeper?" And the answer found in the relationship between George and Lennie is an unmistakable confirmation.

Of Mice and Men is most often read as one of Steinbeck's most pessimistic works, smacking of pessimistic determinism. Fontenrose suggests that the novel is about "the vanity of human wishes" and asserts that, more pessimistically than Burns, "Steinbeck reads, '*All* schemes o' mice and men gan *ever* agley' [my italics]. Howard Levant, in a very critical reading of the novel, concurs, declaring that "the central theme is stated and restated—the good life is impossible because humanity is flawed."[30] In spite of the general critical reaction, and without disputing the contention that Steinbeck allows no serious hope that George and Lennie will ever achieve their dream farm, it is nonetheless possible to read *Of Mice and Men* in a more optimistic light than has been customary. In previous works we have seen a pattern established in which the Steinbeck hero achieves greatness in the midst of, even because of, apparent defeat. In *Of Mice and Men*, Steinbeck accepts, very non-teleologically, the fact that man is flawed and the Eden myth mere illusion. However, critics have consistently undervalued Steinbeck's emphasis on the theme of commitment, which runs through the novel and which is the chief ingredient in the creation of the Steinbeck hero.

The dream of George and Lennie represents a desire to defy the curse of Cain and fallen man—to break the pattern of wandering and loneliness imposed on the outcasts and to return to the perfect garden. George and Lennie achieve all of this dream that is possible in the real world: they are their brother's keeper. Unlike the solitary Cain and the solitary men who inhabit the novel, they have someone who cares. The dream of the farm merely symbolizes their deep mutual commitment, a commitment that is immediately sensed by the other characters in the novel. The ranch owner is suspicious of the relationship, protesting, "I never seen one guy take so much trouble for another guy" (p. 25). Slim, the godlike jerkline skinner, admires the relationship and says, "Ain't many guys travel around together. . . . I don't know why. Maybe everybody in the whole damn world is scared of each other" (p. 43). Candy, the one-handed swamper, and Crooks, the deformed black stablehand, also sense the unique commitment between the two laborers, and in their moment of unity Candy and Crooks turn as one to defend Lennie from the threat posed by Curley's wife. The influence of George and Lennie's mutual commitment, and of their dream, has for an instant made these crippled sons of Cain their brother's keepers and broken the grip of loneliness and solitude in which they exist. Lennie's yearning for the rabbits and for all soft, living things symbolizes the yearning all men have for warm, living contact. It is this yearning, described by Steinbeck as "the inarticulate and powerful yearning of all men,"[31] which makes George need Lennie just as much as Lennie needs George and which sends Curley's wife wandering despairingly about the ranch in search of companionship. Whereas Fontenrose has suggested that "the individualistic desire for carefree enjoyment of pleasures is the serpent in the garden" in this book,[32] the real serpent is loneliness and the barriers between men and between men and women that create and reinforce this loneliness.

Lennie has been seen as representing "the frail nature of primeval innocence"[33] and as the id to George's ego or the body to George's brain.[34] In the novel, Lennie is repeatedly associated with animals or described as childlike. He appears in the opening scene dragging his feet "the way a bear drags his paws" (p. 2), and in the final scene he enters the clearing in the brush "as silently as a creeping bear" (p. 110). Slim says of Lennie, "He's jes' like a kid, ain't he," and George repeats, "Sure, he's jes' like a kid" (p. 48). The unavoidable truth is, however, that Lennie, be he innocent "natural," uncontrollable id, or simply a huge child, is above all dangerous. Unlike Benjy in *The Sound and the Fury* (whom Steinbeck may have had in mind when describing the incident in Weed in which Lennie clings bewildered to the girl's dress), Lennie is monstrously powerful and has a propensity for killing things. Even if Lennie had not killed Curley's wife, he would sooner or later have done something fatal to bring violence upon himself, as the lynch mob that hunted him in Weed suggests.

Steinbeck's original title for *Of Mice and Men* was "Something That Happened," a title suggesting that Steinbeck was taking a purely non-teleological or nonblaming point of view in this novel. If we look at the novel in this way, it becomes clear that Lennie dies because he has been created incapable of dealing with society and is, in fact, a menace to society. Like Pepé in "Flight," Tularecito in *The Pastures of Heaven*, and Frankie in *Cannery Row*, Lennie is a "natural" who loses when he is forced to confront society.

This is simply the way it is—something that happened—and when George kills Lennie he is not only saving him from the savagery of the pursuers, he is, as John Ditsky says, acknowledging that "Lennie's situation is quite hopeless." Ditsky further suggests that Lennie's death represents "a matter of cold hard necessity imposing itself upon the frail hopes of man." Along these same lines, Joan Steele declares that "Lennie has to be destroyed because he is a "loner" whose weakness precludes his cooperating with George and hence working constructively toward their mutual goal."[35] Lennie, however, is not a "loner"; it is, in fact, the opposite, overwhelming and uncontrollable urge for contact that brings about Lennie's destruction and the destruction of living creatures he comes into contact with. Nonetheless, Steele makes an important point when she suggests that because of Lennie the dream of the Edenic farm was never a possibility. Lennie's flaw represents the inherent imperfection in humanity that renders Eden forever an impossibility. Lennie would have brought his imperfection with him to the little farm, and he would have killed the rabbits.

When Lennie dies, the teleological dream of the Edenic farm dies with him, for while Lennie's weakness doomed the dream it was only his innocence that kept it alive. The death of the dream, however, does not force *Of Mice and Men* to end on the strong note of pessimism critics have consistently claimed. For while the dream of the farm perishes, the theme of commitment achieves its strongest statement in the book's conclusion. Unlike Candy, who abandons responsibility for his old dog and allows Carlson to shoot him, George remains his brother's keeper without faltering even to the point of killing Lennie while Lennie sees visions of Eden. In accepting complete responsibility for Lennie, George demonstrates the degree of commitment necessary to the Steinbeck hero, and in fact enters the ranks of those heroes. It is ironic that, in this fallen world, George must reenact the crime of Cain to demonstrate the depth of his commitment. It is a frank acceptance of the way things are.

Slim recognizes the meaning of George's act. When the pursuers discover George just after he has shot Lennie, Steinbeck writes: "Slim came directly to George and sat down beside him, sat very close to him" (pp. 118–19). Steinbeck's forceful prose here, with the key word "directly," and the emphatic repetition in the last phrase place heavy emphasis on Slim's gesture. Steinbeck is stressing the significance of the new relationship between George and Slim. As the novel ends, George is going off with Slim to have a drink, an action Fontenrose mistakenly interprets as evidence "that George had turned to his counter-dream of independence: freedom from Lennie." French suggests that "Slim's final attempt to console George ends the novel on the same compassionate note as that of *The Red Pony*, but Slim can only alleviate, not cure, the situation."[36] Steinbeck, however, seems to be deliberately placing much greater emphasis on the developing friendship between the two men than such interpretations would allow for. Lisca has pointed out the circular structure of the novel—the neat balancing of the opening and closing scenes. Bearing this circularity in mind, it should be noted that this novel about man's loneliness and "apartness" began with two men—George and Lennie—climbing down to the pool from the highway and that the novel ends with two men—George and Slim—climbing back up from the pool to the highway. Had George been left alone and apart from the rest of humanity at the end of the novel, had he suffered the fate of Cain, this would indeed have been the most pessimistic of Steinbeck's works. That George is not alone has tremendous significance. In the fallen world of the valley, where human commitment is the only realizable dream, the fact that in the end as in the beginning two men walk together causes *Of Mice and Men* to end on a strong note of hope—the crucial dream, the dream of man's commitment to man, has not perished with Lennie. The dream will appear again, in fact, in much greater dimension in Steinbeck's next novel, *The Grapes of Wrath*.

Notes

29. Fontenrose, *John Steinbeck: An Introduction and Interpretation*, p. 59; Lisca, *John Steinbeck: Nature and Myth*, p. 82; Donald Pizer, "John Steinbeck and American Naturalism," *Steinbeck Quarterly* 9 (Winter 1976): 13.

30. Fontenrose, *John Steinbeck: An Introduction and Interpretation*, p. 57; Levant, *The Novels of John Steinbeck*, p. 134.

31. Steinbeck is quoted in Fontenrose, *John Steinbeck: An Introduction and Interpretation*, p. 57.

32. Ibid., p. 59.

33. Astro, *Steinbeck and Ricketts*, p. 104.

34. Lisca, *John Steinbeck: Nature and Myth*, pp. 78–79.

35. John Ditsky, "Ritual Murder in Steinbeck's Dramas," *Steinbeck Quarterly* 11 (Summer–Fall 1978): 73; Joan Steele, "A Century of Idiots: *Barnaby Rudge* and *Of Mice and Men*," *Steinbeck Quarterly* 5 (Winter 1972): 16.

36. Fontenrose, *John Steinbeck: An Introduction and Interpretation*, p. 57; French, *John Steinbeck*, 2d ed., p. 91.

HOWARD LEVANT

John Steinbeck's The Red Pony:
A Study in Narrative Technique

The Red Pony is a very early and a completely successful instance of the organic relationship between structure and materials which distinguishes Steinbeck's most important fiction.[1] It is set off from much of Steinbeck's work by a relative absence of extraneous devices intended to force order into the work of art.

This long short story consists of three episodes: "The Gift," "The Great Mountains," and "The Promise." The structure is panoramic with a strong thematic unity which binds the three episodes together. Their shared reference is to one important experience, the process of growing up, and their shared focus is on one character, the boy Jody. The episodes provide concrete evidence that the meaning of growing up is chiefly a development of a sense that life and death are involved in each other; this awareness is equated with a growth of a sense of tragedy. Detail is presented consistently in terms of Jody's progressive awareness of the reality of death. The objective events and their implied meanings are self-contained.

Because Jody's is the point of view, we tend to accept his innocence as our own. The events are developed so that each episode is an objective record of Jody's experience and deepening awareness. One episode flows into the next, and the last episode fuses with the first because it ends as the

From the *Journal of Narrative Technique*. Reprinted in *The Short Novels of John Steinbeck*, pp. 84–94. © 1990 by Duke University Press.

first begins, with the present of a pony for Jody; but any sense of a purely mechanical progression is subordinated to Jody's innocent point of view.

There are some minor mechanical connections between characters and events which serve only to tighten the story. Thus, each episode begins with a focus on Jody's childish faith in adults or a child's game or daydream, but an adult problem intrudes and absorbs the child's world. The specific content in the process is that death and imperfection are everywhere, and that people try to conquer death and overcome imperfection in spite of their failures, while nature is a merely neutral element.

Death is a natural and fairly innocent presence in the opening division of "The Gift." Jody's world is ordered by kindly and severe adults, but contains cows and pigs that are to be butchered, a dog that has killed a coyote and been lamed, unseen dead animals, and highly visible buzzards. At night Jody hears owls hunting mice. Of all the evidence of death, Jody hates only the buzzards "as all decent things hate them" (p. 206). They are natural enough, and so necessary "they could not be hurt" (p. 207). Yet, in feeding on carrion, buzzards mark the point at which death becomes an ugly imperfection that cannot be accepted serenely. Buzzards prove that nature feeds on nature. They dramatize the ugly fact. And, within Jody's experience, their realistic function connotes their symbolic role at the conclusion—as the ultimate images of Death.

Into this flawed ranch world, and into Jody's formless innocence, Jody's father brings the red pony. In keeping with the theme, the pony is not quite perfect. He is untrained, acquired at an auction after the bankruptcy of a "show." The red saddle he comes with is too frail for ordinary use, and he has been paid for by money from the butchered cows. Also this random gift emphasizes Mr. Tiflin's own imperfection. Jody's father is a stern disciplinarian, implicitly afraid to express his affection for Jody (p. 205). Mr. Tiflin's materialistic gift and his claim that the pony will be useful mask his effort to express a love for Jody that he cannot express in words. The ironies increase. Once he sees the red pony, Jody is filled with wonder and affection for it, not for Mr. Tiflin, but the pony bites Jody's hand.

These narrative details suggest a weight of imperfection, but, for the moment, that weight is lifted by Jody's happiness. He loves the stylish red saddle and feels that biting proves the pony's high spirits. Even the doubts of his playmates, when they learn the pony is untrained, fail to diminish Jody's happiness. He even rises somewhat out of childhood. When his friends leave, he speaks to the pony "in a deep voice," and directs all of his attention to this new love; and his mother points to this development when she feels "a curious pride rise up in her" as she sees Jody falling in love with the pony (pp. 214–15).

The pony's training can be read in abstract terms as the bending of nature to man's will, or paralleled with Jody's growing up, but the specific details of the training carry their own conviction. The fact is that Billy Buck, the kindly stable hand, teaches the pony with Jody's help; implicitly, Billy teaches Jody how to be a man by way of using a horse without showing fear. Still, the first time that Jody thinks of riding the pony as a fact, he is afraid of being hurt if the pony should fall. This reality merges with Jody's distanced fantasies of imperfection, for he imagines at times that the pony has been hurt, but only to indulge the childish luxury of self-torture. The final sentence in this passage sets aside fears and fantasies; Jody's happiness is predominant: "When the two came back from an expedition they smelled of the sweet sage they had forced through" (p. 222). Nonetheless, happiness and imperfection are so mingled in the details of this episode that very often they cannot be separated. Jody's mother speaks "irritably" and his father "crossly" to Jody on the morning he gets the pony, since they do not know how to express the love or joy that they do feel (pp. 209–11). Jody's mother says to Carl Tiflin, "Don't you let it keep him from school," and his father "walked up a side-hill to be by himself, for he was embarrassed" (pp. 210–11). Yet the objective narrator, not Jody, records these details. Again, the pony connotes power, quite as strongly as love, as when the visiting boys are awed: "They knew instinctively that a man on a horse is spiritually as well as physically bigger than a man on foot" (p. 213). And love is balanced by the mixed stages of the training; the carrots and the petting occur in a context of details such as this: "The first time the pony wore the bridle he whipped his head about and worked his tongue against the bit until the blood oozed from the corners of his mouth . . . and his eyes turned red with fear and with general rambunctiousness. Jody rejoiced, for he knew that only a mean-souled horse does not resent training" (p. 220).

The illness and death of the pony occur in this context of imperfection that even happiness does not negate. The central human fact is that Jody tends to transfer an implicit belief in his father's perfection to the less awesome Billy Buck, who is aware that he cannot bear to seem fallible to Jody. Partly because of this self-knowledge, Billy claims too much good sense, and he is badly mistaken on three occasions. The pony gets wet because Billy misjudges the weather (by quiet irony it is near Thanksgiving, when Jody can ride the pony); the pony gets sick in spite of Billy's assurance that he will not; and the pony fails to get better in spite of Billy's careful doctoring. To complete the round, Jody's need to place the whole blame for human imperfection on Billy dissolves when Jody goes to sleep in the stable, while the pony might yet recover, and wakes up to find that the pony has wandered outdoors into the chilly night. Jody does not mention this lapse, but he falls asleep again and lets the pony wander off to its death.

Carl Tiflin, Billy Buck, and Jody Tiflin are imperfect, then, in their various human ways. But the ultimate fusion of death with imperfection (and a human striving after perfection) is presented in one brilliant narrative image in the final division of the episode, in Jody's fight with the buzzard. When Jody finds the pony's body, he catches one buzzard and beats it to death. Jody wishes to protect the dead pony because he was unable to protect the sick, living pony, but his "punishment" of the carrion eater is worse than futile. The imagery indicates that nature is an indifferent process to which men assign meaning. The buzzard cannot be hurt even by its death, for it is not human; as Jody struck, "the red fearless eyes still looked at him, impersonal and unafraid and detached" (p. 238). Carl Tiflin cannot understand Jody's act (or, probably, the foregoing image), so, in the last paragraph of the episode, Billy Buck expresses Jody's feelings: "His father moved the buzzard with his toe. 'Jody,' he explained, 'the buzzard didn't kill the pony. Don't you know that?' 'I know it,' Jody said wearily. It was Billy Buck who was angry. He had lifted Jody in his arms, and had turned to carry him home. But he turned back on Carl Tiflin. 'Course he knows it,' Billy said furiously, 'Jesus Christ! man, can't you see how he'd feel about it?'" (p. 238). There is no loading of meaning; the passage's intensity and the shifts in tone are implicit in the objective narrative, as a sequence of human responses on the basis of everything that has gone before. Jody has learned that nothing can be blamed, given human imperfection and uncaring nature. The fallible but fatherly Billy Buck—Jody in his arms—being closer to nature, and more involved in Jody, can understand better than the well-meaning but detached Carl Tiflin, who presumes that Jody is inwardly as young as his physical age. The one positive touch is that Jody and Billy Buck share an awareness of human imperfection and of an impersonal nature.

So, by a completely unspoken implication, Jody leaps into the sense of tragedy that defines manhood. As silently, that leap is an ironic by-product of the circumstances of the pony's illness and death. More than in much of his later work, Steinbeck is willing here to let an extensive texture of imagery, events, and characters produce their own implicit meanings. Steinbeck's later concept of "is" thinking (nonteleological observation) is intended to produce a precise language; that precision is organically justified here because many of the details of the pony's training, illness, and death are new to Jody. And those details serve implicitly to indicate Jody's development from childish innocence to a mature, tragic awareness; they are not merely an aspect of Steinbeck's technique. Particularly Steinbeck avoids any suggestion of the allegory that is so common in the later novels. For example, the buzzards are really, and therefore organically, the chief images of Death that a country boy would know about. The imagistic richness of the Death figure is precisely its natural quality, which corresponds perfectly with its larger meaning. A buzzard is a natural and necessary beast, and a terrible one, and in these qualities it approximates our feelings about death itself. Hence the image grows out of its surroundings and fulfills its own nature; its objectivity precludes allegorical pumping.

The second episode, "The Great Mountains," is an interlude that continues a development of the themes of Death, imperfection, and a sense of tragedy, but with some decline of narrative intensity.

The episode begins with a seemingly aimless introduction. Jody plays around the ranch—he tortures the lamed dog that he had kissed and relieved of a tick during the pony's illness; he kills a "little thrush" with a slingshot, cuts it up because he is ashamed, and finally throws the parts away; and he asks his father, mother, and Billy about the large seaward mountains that suggest death to him in contrast with the "jolly" landward mountains, the Gabilans (pp. 200, 242). The key to Jody's play is his fascination with death. Having become aware of it, he must understand its human meaning. He poses "the possibility of ancient cities lost in the mountains" to justify his deeper fascination (p. 242). "Ancient cities" is an impossible fantasy, but the mountains become even more suggestive to Jody as a strictly private image; they are "dear to him, and terrible" in their mystery (p. 242). Jody's secret fascination is drawn to one imagistic point by the appearance of Gitano, an old paisano, who comes back to his birthplace to die. After learning that the family adobe hut has washed away, and after staying a day and night with the Tiflins, Gitano travels into the great mountains that rim the Pacific, and he takes the old, useless horse, Easter; for the journey is to death.

All of this is a little too contrived. Nonetheless, it is made clear that Jody's mind works as a child's mind often does, through symbols in its preoccupation. That explains why Jody is so excited when Gitano appears. Jody can sense the painful reality of Gitano's wish to die, having learned about death in his own right, and he feels a kinship because he senses that Gitano's thoughts are like his own. Jody feels "irresistibly drawn" to the bunkhouse where Gitano is put up, since, in Jody's mind, Gitano's wish to die is associated with the seaward mountains (p. 252). Indirectly but clearly, the narrative moves forward in a subsequent action, a fusion of the question that death raises with the theme of fatherhood. Jody finds Gitano with a rapier, and Gitano's initial anger at being spied on is changed to sympathy as he realizes the boy's need: "Jody put out his hand, 'Can't I see it?' Gitano's eyes smouldered angrily and he shook his head. 'Where'd you get it? Where'd it come from?' Now Gitano regarded him profoundly, as though he pondered. 'I got it from my father'" (p. 253). Jody understands in turn that Gitano's reply is a sudden insight—the end of his search for a place to die. The privacy

of the insight is shared in the objective fact of the rapier: "Jody knew . . .
he must never tell anyone about the rapier. It would be a dreadful thing to
tell anyone about it, for it would destroy some fragile structure of truth. It
was a truth that might be shattered by division" (p. 254). The truth seems
to be that death is only a natural fact, and it is natural because it is really a
search for origins, for one's father. It is quite to the point that Jody's earlier
eager questioning about treasure cities in the mountains forces Gitano to
understand that his own search is really for a place to die that is his father's;
for, as Jody questions, Gitano remembers that his father had taken him into
the mountains once when he was a boy, and he comes to feel that only the
mountains belong now to his father. This range of insight is not limited to
the supporting phallic symbolism (mountains, rapier), or to the socially apt
suggestion that Mr. Tiflin is not a warm father (a real father?) to Jody, or
to the religious implications of "father," although all of these elements are
relevant to the fragile structure of truth, which cannot be expressed simply.

Steinbeck is perhaps too simple at the climax of the episode, in the
report the next morning that a neighbor has seen Gitano going into the
seaward mountains, leading Easter and carrying a sword. Until that moment,
the episode is developed surely.

Gitano's father contrasts sharply with Carl Tiflin. Gitano's father was
a great man and was loved by his son, but Carl Tiflin is a fool. Interestingly,
Steinbeck uses a version of his later allegorical method at its worst to suggest
Mr. Tiflin's inability to sense that Gitano wishes to die. Mr. Tiflin is afraid
of having to support the old man, and parallels him with Easter in a bad
associative joke, suggestive of narrow stupidity, although Mr. Tiflin likes
the joke so much (it is typical of him) that he repeats it: "Jody's father had a
humorous thought. He turned to Gitano. 'If ham and eggs grew on a side-
hill I'd turn you out to pasture too,' he said. 'But I can't afford to pasture you
in my kitchen'" (pp. 249–50). Having innocently set off this exchange, Jody
listens. Later, in the scene in the bunkhouse, Gitano is given the insight that
Jody lacks a father he can respect fully. Still later, Gitano senses Jody's feeling
that the rapier is a secret. And, for Jody, keeping the secret means keeping it
especially from his father. Jody's lack of a respected father is emphasized—by
ironic reversal—when Gitano goes into the mountains to find a place he can
associate with his father. These narrative details draw together at the close.
Mr. Tiflin thinks that Gitano has robbed him by taking Easter, but, with a
deeper understanding, Jody walks out alone to look at the great mountains
and to think about Gitano: "He lay down in the green grass . . . covered his
eyes with his crossed arms . . . and he was full of a nameless sorrow" (p. 256).
Jody's sorrow is for Gitano, for his probable death, and for the mystery of
it. Even more, it is the sorrow of self-discovery, that imperfection is worse
than death. Thus, Jody passes from a fascination with death, even from an

older sorrow for the death of the red pony, to the profounder sorrow of recognizing that his father's limitations create or reveal imperfection at such close hand.

Clearly this episode is superior narrative work. Its relative inferiority to the surrounding episodes is due to some narrative strain. Mr. Tiflin's lack of sensibility is a much smaller point than the reality of death, and Mr. Tiflin's jovial stupidity cannot be elevated into a perfect correlation with Gitano's passion for his father. And the parallel between Gitano and Easter is much too self-conscious and slick in its surface emphasis. These imperfections keep "The Great Mountains" from attaining a thorough organic unity. The strength of the episode is in its success as an interlude, and its somewhat mechanical quality may have been intended precisely to relax the narrative tension to some extent. Certainly it occupies the mid-position between two very intense episodes. Finally, there is a thorough success in Steinbeck's transfer of Jody's awareness of death from the animal to the human sphere.

The third episode, "The Promise," is absolutely an organic unity. It is one of Steinbeck's most impressive works. "The Promise" opens with a series of games that Jody plays by himself on the way from school. The games modulate from pure fantasy into the real world, from leadership of "a phantom army with great flags and swords, silent but deadly," through a batch of small animals that Jody stores, "moist and uncomfortable" in his lunch pail, to his eager collection of the mail from the box in front of the ranch, and finally to his mother's news that his father wants to see him (pp. 256–58). Here the real world intrudes clearly, and the game becomes adult— a game of creation that is "silent but deadly," that involves pain, yet more new experience than a weekly paper or a mail catalog can provide.

Mr. Tiflin has been convinced by Billy Buck that one of the ranch mares, Nellie, should be bred; her colt will replace the red pony. Mr. Tiflin masks the idea with a typical coldness; his offer is based on Jody's previous good behavior, and his condition is that Jody must earn the five-dollar stud fee by work around the ranch. Jody's response is a joyful fearfulness and respect for the stern father, and "a sudden warm friendliness" for Billy Buck as he realizes that the idea is Billy's (p. 260). A forward movement containing the emotional content of the earlier episodes is clear now: Billy becomes Jody's substitute father, and Mr. Tiflin is allowed only a minimal role. Billy's stake is that he loves Jody as a father might; his benevolent idea is to let Jody help to create the new pony in the sense of helping at the birth of Nellie's colt, Mr. Tiflin's love is more objective and abstract. It is rooted in the virtue of duty and the value of money. So the idea is enmeshed from the beginning in Mr. Tiflin's private imperfections as a father and as a man.

Events deepen this suggestion. Jody brings Nellie to a neighbor who has a stallion; imagery controls the result:

The stallion came on so fast that he couldn't stop when he reached the mare. Nellie's ears went back; she whirled and kicked at him as he went by. The stallion spun around and reared. He struck the mare with his front hoof, and while she staggered under the blow, his teeth raked her neck and drew an ooze of blood. Instantly, Nellie's mood changed. She became coquettishly feminine ... Jess Taylor sat the boy behind him on the horse. "You might have got killed," he said. "Sundown's a mean devil sometimes. He busted his rope and went right through a gate." (p. 263)

Nellie's mild injury, Jody's very probable danger, and the natural violence of the breeding, all presented from Jody's point of view, engender a train of imagery suggesting that violence, joy, and the chance of death are involved in creation—in an event more complex than a stud fee would imply through its reduction of the event to a calculated price. Mr. Tiflin, and Jody through him, tends to deny this complexity in the rationality of work. Jody's grinding schedule, set by Mr. Tiflin, repays the stud fee and pays for Nellie's special diet. As metaphor, father and son presume the colt's life has been paid for beforehand, hence assured, and Jody is his father's son to the extent that he expects the rational bargain to be kept.

But at birth the colt is twisted around in the womb; Billy has to kill Nellie to save the colt. Thus human and natural imperfection continue, and death remains the price of life.

The episode reaches a tragic plane, a heightening of the irony that we cannot buy a life, through Jody's shared awareness of Billy's suffering. Billy does what is "right" because he is determined to keep his promise to give Jody a colt, and he knows the mare has to die if the colt is to live. "Right" as it is, Billy's act is as bad, in effect, as the fact of a buzzard's endless hunger. Billy knows this; therefore he is stricken with guilt. A buzzard feels no guilt, nor does a man as unsubtle as Mr. Tiflin. The forward narrative movement from the first episode is in Billy's tragic awareness that the best he can do is imperfect, and Jody is able to comprehend this scale of moral awareness because it echoes his own earlier experience. Thus the narrative movement is completely organic and self-contained.

Steinbeck is very careful about this. Jody's point of view remains constant; it is through his essentially innocent perception that we realize the depth of Billy's sense of guilt. Always Jody's understanding is the center of the action, not the violence of birth in its bloody detail. And Jody's point of view is justified. He tends to substitute Billy Buck for his father, as human warmth for inhumanly chilly abstraction, but that does not lull his conviction that Billy is a fallible man. Hence, Jody wants to be certain that everything goes well. He makes Billy promise "you won't let anything happen" to the colt, and he insists on attending the birth (p. 275). The price that Jody pays is a vision of Billy's self-torment. Billy's strain as the birth develops badly is established through his increasingly violent way of speaking to Jody. In the final sentence, Jody's concentration on having the colt he has paid for and arranged to have is shifted completely under these influences to Jody's awareness of Billy's torment: "He tried to be glad because of the colt, but the bloody face, and the haunted, tired eyes of Billy Buck hung in the air ahead of him" (p. 279). So, fusing natural imperfection, death, and fatherhood, the episode ends in a human environment that is more significant than the colt, given Jody's established point of view. Human relevance is at one with the clarity of the narrative.

Like "The Gift," "The Promise" is an organic whole. Its events and characters imply a larger meaning that is implicit without strain in the narrative. There are no purely mechanical links, as there are in "The Great Mountains." Certain mechanical connections are evident, as in "The Gift," but they remain minor details that only tighten the events. Thus, Jess Taylor, who saw Gitano going away, owns the stallion in "The Promise." Jody's colt is intended to replace the red pony. A year passes and Jody thinks he will be too old before he can ride the new colt. In fact, he is growing mature enough to comprehend tragedy, not merely death. The major themes are always kept in view and focus the organic development of the narrative. In brief, details are not ends in themselves; they support the whole.

Clearly, then, *The Red Pony* can stand with *In Dubious Battle*, much of *The Grapes of Wrath*, and *The Pearl* as among Steinbeck's most impressive successes in the art of narrative.

NOTE

1. John Steinbeck, *The Long Valley* (New York: Viking Press, 1938). All later page references are to this edition. Several parts of *The Red Pony* were published during the winter of 1933.

NELLIE Y. McKAY

"Happy[?]-Wife-and-Motherdom"[1]: *The Portrayal of Ma Joad in John Steinbeck's* The Grapes of Wrath

Women's social roles in western culture are central concerns in contemporary feminist criticism. The discourse focuses on the idea that our society is organized around male-dominated sex–gender systems that admit two genders, that privilege heterosexual relationships, and that embrace a sexual division of labor in which wife and mother are the primary functions of women.[2] In such works as *Of Woman Born* by Adrienne Rich,[3] *Man's World, Woman's Place* by Elizabeth Janeway,[4] *The Reproduction of Motherhood: Psychoanalysis and the Sociology of Gender* by Nancy Chodorow,[5] and *Contemporary Feminist Thought* by Hester Eisenstein,[6] critics argue that, in spite of prevailing social dogma to the contrary, the biological functions of childbearing and lactation (motherhood), and the cultural one of nurturing (mothering) are divisible. Whereas one is restricted to women, the other need not be. Parenting, in place of mothering, is not biologically determined, and there is no proof that men are less capable of nurturing children than women, or that children would suffer adverse effects if women were not their primary caretakers. However, female oppression under patriarchy dictates an institution in which the heterosexual family is at the center of the social system; woman, wife, motherhood, and mothering are synonymous; and sex-role stereotyping separates the social expectations of women from those of men. From

---

From *New Essays on the Grapes of Wrath*, pp. 47–69. © 1990 by Cambridge University Press.

this institution, "Happy-Wife-and-Motherdom" assumes woman's ideal social, emotional, and psychological state.

The success of such sex-role stereotyping depends on establishing socially acceptable clusters of behavioral attitudes that define male and female gender identities differently from the biological (sex-based) identities of women and men. To function properly, these behaviors require social placement on a hierarchical scale of dominant versus submissive, strong versus weak, independent versus dependent, in favor of men.[7] Consequently, women are conditioned toward passivity while men are rewarded for more aggressive behavior. For women, the expressive traits (affection, obedience, sympathy, and nurturing) are hailed and rewarded as "normal" behavior; men are expected to be aggressive, tenacious, ambitious, and responsible. Objecting to psychological impositions that render women subordinate to men, Elizabeth Janeway, among others, speaks out against social scientists like Freud and Eric Erickson who, in defense of the status quo, made it their business to substitute *"prescription"* for *"description,"* as they tried to explain how women ought to be, rather than how they are.[8] She argues that there is no scientific basis for the male-constructed definition of women's nature, and that opinions on the biological aspects of women's inabilities to perform as well as men in some areas, and vice versa, are not facts, but are, rather, social mythology based on beliefs and practices that shape social life according to a particular set of values.[9] This social mythology of women's nature enables men to define the "natural" capabilities of women in ways that make women socially and economically dependent on men.

The image of woman/wife/mother with children as the "core of domestic organization is implicit in patriarchal sex–gender systems."[10] Traditionally, men perform in the public sphere, while women's place is in the home, where they loom large and powerful, although, in the larger world, they remain under the control of husbands and fathers. Nor are women innocent in the development of these systems. Several feminist critics now argue that sex-role differentiation originated partly in male propaganda, and partly because women found certain of its elements sufficiently attractive willingly to give up intellectual, economic, and political power in exchange for private power in the domestic sphere. As women/wives/mothers, they are able to hold sway over the lives of their children, and to manipulate their husbands in the sexual arena.[11] This arrangement frees men from domestic responsibilities and permits them to focus their lives primarily in the public sphere: the masculine world of social and political control that determines the lives of men and women. The husband/father assumes the socially approved masculine responsibility to make important decisions and provide monetarily for his family, while the wife/mother agrees to accept a variety of unspecified familial obligations, including constant attunement to the needs of her husband and children. His support is expected to be largely material; hers, emotional. Nor are the rewards equal. By society's standards, his contributions to the family are perceived greater; hers are lesser. He articulates his family and gives it a place in the larger world; she is bound by that articulation.[12]

Until recently, literary representations of women, especially by men, subscribed almost exclusively to the ideology of locating women's place in the domestic world. Women who moved outside of their designated boundaries in search of authority over their own lives were stigmatized as unfeminine, bad mothers and wives, and social deviants. The most well-known positive image in the category of the good woman is the Earth Mother, who, engaged in selfless mothering, dedicates her entire being to the welfare of her husband and children. In *The Lay of the Land*, Annette Kolodny reminds us of how powerful the representation of a symbiotic relationship between femaleness and the land (the earth) is in the national consciousness. The desire for harmony between "man" and nature, based on an experience of the land as woman/mother—the female principle of "receptivity, repose, and integral satisfaction," is one of our most cherished American fantasies, she tells us.[13] In her analysis of seventeenth- and eighteenth-century writings by early settlers in America, Kolodny writes that the members of this group carried with them a yearning for paradise, and perceived the New World as a "maternal 'garden,' receiving and nurturing human children."[14] Furthermore, she asserts that for these settlers there was

> a *need* to experience the land as a nurturing, giving maternal breast.... Beautiful, indeed, that wilderness appeared—but also dark, uncharted, and prowled by howling beasts.... Mother was ready to civilize it ... [to make] the American continent ... the birthplace of a new culture ... with new and improved human possibilities ... in fact as well as metaphor, a womb of generation and a provider of sustenance.[15]

This equation of the American land with woman's biological attributes did much to foster the widespread use of literary images of women as one with the "natural" propensities of a productive nurturing earth, and to erase, psychologically, the differences between the biological and the social functions of women.

Fully immersed in this tradition, men, male vision, and the relationships of men to each other and to the rest of the world dominate the works of John Steinbeck, whereas women, without whom the men would have no world, have no independent identity of their own. The social and economic conditions in the lower working-class milieu in which many of these women appear can easily give rise to what on the surface seems to represent a very different relationship to the social structure from that of women in other strata. On the contrary, the ideology that woman's place is rooted in her interests in others, preferably those of husbands and children, remains the same. Steinbeck's women seldom need seek the right to work outside of their homes, or to choose careers equal to those of men. They have no connections to the "gentle-companions" female identity or to the ideology of femininity that became popular in the nineteenth century. Work, as hard as that of farm men, or lower class men struggling for survival outside of the agrarian economy, occupies a great deal of their time. In the words of Tom Joad, "Women's always tar'd, . . . that's just the way women is, 'cept at meetin' once an' again."[16] They are always tired because they are always attending to the needs of everyone but themselves. Even domestic violence against these women is socially acceptable within the group.[17] Only race privilege protects them from the barbarous abuse of others outside of their community that women of color in similar situations experience. Yet, the most they can achieve and hold onto with social dignity is the supportive nurturing role of woman's place in a man's world.

The centrality of women to the action of *The Grapes of Wrath* is clear from the beginning as well. For one thing, not only among the Joads, the main characters in this novel, but in all the families in crisis, the children look to the women for answers to their immediate survival: "What are we going to do, Ma? Where are we going to go?" (47) the anonymous children ask. In male-dominated sex–gender systems, children depend on their mothers for parenting, and their stability rests mainly on the consistency and reliability with which women meet their needs. There is no question that in this model the woman/wife/mother makes the most important contributions to family stability. This chapter does not challenge Steinbeck's understanding of the value of women's roles in the existing social order. I attempt, however, to place his vision of those roles within the framework of an American consciousness that has long been nourished by gender myths that associated women with nature, and thus primarily with the biological and cultural functions of motherhood and mothering, whereas men occupy a separate masculine space that affords them independence and autonomy. By adopting Robert Briffault's theory that matriarchy is a cohesive, nonsexually dominating system,[18] Steinbeck assures us that the family can survive by returning to an earlier stage of collective, nonauthoritarian security while the larger society moves towards a socialistic economy. As he sees it, in times of grave familial or community need, a strong, wise woman like Ma Joad has the opportunity (or perhaps the duty) to assert herself and still maintain her role as selfless nurturer of the group. In this respect, she is leader and follower, wise and ignorant, and simple and complex, simultaneously.[19] In short, she is the woman for all seasons, the nonintrusive, indestructible "citadel" on whom everyone else can depend.

This idealistic view of womanhood is especially interesting because, although there are qualities in Steinbeck's work that identify him with the sentimental and romantic traditions, as a writer with sympathies toward socialism he also saw many aspects of American life in the light of harsh realism. His reaction to the plight of the Oklahoma farmers in this novel moved him to a dramatic revision of the frontier patriarchal myth of individual, white-male success through unlimited access to America's abundant and inexhaustible expanses of land. He begins with the equivalent of a wide-lens camera view that portrays the once-lush land grown tired and almost unyielding from overuse, and then follows that up with vivid descriptions of farmers being brutally dispossessed by capitalist greed from the place they thought belonged to them. His instincts are also keen in the matter of character development; unanticipated circumstances alter the worldview that many of the people in the novel previously held, and their changes are logical. As they suffer, the Joads, in particular the mother and her son Tom (the other Joad men never develop as fully), gradually shed their naïveté and achieve a sound political consciousness of class and economic oppression. This is a difficult education for them, but one which they eventually accept. Through it all, without the unshakable strength and wisdom of the mother, who must at times assert her will to fill the vacuum of her husband's incapability, nothing of the family, as they define it, would survive. Still, she never achieves an identity of her own, or recognizes the political reality of women's roles within a male-dominated system. She is never an individual in her own right. Even when she becomes fully aware of class discrimination and understands that the boundaries of the biological family are much too narrow a structure from which to challenge the system they struggle against, she continues to fill the social space of the invincible woman/wife/mother.

Critics identify two distinct narrative views of women in Steinbeck's writings. In one, in novels such as *To a God Unknown* (1933) and *The Grapes of Wrath* (1939), the image is positive and one-dimensional, with female significance almost completely associated with the maternal roles that Kolodny and others decry. In the other, for example *Tortilla Flat* (1935), *Of Mice and Men* (1937), *East of Eden* (1952), and several of the short stories in *The Long Valley* (1938), the portraiture is socially negative. Whores, hustlers, tramps, or madams are the outstanding roles that define the majority of these women. More graphically stated by one critic, these women "seem compelled to choose between homemaking and whoredom."[20] Interestingly, in spite of their questionable behavior, women within this group are often described as "big-breasted, big-hipped, and warm," thus implying the maternal types.[21] In his post-1943 fiction, after he moved to New York City, sophisticated women characters who are jealous, vain, and cunning—the opposite of the women in his earlier works—appear (as negative portrayals) in Steinbeck's work. Furthermore, Steinbeck's "positive" women are impressively "enduring," but never in their own self-interests. Their value resides in the manner in which they are able to sustain their nurturing and reproductive capabilities for the benefit of the group. As Mimi Reisel Gladstein notes,

> they act as the nurturing and reproductive machinery of the group. Their optimistic significance lies, not in their individual spiritual triumph, but in their function as perpetuators of the species. They are not judged by any biblical or traditional sense of morality.[22]

In conjunction with their ability to endure and to perpetuate the species, they are also the bearers of "knowledge—both of their husbands and of men generally," knowledge which enables them to "come . . . [closer than men] to an understanding of the intricacies of human nature and the profundities of life in general."[23]

Since its publication in 1939, *The Grapes of Wrath*, one of Steinbeck's most celebrated works, has been the subject of a variety of controversial appraisals. Seen by some as "an attempted prose epic, a summation of national experience at a given time,"[24] others belabor its ideological and technical flaws. The disagreements it continues to raise speak well for the need to continue to evaluate its many structural and thematic strands.

The novel opens on a note that explodes the American pastoral of the seventeenth and eighteenth centuries that Kolodny describes in her work. The lush and fertile lands that explorers in Virginia and the Carolinas saw give way to the Oklahoma Dust Bowl, where ". . . dawn came, but no day. In the gray sky a red sun appeared, a dim red circle that gave a little light, like dusk; and as that day advanced, the dusk slipped toward darkness, and the wind cried and whimpered over the fallen corn" (5). The impotence and confusion of a bewildered group of displaced people replace the assuredness and confidence of the nation's early settlers. In this world where nature is gone awry, and human control lies in the hands of men greedy for wealth and in possession of new technology that enhances their advantages, the men, women, and children who have, until now, lived on the land are helpless against an unspeakable chaos.

Feeling completely out of control in a situation they cannot comprehend, the men stand in silence by their fences or sit in the doorways of the houses they will soon leave, space that echoes loudly with their impotent unspoken rage, for they are without power or influence to determine their destinies.

Even more outrageous for them is their profound sense of alienation. Armed with rifles, and willing to fight for what they consider rightfully theirs, there is no one for them to take action against. They can only stare helplessly at the machines that demolish their way of life. They do not understand why they no longer have social value outside of their disintegrating group, and they do not know how to measure human worth in terms of abstract economic principles. "One man on a tractor can take the place of twelve or fourteen families," the representatives of the owner men explain to the uncomprehending displaced farmers. That some of their own people assist the invaders leaves them more befuddled.

> "What are you doing this kind of work for—against your own people?"

a farmer asks the tractor-driver son of an old acquaintance. The man replies:

> [for] "three dollars a day. . . . I got a wife and kids. We got to eat . . . and it comes every day."
> "But for three dollars a day fifteen or twenty families can't eat at all,"

the farmer rebuts, and continues:

> "nearly a hundred people have to go out and wander on the roads for your three dollars a day. Is that right?" . . . And the driver says, "Can't think of that. Got to think of my own kids. Three dollars a day, and it comes in every day. Times are changing, mister, don't you know? Can't make a living on the land unless you've got two, five, ten thousand acres and a tractor. Crop land isn't for little guys like us anymore. . . . You try to get three dollars a day some place. That's the only way." (50)

The quality of the frustration and level of the ineffectiveness that the men feel is displayed in the actions of Grampa, the patriarch of the Joad clan. He fires a futile shot at the advancing tractor, but succeeds only in "blow[ing] the headlights off that cat, . . . [while] she come on just the same" (62). The march of technology and the small farmers' distress go hand in hand.

Deprived of traditional assertive masculine roles, for the most part, the helpless, silent men seldom move; only their hands are engaged—uselessly—"busy," with sticks and little rocks as they survey the ruined crops, their ruined homes, their ruined way of life, "thinking—figuring," and finding no solution to the disintegration rapidly enveloping them. Nor do the women/ wives/mothers precipitously intrude on their shame. They are wise in the ways of mothering their men; of understanding the depth of their hurt and confusion, and in knowing that at times their greatest contribution to the healing of the others' psychic wounds lies in their supportive silence. "They knew that a man so hurt and so perplexed may turn in anger, even on people he loves. They left the men alone to figure and to wonder in the dust" (7). Secretly, unobtrusively, because they are good women, they study the faces of their men to know if this time they would "break." Also furtively, the children watch the faces of the men and the women. When the men's faces changed from "bemused perplexity" to anger and resistance, although they still did not know what they would do, the women and children knew they were "safe"—for "no misfortune was too great to bear if their men were whole" (7).

In the face of such disaster, enforced idleness is the lot of men. Their work comes to a halt. The women, however, remain busy, for the housewife's traditional work, from which society claims she derives energy, purpose, and fulfillment, goes on. In addition, as conditions worsen and the men further internalize impotence, the women know they will be responsible for making the crucial decisions to lead their families through the adjustment period ahead. Critic Joan Hedrick explains the dynamics of the division of labor in sex–gender-differentiated systems this way, rather than as women's "nature":

> Though there are no crops to be harvested, there are clothes to mend, cornmeal to stir, side-meat to cut up for dinner. In a time of unemployment, women embody continuity, not out of some mythic identity as the Great Mother, but simply because their work, being in the private sphere of the family, has not been taken away. . . .[25]

According to critics Richard Astro and Warren Motley, Steinbeck's philosophy of women was deeply influenced by his readings of Robert Briffault's *The Mothers: The Matriarchal Theory of Social Origins* (1931), a work they include in a group that "strove to heal the . . . post-Darwinian split between scientific thinking and ethical experience."[26] Although Briffault saw matriarchy (historically antecedent to patriarchy) as a primitive and regressive order, he felt it described a "relationship based on cooperation rather than power," and fostered an "equalitarian" society to which "authority" and "domination" were foreign. As Motley sees it, Steinbeck did not believe that matriarchy was regressive, but he was convinced that the shock of dispossession undermined the patriarchal authority (based on male economic dominance) of the Joad men and the other farmers to such an extent that they were forced to turn back to matriarchy, the more positive social organization force, epitomized by Ma Joad's "high calm," "superhuman understanding," and selfless concern for her family, as the hope for a better future.[27] Matriarchy, divested of the threat of authority and domination over men, was a system that suited Steinbeck's purpose in this novel.

The Grapes of Wrath delineates the tragedy of an agrarian family in a world in which capitalist greed and the demands of rapidly advancing technology supersede human needs and extenuating financial circumstances. Different in their attitudes from other white groups who seek the American Dream in social and economic mobility, the hard-working Joads, once tenant farmers, now reduced to sharecropper status, lived contentedly on the land in a community of like others, for three generations. They asked little of anyone outside of their world. Solid Americans, as they understand that term, they wanted only to live and let live. For instance, oblivious to the implications of his racial politics, the tenant man proudly explains his family's contributions to the pioneer history of white America. His grandfather arrived in frontier Oklahoma territory in his youth, when his worldly possessions amounted to salt, pepper, and a rifle. But before long, he successfully staked out a claim for his progeny:

> Grampa took up the land, and he had to kill the Indians and drive them away. And Pa was born here, and he killed weeds and snakes. . . . An we [the third succeeding generation] was born here. . . . And Pa had to borrow money. The bank owned the land then, but we stayed and got a little bit of what we raised. (45)

Unfortunately, the irony of their helplessness in confrontation with the power of the banks, with the absent, large land owners, and with the great crawling machines versus the fate of the Indians (to the farmer, of no greater concern than the comparison he makes of them to snakes or weeds) completely escapes the present generation. The subsequent education in class politics might have come sooner and been less psychologically devastating to the Joads and their friends if they had been able to recognize the parallels between racial and economic hegemony.

Three characters drive the action in *The Grapes of Wrath*: Jim Casy, a country preacher turned political activist; Tom Joad, the eldest son, ex-convict, and moral conscience of the family; and the indestructible Ma Joad, who holds center stage. At times she assumes mythic proportions, but her portraiture is also realistic and she acts with wisdom. Impressionistically, she is firmly planted in the earth, but she is more dependable than the land, which could not withstand the buffeting of nature or the persistent demands of small farmers or the evil encroachment of technology and corporate power. Her position is established at the beginning of the novel:

> Ma was heavy, but not fat; thick with child-bearing and work . . . her strong bare feet moved quickly and deftly over the floor. . . . Her full face was not soft; it was controlled, kindly. *Her hazel eyes seemed to have experienced all possible tragedy and to have mounted pain and suffering like steps into a big calm and superhuman understanding. She seemed to know, to accept, to welcome her position, the citadel of the family.* (99–100—italics mine)

Unless she admitted hurt or fear or joy, the family did not know those emotions; and better than joy they loved her calm. They could depend on her "imperturbability." When Tom, Jr., returns from prison to find no homestead, the house pushed off its foundations, fences gone, and other signs of living vanished, his first thought is "They're gone—or Ma's dead" (56). He knows that under no circumstances would she permit the place to fall into such ruin if she were there. His is not a casual observation, but a statement fraught with anxiety. As Nancy Chodorow points out, in the sex–gender system, the absent mother is always the source of discomfiture for her children. Tom Joad closely associates the physical deterioration of his home with a missing mother, a signal for him of the catastrophe of which he is yet unaware.[28]

There is no question that Steinbeck had, as Howard Levant stresses, "profound respect" and "serious intentions" for the materials in *The Grapes of Wrath*. His sympathies are with a group of people who, though politically and economically unaggressive by other traditional American standards, represented an important core in the national life.[29] His portrayal of the misfortunes and downfall of this family constitutes a severe critique of a modern economic system that not only devalues human lives on the basis of class but, in so doing, that violates the principles of the relationship between hard work and reward and the sanctity of white family life on which the country was founded. In light of the brutal social and economic changes, and the disruptions of white family stability, there is no doubt that Steinbeck saw strong women from traditional working-class backgrounds as instrumental in a more humane transformation of the social structure. Of necessity, women are essential to any novel in which the conventional family plays a significant role. Here, he gives the same significance to the destruction of a family-centered way of life that one group had shaped and perpetrated for generations as he does to the economic factors that precipitated such a dire situation. Furthermore, through female characters in *The Grapes of Wrath*, Steinbeck's sensitivities to the values of female sensibilities demonstrate a point of view that supports the idea of humanitarian, large-scale changes that would make America, as a nation, more responsive to larger social needs.

In this respect, in spite of the grim reality of the lives of the Joads and their neighbors, *The Grapes of Wrath* is optimistic in favor of massive social change. We can trace this optimism from the beginning of the book, in which, unlike traditional plots of the naturalistic novels of its day, events unfold through the consciousness of the characters in such a way as to permit them to envision themselves exercising free will and exerting influence on their social world. In addition, as a result of his economic politics, Steinbeck reinforces the idea that the situation is not the dilemma of an isolated family, but of an entire group of people of a particular class. If sufficiently politicized, they can and will act. The novel chronicles the misfortunes and political education of the Joad family, but they represent the group from which they come, and share the feelings of their like-others. For example, also at the beginning, an unnamed farmer, recognizing his individual impotence in the face of capitalism and the technological monster, protests: "We've got a bad thing made by man, and by God that's something *we* can change" (52—italics mine). While neither he nor his fellow farmers can comprehend the full meaning of that statement at the time, the end of the novel suggests that those who survive will come to realize that group action can have an effect on the monstrous ideology that threatens their existence. But first they must survive; and the women are at the center of making that survival possible.

The first mention of Ma Joad in the novel occurs when Tom, recently released from jail after serving four of a seven-year sentence for killing a man in self-defense, returns to the homestead to find it in ruin. During his absence, he had almost no contact with his family, for, as Tom observes to his friend Casy: "they wasn't people to write" (57). Two years earlier, however, his mother sent him a Christmas card, and, the following year, the grandmother did the same. His mother's appears to have been appropriate; his grandmother's, a card with a "tree an' shiny stuff [that] looks like snow," with an embarrassing message in "po'try," was not:

Merry Christmus, purty child,
Jesus meek an' Jesus mild,
Underneath the Christmus tree
There's a gif' for you from me. (35)

Tom recalls the teasing of his cellmates who saw the card. Subsequently, they call him "Jesus Meek."

Given the living situation within the Joad community—the hard work and frustration over the yield of the land and the absence of genteel rituals, especially in such hard times—the fact that both women sent Christmas cards to the incarcerated young man is testimony to the quality of their commitment to mothering. Granma's card, however, is not appropriate for the young man confined involuntarily among men for whom only masculine symbols and behavior are acceptable. Nevertheless, Tom does not hold this against her. He understands and accepts her impulse and her motive. He believes she liked the card for its shiny exterior and that she never read the message, perhaps because, having lost her glasses several years before, she could not see to read. Symbolically, Granma may have good intentions, but she lacks the perception to fill successfully the present or future needs of her family. Later, when both grandparents die en route to California, the family realizes that they were too old to make the transition from one way of life to another. On the other hand, although there is no mention of the nature of Ma Joad's card, we can assume that it was not a cause of embarrassment for her son. She is the woman of wisdom who knows how to use her talents to comfort her family in its moments of greatest distress. The differences in the two Christmas cards set the stage for understanding that Ma Joad is the woman who will be the significant force in the life of the family in the difficult times ahead.

Critics of Steinbeck's women often note that the first time we come face to face with Ma Joad she is engaged in the most symbolic act of mothering—feeding her family. I add that the second time we see her, she is washing clothes with her arms, up to her elbows, in soapsuds, and the third time, she is trying to dress the cantankerous grandfather who is by now incapable of caring for his own basic needs. Occurring in quick succession on a busy morning, these are the housewife's most important tasks: feeding the family, keeping them clean, and tending to the needs of those too young or too old to do so for themselves. In these earliest scenes with Ma Joad, the family is making its final preparations for the journey to California, and women's work not only goes on almost uninterruptedly, but increases in intensity. The adults, though full of apprehensions, have high hopes that steady work and a return to stability await them at the end of the trip. They have seen handbills calling for laborers to come to California to reap the harvests of a rich and fruitful land. They believe the handbills, for who would go to the expense of printing misrepresentations of the situation?

Although at all times the Joads have very little or almost no money; and, while in Oklahoma, no realistic appraisal of how long the trip to California will take in their dilapidated vehicle; and, in California, no assurances of how soon they will find work or a place to settle or know the nature of their future; an interesting aspect of Ma Joad's mothering psychology surfaces in different locations. On one hand, through most of the novel, she insists that her considerations are mainly for her family; on the other, she is willing to share the little food she has, to nurture whoever else is in need and comes along her way. We see this for the first time in Oklahoma, on first meeting her. Tom and his friend Casy arrive just as she completes the breakfast preparations on the day before the long, uncertain journey begins. Before she recognizes who they are, she invites them to partake of her board. Most notably, evidence of her largesse occurs again under more stressful circumstances, when she feeds a group of hungry children in California, although there is not sufficient food even for her family.

Another extension of Ma Joad's mothering precipitates her into a new and unaccustomed position of power within the family when she insists that Casy, with no family of his own, but who wishes to travel with them, be taken along. This is her first opportunity to assert herself outside of her housewife's role, to claim leadership in important decision making, whereas previously only the men officiated. Casy travels with the Joads only because Ma Joad overrides the objections of her husband, whose concerns for their space needs, and the small amount of money and little food they have, lead him to think it unwise to take an extra person, especially an outsider to the family, on the trip. Questioned on the matter, Ma replies:

> It ain't kin we? It's will we? . . . As far as 'kin,' we can't do nothin', not go to California or nothin'; but as far as 'will,' why, we'll do what we will. (139)

When the conversation ends, Casy has been accepted and she has gained new authority. She accepts this unpretentiously and with an absence of arrogance that will accompany her actions each time she finds it necessary to assert her will in the weeks and months ahead. And always, she asserts herself only for the good of the family. Two incidents that illustrate the group's understanding and acceptance of her wisdom and good judgment are especially noteworthy in this context. One occurs when the car breaks down during the journey and she refuses to agree to split up the family in order to hasten the arrival of some of its members in California. When her husband insists that separating is their better alternative, she openly defies him and, armed with a jack handle, challenges him to "whup" her first to gain her obedience to his will (230).[30] The second incident takes place in California, when, after weeks of the groups' unsuccessful search for work and a decent place to settle down, she chides the men for capitulating to despair. "You ain't got the right to get discouraged," she tells them, "this here fambly's goin' under. You jus' ain't got the right" (479).

But these situations, in which Ma's voice carries, also illustrate the tensions between men and women, in sex–gender-role systems, when women move into space traditionally designated to men. Each time Ma asserts her leadership she meets with Pa's resentment, for, regardless of her motives,

he perceives that she usurps his authority. In the first instance, when Casy
is accepted into the group, "Pa turned his back, and his spirit was raw from
the whipping" her ascendancy represented to him (140). She, mindful of her
role, leaves the family council and goes back to the house, to women's place,
and women's work. But nothing takes place in her absence, the family waits
for her return before continuing with their plans, "for she was powerful in the
group" (140). During the trip (when Ma challenges Pa to "whup" her), after
several suspenseful minutes, as the rest of the group watch his hands, the
fists never form, and, in an effort to salvage his hurt pride, he can only say:
"one person with their mind made up can shove a lot of folks aroun'!" (230).
But again she is the victor and the "eyes of the whole family shifted back to
Ma. She was the power. She had taken control" (231). Finally, in California,
when Ma has her way once more in spite of Pa's opposition, and the family
will move from a well-kept camp that had been a temporary respite from the
traumas of the journey and their stay in Hooverville, but that placed them in
an area in which they could find no work,

> Pa sniffled. "Seems like times is changed," he said sarcastically.
> "Time was when a man said what we'd do. Seems like women
> is tellin' now. Seems like it's purty near time to get out a stick."
> (481)

But he makes no attempt to beat her, for she quickly reminds him that men
have the "right" to beat their women only when they (the men) are adequately
performing their masculine roles.

> "You get your stick Pa," she said. "Times when they's food an'
> a place to set, then maybe you can use your stick an' keep your
> skin whole. But you ain't a-doin' your job, either a-thinkin' or
> a-workin'. If you was, why, you could use your stick, an' women
> folks'd sniffle their nose an' creep-mouse aroun'. But you jus' get
> you a stick now an' you ain't lickin' no woman; you're a fightin',
> 'cause I got a stick all laid out too." (481)

In each of the instances mentioned here, once the decision is made
and Ma's wise decision carries, she returns to women's place and/or displays
stereotypical women's emotions. After her first confrontation with Pa over
Casy, she hastens to tend the pot of "boiling side-meat and beet greens"
to feed her family. Following the second, after she has challenged Pa to a
fight and wins, she looks at the bar of iron and her hand trembles as she
drops it on the ground. Finally, when she rouses the family from despair,
she immediately resumes washing the breakfast dishes, "plunging" her hands

into the bucket of water. And, to emphasize her selflessness, as her angry husband leaves the scene, she registers pride in her achievement, but not for herself. "He's all right," she notes to Tom. "He ain't beat. He's like as not to take a smack at me." Then she explains the aim of her "sassiness."

> Take a man, he can get worried an' worried, an' it eats out his liver, an' purty soon he'll jus' lay down and die with his heart et out. But if you can take an' make 'im mad, why, he'll be awright. Pa, he didn't say nothin', but he's mad now. He'll show me now. He's awright. (481)

Only once does Ma come face to face with the issue of gender roles, and the possibilities of recognizing women's oppression within the conventions of the patriarchal society, and that is in her early relationship with Casy, when, in her psychological embrace of him, he is no longer a stranger, or even a friend, he becomes one of the male members of the family. He thanks her for her decision to let him accompany them to California by offering to "salt down" the meat they will carry with them. To this offer, she is quick to point out that the task is "women's work" that need not concern him. It is interesting that the only crack in the ideology of a gender-based division of labor to occur in the novel is in Casy's reply to Ma, and his subsequent actions: "It's all work. . . . They's too much to do to split it up to men's and women's work. . . . Leave me salt the meat" (146). Although she permits him to do it, apparently, she learns nothing from the encounter, for it never becomes a part of her thinking. On the other hand, Casy's consciousness of the politics of class is in formation before we meet him in the novel and he is the only character in the book to realize that women are oppressed by the division of labor based on the differentiation of sex–gender roles.

If the wisdom that Steinbeck attributes to women directs Ma to step outside of her traditional role in times of crisis, as noted above, her actions immediately after also make it clear that she is just as willing to retreat to wifehood and motherdom. In this, she supports Steinbeck's championing of Briffault's theory that, in matriarchy, women do not seek to have authority over men. In her case, not even equality of place is sought, only the right to lead, for the good of the group, when her man is incapable of doing so. And Steinbeck suggests why women are better equipped to lead in time of great social stress: They are closer to nature and to the natural rhythms of the earth. When family morale is at its lowest point, Ma continues to nurture confidence: "Man, he lives in jerks—" she says, "baby born an' a man dies, an' that's a jerk—gets a farm an' loses his farm, an' that's a jerk." But women are different. They continue on in spite of the difficulties. "Woman, its all one flow, like a stream, little eddies, little waterfalls, but the river, it goes right on. Woman looks at it like that" (577). In times of crisis, Steinbeck suggests, the survival of the family and, by extension, the social order, depends on the wisdom and strength of the mother, whose interests are always those of her husband and children.

The long trek from Oklahoma to California provides many instances that demonstrate Ma's selfless nurturing, her wisdom, her leadership abilities, and, above all, her centeredness in the family. An important illustration of the latter occurs at the time of the death of the grandmother on the long night in which the family makes an incredibly precarious desert crossing into California. Lying with the dead old woman all night to conceal this partially unforeseen mishap from the rest of the group, Ma Joad's only thought during the ordeal is: "The fambly hadda get acrost" (312). Alone with her secret of the true state of the old woman's condition, her considerations for the other members of the family, in this case particularly for the future of the younger children and for her daughter's unborn child, take precedence over the tremendous emotional cost to herself. Her determination to protect the family is almost ferocious, as she stands up to the officials at the agricultural inspection station on the California border to prevent them from discovering the dead woman by making a thorough check of the contents of the truck.

> Ma climbed heavily down from the truck. Her face was swollen and her eyes were hard. "Look, mister. We got a sick ol' lady. We got to get her to a doctor. We can't wait." She seemed to fight with hysteria. "You can't make us wait." (308)

Her apparent distress over the welfare of the old woman's health is convincing. One inspector perfunctorily waves the beam of his flashlight into the interior of the vehicle, and decides to let them pass. "I couldn' hold 'em" he tells his companion. "Maybe it was a bluff," the other replied, to which the first responded: "Oh, Jesus, no! You should of seen that ol' woman's face. That wasn't no bluff" (308). Ma is so intent on keeping the death a secret, even from the rest of the group as long as their overall situation remains threatening, that, when they arrive in the next town, she assures Tom that Granma is "awright—awright," and she implores him to "drive on. We got to get acrost" (308). She absorbs the trauma of the death in herself, and only after they have arrived safely on the other side of the desert does she give the information to the others. Even then she refuses the human touch that would unleash her own emotional vulnerability. The revelation of this act to protect the family is one of the most powerful scenes in the novel. The members of the family, already almost fully dependent on her emotional stamina, look at her "with a little terror at her strength" (312). Son Tom moves toward her in speechless admiration and attempts to put his hand on her shoulder to comfort her. "'Don' touch me,' she said. 'I'll hol' up if you don' touch me. That'd get me'" (312). And Casy, the newest member of the family, can only say: "there's a woman so great with love—she scares me" (313).

In Steinbeck's vision of a different and more humane society than capitalistic greed spawned, he also believed that efforts like Ma Joad's, to hold the family together in the way she always knew it (individualism as a viable social dynamic), were doomed to failure. Although she is unconscious of it at the time, her initial embrace of Casy is a step toward a redefinition of family, and, by the time the Joads arrive in California, other developments have already changed the situation. Both Grampa and Granma are dead. Soon after, son Noah, feeling himself a burden on the meager resources at hand, wanders away. In addition, Casy is murdered for union activities; Al, whose mechanical genius was invaluable during the trip, is ready to marry and leave; Connie, Rose of Sharon's husband, deserts, and her baby is stillborn; and Tom, in an effort to avenge Casy's death, becomes a fugitive from the law and decides to become a union organizer, to carry on Casy's work. Through these events, first Tom, and then Ma, especially through Tom's final conversation with her, achieve an education in the politics of class oppression, and realize that the system that diminishes one family to the point of its physical and moral disintegration can only be destroyed through the cooperative efforts of those of the oppressed group. "'Use' ta be the fambly was fust. It ain't so now. It's anybody," Ma is forced to admit toward the end of the novel (606).

But, although the structure of the traditional family changes to meet the needs of a changing society, in this novel at least, Steinbeck sees "happy-wife-and-motherdom" as the central role for women, even for those with other significant contributions to make to the world at large. Ma Joad's education in the possibilities of class action do not extend to an awareness of women's lives and identities beyond the domestic sphere, other than that which has a direct relationship on the survival of the family. The conclusion of the novel revises the boundaries of that family. In this scene, unable physically to supply milk from her own breasts to save the old man's life, she initiates her daughter into the sisterhood of "mothering the world," of perpetuating what Nancy Chodorow calls "The Reproduction of Mothering." Ma Joad is the epitome of the Earth Mother. Critics note that Steinbeck need give her no first name, for she is the paradigmatic mother, and this is the single interest of her life. The seventeenth- and eighteenth-century metaphor of the fecund, virgin American land (women) gives way to that of the middle-aged mother (earth), "thick with child-bearing and work," but Steinbeck holds onto the stereotypical parallels between woman and nature. In our typical understanding of that word, Ma may not be happy in her role, but "her face . . . [is] controlled and kindly" and she fully accepts her place. Having "experienced all possible tragedy and . . . mounted pain and suffering like steps into a high calm," she fulfills her highest calling in the realm of wife and motherdom.

Notes

1. I borrow from a phrase in Elizabeth Janeway's *Man's World, Woman's Place* (New York: William Morrow & Company, 1971), p. 151.

2. See Nancy Chodorow, *The Reproduction of Mothering: Psychoanalysis and the Sociology of Gender* (Berkeley: The University of California Press, 1978), p. 9.

3. Adrienne Rich, *Of Woman Born* (New York: W. W. Norton and Company, 1976).

4. See Note 1.

5. Nancy Chodorow, *The Reproduction of Motherhood: Psychoanalysis and the Sociology of Gender* (Berkeley: The University of California Press, 1978).

6. Hester Eisenstein, *Contemporary Feminist Thought* (Boston: G. K. Hall, 1983).

7. Eisenstein, p. 7. This is a point of view also expressed by almost all feminist critics.

8. Janeway, p. 13.

9. Ibid.

10. Chodorow, p. 9.

11. Janeway, pp. 192–208.

12. Chodorow, p. 179.

13. Annette Kolodny, *The Lay of the Land: Metaphor as Experience and History in American Life and Letters* (Chapel Hill: University of North California Press, 1975), p. 4.

14. Kolodny, pp. 5–9.

15. Ibid., p. 9.

16. John Steinbeck, *The Grapes of Wrath*, Peter Lisca, ed. (New York: Viking, 1972), p. 147. Subsequent references to this work are taken from this text.

17. See the scenes in which Ma Joad explains the conditions under which wives will allow themselves to be beaten without fighting back: pp. 230, 479.

18. Robert Briffault, *The Mothers: The Matriarchal Theory of Social Origins* (New York: Macmillan, 1931). Cited from Warren Motley, "From Patriarchy to Matriarchy: Ma Joad's Role in *The Grapes of Wrath*, *American Literature*, Vol. 54, No. 3, October 1982, pp. 397–411.

19. Mimi Reisel Gladstein, *The Indestructible Woman in Faulkner, Hemingway, and Steinbeck* (Ann Arbor, MI: University of Michigan Research Press, 1986), p. 79.

20. Peter Lisca, *The Wide World of John Steinbeck* (New Brunswick, NJ: Rutgers University Press, 1958), pp. 206–7. Quoted from Sandra Beatty, "A Study of Female Characterization in Steinbeck's Fiction," in Tetsumaro Hayashi, *Steinbeck's Women: Essays in Criticism* (Muncie, IN: The Steinbeck Society of America, 1979), p. 1.

21. Even though this is the prevailing opinion among critics of Steinbeck's women, I repeat it here to emphasize my basic agreement with this reading of the female characters. Steinbeck, like many male authors, sees a close link between woman as mother, nature, and the American land.

22. Gladstein, p. 76.

23. Sandra Falkenberg, "A Study of Female Characterization in Steinbeck's Fiction," in *Steinbeck Quarterly*, Vol. 8(2), Spring 1975, pp. 50–6.

24. Howard Levant, "The Fully Matured Art: *The Grapes of Wrath*," in *Modern Critical Views* edited and with an introduction by Harold Bloom (New York: Chelsea House Publishers, 1987), p. 35.

25. Joan Hedrick, "Mother Earth and Earth Mother: The Recasting of Myth in Steinbeck's *Grapes of Wrath*," in The Grapes of Wrath: *A Collection of Critical Essays*, Robert Con Davis, ed. (Englewood Cliffs, NJ: G. K. Hall, 1982), p. 138.

26. Motley, p. 398.

27. Ibid., p. 405.

28. Chodorow, pp. 60–1.

29. See Kolodny, pp. 26–28 for an account of the high regard men like Thomas Jefferson had for the small farmer. In spite of the benefits of large-scale farming, he advocated the independent, family-size farm, and believed that those who tilled the earth gained "substantial and genuine virtue."

30. Ma Joad's challenge to her husband is that she be "whupped," not beaten. A woman may be beaten if her husband thinks she deserves it, and she accepts it without resistance. To be whipped indicates that she will fight back, and that he must win the fight in order to claim that he has whipped her.

JAY PARINI

The Front Line of Poverty

"I shall never learn to conceive of money in larger quantities than two dollars."
—Steinbeck to Elizabeth Otis, January 27, 1937

By the mid-thirties the genteel tradition of American fiction had to make room for what might, for lack of a better term, be called, political fiction. To be sure, the muckraking and semidocumentary novels of writers like Sherwood Anderson, Upton Sinclair, and Theodore Dreiser had acquired a readership some years before. "I am accepted by working people everywhere as one of themselves and I am proud of that fact," Anderson had famously, if somewhat fantastically, remarked. But the subject of politics was now pushed to the front by the sharp economic and social inequities of American life, and many younger writers began to think of themselves as activists.

The Depression played a key role in this shift of consciousness. Magazines like *New Masses* and the *New Republic* called for "author-fighters" and "worker-correspondents" to join in the cause, which was conceived in rather conventional Marxist terms as "owners of the means of production" versus "workers." Novelists like Jack Conroy, himself a steelworker, came into temporary vogue. Richard Wright, the black writer who would later gain a lasting audience, began to find readers. Henry Roth's vivid portrait of growing up on New York's Lower East Side, *Call It Sleep*, appeared in 1934

From *John Steinbeck: A Biography*, pp. 162–188. © 1995 by Jay Parini and was warmly praised and widely read. Michael Gold's novel *Jews Without Money* attracted a small but sympathetic audience, as did Edward Dahlberg's vividly polemical *Bottom Dogs*. Another populist novel, one that anticipates Steinbeck's *In Dubious Battle*, is *Strike!* by Mary Heaton Vorse. The political novels of Frank Norris, which were written at the turn of the century, were suddenly popular again, and they were especially important for Steinbeck, who avidly reread *McTeague* (1899) in the early thirties.

A well-publicized organization of the day was the John Reed Club, which took as its slogan "Art Is a Class Weapon." The idea was that paintings and novels and poems should be used to influence people, to change their minds and create class solidarity among the workers. Thirty "cells" of this club had formed by 1935, and the New York chapter founded a literary magazine called the *Partisan Review* to promote its ideas. Its politics, similar to those of the first American Writers' Congress of 1935, were (roughly speaking) Stalinist, although followers of Leon Trotsky could be found scattered among the Stalinists. The surge toward radicalism peaked in the mid-thirties, just when Steinbeck was writing *In Dubious Battle*, and it would slow down after the infamous Moscow show trials of 1937, when it became obvious that Stalin was a vicious totalitarian dictator. (The signing of the Soviet–Nazi pact in 1939 was, for most intellectual Marxists of the thirties, the last straw, though some stragglers did not depart the ranks of the Communist Party until the 1956 invasion of Hungary.)

Covici-Friede brought out *In Dubious Battle* on January 15, 1936, and the response was predictably strong, building upon the interest in Steinbeck's work that had been growing in the aftermath of *Tortilla Flat*, which was still on many bestseller lists throughout the country. Reviewers generally liked the book, although many complained about Steinbeck's use of violence: a complaint that would surface frequently in critical responses to Steinbeck's work of the thirties. "It seems that violence in itself has an inherent fascination for Steinbeck," wrote one critic in a typical mode, "that its appeal lies merely in the glitter of the knife, the tearing of the flesh, the hangings, shootings, mutilations with which his work is filled."[1]

Another prominent dissenting voice was Mary McCarthy, who would go on to considerable fame herself as a novelist and critic; she was then a young Vassar graduate, and she reviewed the novel for the *Nation*, calling it "academic, wooden, inert."[2] She complained that the "dramatic events take place for the most part off-stage and are reported, as in the Greek drama, by a breathless observer." With a bravura often found in young reviewers, she passes resounding final judgment on the capacities of John Steinbeck: "He may be a natural story-teller; but he is certainly no philosopher, sociologist, or strike technician."

The violence in the novel, which upset so many critics at the time, was hardly exaggerated, as this account of a strike in the lettuce fields around Salinas suggests, attesting to the level of brutality that was commonplace in this era:

> In 1936 a strike by lettuce packing shed workers was crushed at a cost of around a quarter of a million dollars. Civil liberties, local government, and normal judicial processes were all suspended during the strike and Salinas was governed by a general staff directed by the Associated Farmers and the big lettuce growers and shippers. The local police were bossed by a reserve army officer imported for the job and at the height of the strike all male residents between 18 and 45 were mobilized under penalty of arrest, were deputized and armed. Beatings, tear gas attacks, wholesale arrests, threats to lynch San Francisco newspapermen if they didn't leave town, and machine guns and barbed wire all figured in the month-long struggle which finally broke the strike and destroyed the union.[3]

"I remember that strike," says Willard Stevens, whose father was a strike leader.[4] "John Steinbeck met with my father and the others. He didn't say much, but he stood by the farmers. He knew a senator in Washington and he said he was going to get the federal authorities involved. The way the police were acting made him mad." Stevens adds: "I remember how my father claimed the feds wouldn't do a damn thing for the strikers, that they were on the other side, in fact. He told Steinbeck they were the problem, not the solution." In fact, Steinbeck was skeptical of both extremes and eager to create a balanced impression in his novel, although his sympathies lay with the strikers. Once again, his interest focused on group man; he notes that once the farmers got themselves organized, they became a separate and formidable entity. The influence of Ed Ricketts continues to make itself felt, but Steinbeck's sympathies occasionally seem at odds with Doc, his Ricketts surrogate in the novel; it is as if the afternoon debates that took place in the lab at Pacific Biologicals in Monterey are being played out in the context of this fictional narrative.

The relationship between the individual and the group continued to interest him, as it did many novelists and thinkers in the first half of this century (such as D. H. Lawrence, whose ideas were terribly important for Steinbeck); as a westerner, he could almost not help but celebrate the rugged individual who stands apart from the masses. His early interest in Malory yielded a lifelong commitment to the notion of heroism and the nature of moral action and its effects upon a community. *In Dubious Battle* thus follows the political adventures of one man: Jim Nolan, who quite literally wakes up and smells the bacon. He has been sitting in a chair, stupefied, for a long time as the novel opens. One of American literature's classic *isolatos*, he is a man without a past, having no family, no property, and no visible attachments. He abandons his few connections to the people in the boardinghouse where he lives and takes to the road, having made the firm decision to join "the Party." "I feel dead," he tells the recruiter who has talked him into joining. "I thought I might get alive again."

What he gets, finally, is dead. But in the meantime there is a great deal of life to be had through his experience with the group. Nolan is sent on the road with Mac, an experienced Party man, to organize strikers. They soon arrive in the Torgas Valley, where the task is to mobilize some migrant apple pickers. Nolan watches with amazement as Mac delivers a baby at a makeshift campsite where these "crop tramps" are living like animals, hand-to-mouth. Mac has no right to deliver a baby, of course: he is not a doctor; but he sees this act as a way to enlist the sympathies of the young woman's father-in-law, London, a leader among the migrants. He explains his rationale to Nolan:

> We've got to use whatever material comes to, us. That was a lucky break. We simply had to take it. 'Course it was nice to help the girl, but hell, even if it killed her—we've got to use anything. . . . With one night's work we've got the confidence of the men and the confidence of London. And more than that, we made the men work for themselves, in their own defense as a group. That's what we're here for anyway, to teach them to fight in a bunch. Raising wages isn't all we're after.

Steinbeck summons a sequence of minor characters on the side of the apple pickers: Al Anderson, the owner of a local diner; Dick, the "bedroom radical" who has a unique ability to gather funds from local Party sympathizers; and London himself, whose good standing in the community is crucial to his general usefulness and influence. Mac teaches these men to get themselves "elected" as strike leaders. (The fact that "democracy" is being manipulated does not bother Mac, who is cavalier about ends and means. Nothing concerns him but getting the job done.)

The Torgas Valley Growers' Association gathers the bad guys under one rubric, and they are a spiteful bunch. They line up the authorities behind them, including the banks, the courts, the police, and most of the "respectable" local citizenry. The association is flush with money for bribes, and it doesn't hesitate to use this cash to oppose the migrant workers. A violent chain reaction begins when a sniper's bullet kills Joy, who has been a good friend to Mac and Jim. This gives Mac his martyr, and the conflict really gets underway. An orgy of recrimination and mob action occurs as the phalanx spins out of control on both sides.

Jim Nolan is, as one might expect, lost in the sweep of events. When he shows signs of "weakening," Mac says: "Don't you go liking people, Jim. We can't waste time liking people." Near the end, when Nolan is torn to shreds by shotgun fire, Mac props the lifeless body near a strikers' camp as a symbol of martyrdom, a call to arms for another round of violence. Steinbeck parts company firmly with Mac here. The reader's sympathies inevitably lie with the poor strikers, the apple pickers, who are ruthlessly mistreated by everyone, but Steinbeck is careful not to idealize them; he also goes a long way not to idealize the Party organizers, who use methods of group manipulation that chill the reader's blood. The strikers are generally not so violent as their opponents, but that is probably a result of their lack of weapons and nothing else. They bite, kick, pound, stomp, screech, and burn, flailing at the authorities who oppress them so cruelly.

The characters in this drama are locked, as the line from *Paradise Lost* suggests, "In dubious battle on the plains of heaven." Critics have drawn the appropriate parallels between Milton's epic and Steinbeck's novel, seeing the Party as Satan (red is the Devil's color, with London serving as Beelzebub, Satan's right-hand man. Dick, the "bedroom radical," is Belial, and so forth. The debates about how to proceed against "the authorities" echo similar debates among the fallen angels of Milton's epic.

The Christ symbolism seen in *To a God Unknown* is present again in this novel, too obviously so, with Jim Nolan standing in as Jesus, the figure who appears from nowhere with a passion for the outcast and down-trodden; he ultimately sacrifices himself—quite literally—for the sake of "his people." Steinbeck reinforces these associations in several ways: near the end of Chapter 13 one hears roosters crowing; when Jim is suffering from his wound, he asks for water, in the last chapter we are told that Nolan's "face was transfigured. A furious light of energy seemed to shine from it." And after Nolan's murder, Mac says of him: "This guy didn't want nothing for himself," emphasizing his Christlike nature.

Typically, Steinbeck multiplies the levels of mythical reference, a technique that, in this novel, seems rather crude. Warren French, however, admires the novel's texture and sees the Arthurian legend emerging once more, he notes "a remarkable psychological similarity between Jim Nolan, the central character of the novel, and one of the principal knights of the Round Table, Perceval or Parsifal as he is best known. . . ."[5] Nolan is "a modern exemplar of the chivalric ideals of adventurousness (he longs for action and is finally killed by his impetuousness), selflessness, and chastity."

Steinbeck uses myth in a familiar way to organize his ideas and ground his work in archetypal patterns, while never losing sight of the need to summon a reality that is fresh and concrete. Evoking the lives of its characters in all their gritty particularity, the novel moves beyond a study of social unrest and the oppression of the poor to the contemplation of what one critic, Julian N. Hartt, has called "eschatological man."[6] Hartt suggests that *In Dubious Battle* "deals seriously with eschatological man. Eschatological man so imaged is a creature with a terrible duality of motivations: violent resentment of the social forces which have cheated him out of his rights; and passionate attachment to a splendid vision of an age to come when the furious conflict generated by injustice will have been resolved forever into the peace of a classless community."

One senses this duality of attachments in Steinbeck himself. He had a peculiar and noble sympathy for those who were cheated out of their natural birthright and dignity. Injustice drove him wild; as his sister Beth says, "Even as a child John sided with the underdog." These radical or, more precisely, liberal sympathies bound him, psychologically, to the present struggle, whatever it might be; on the other hand, his philosophical and spiritual drive led him to posit a utopian moment, "the peace of a classless community." All progressive politics depend on this duality, and Steinbeck (in his most activist period) seems to have drawn great energies from this unusually generative conflict.[7]

* * *

Having had good luck in selling *Tortilla Flat* to Paramount, Elizabeth Otis set to work to get a film offer for *In Dubious Battle*. Hollywood was not interested, but Otis soon struck a deal with Herman Shumlin, a Broadway producer, who contracted John O'Hara to adapt the novel for the stage. O'Hara was at this point a much-admired writer of short stories for *The New Yorker* and other magazines, although he had very little experience in writing for the stage. Steinbeck reported to Otis: "Now for the dramatic thing. John O'Hara stopped on his way to San Francisco. I do not know his work, but I liked him and his attitude. I think we could get along well. I do not believe in collaboration. If he will maintain the intention and theme of the book (and I am convinced that he will) I shall not interfere with him at all. He said he would come up in a month with some script to go over. I am pleased with him as the man to do the job."[8]

O'Hara later recalled that visit to Pacific Grove, saying that Steinbeck "had kept him up all night with talk of the phalanx." During this encounter O'Hara firmly insisted that anybody with Steinbeck's gift for narrative and dialogue would be able to write plays and screenplays in his sleep. This conversation further stimulated Steinbeck's interest in the theater, and it set him thinking. He eagerly awaited the O'Hara script, but nothing came of the project. When several months passed with no word from O'Hara, Steinbeck in frustration sat down to try to write the play adaptation for Shumlin himself. This, too, came to nothing, although it did get him thinking about his next novel in terms of a play.

Meanwhile, the Steinbecks came back from Mexico and settled into the house on Eleventh Street in January 1936. The weather was drizzly and cold, and Carol's sinuses began to act up. For some time she had been eager to leave Pacific Grove, and now she argued that it was time to move somewhere consistently hot and dry. The old cottage was too small, she complained; now that they had some money—quite a lot of money, by their standards— shouldn't they move into a bigger house? Should they not buy something of their own? (Ownership of the cottage had been divided among the children by John Ernst and Olive Steinbeck.)

Steinbeck had mixed feelings about his new prosperity. The memory of what it was like to live close to the poverty line persisted; indeed, it was but a few months before this period that he had wondered if he could even make it through the year without taking a job that paid a salary. He was also afraid that if the money continued to roll in (as it would) he would lose something of himself, and that this would adversely affect his writing. A sense of writing from poverty felt like an essential aspect of his creativity, which was grounded in a defiance of his parents' bourgeois attitudes. "The subject of money drove him kind of crazy," Toby Street later recalled, "and this was true even after money was no longer an issue, when he was in reality a wealthy man. He needed to think he was poor."[9]

In April, Carol found a piece of land that ran along a gorgeous canyon in a thickly wooded area some fifty miles north of Monterey near Los Gatos. She convinced her husband to buy the two-acre parcel and to let her build a house there, something that would genuinely be theirs and not a hand-me-down from the Steinbeck family. She was also eager to get away from Ed Ricketts, who tended to keep her husband to himself and to ignore her. (Doubtless, the affair with Joseph Campbell was still troubling her, and the Monterey setting may have reminded her of him.) A local carpenter-contractor who had worked on previous occasions for Carol's father was hired to supervise the construction, and Carol stayed with a friend nearby to oversee the project. The architectural plans were almost entirely Carol's, although Steinbeck sketched in a version of the room that would be his study: a workroom not unlike the one in Pacific Grove. He wanted isolation, and he insisted on having a cot in the room because when he was working intensely he liked to sleep in the same room where he wrote; this somehow bound him, emotionally, to the project. It may also have helped to erase the borders between reality and fiction. The world of the text became everything.

Because of its remoteness, the house near Los Gatos did not yet have access to electricity or telephone lines, and Steinbeck liked these "deficiencies." Although he was not yet besieged for interviews, he had experienced enough of this pressure to convince him that sanity lay in avoiding the press, at least he could be certain that the phone would not ring. The remote setting also recalled the compound at Lake Tahoe where *Cup of Gold* had been written, and this isolation stimulated his imagination.

Back in Pacific Grove, Steinbeck continued working on a story originally intended for children that would soon turn into *Of Mice and Men*, his most popular novella. For some time now the idea that he should be writing plays or screenplays had been floating through his head, and to one friend he said, "Between us I think the novel is painfully dead. I've never liked it. I'm going into training to write for the theater, which seems to be waking up. I have some ideas for a new dramatic form which I'm experimenting with."[10] He fiddled with this "experimental" work for several months, and he had a substantial manuscript in hand when, in early May, his new puppy (a setter called Toby) decided that his master's book would make a good lunch. Steinbeck told Elizabeth Otis that the dog had "made confetti of about half of my ms. book," leaving him with "two months work to do over again." With considerable optimism, he estimated that by the beginning of the summer his "new little manuscript," which he called *Something That Happened*, would be ready for publication.

In early July, with the novel still unfinished, the Steinbecks moved their relatively few belongings to the new house. (In the reshuffle, Steinbeck found an early draft of *The Red Pony* that he had been panicked about having lost. The Los Gatos ranch suited the Steinbecks very well, and Carol was relieved to have her husband all to herself, away from "the boys at the lab," as she called them. She often complained that her husband had fallen "too much under the sway of Ed Ricketts" and his friends; indeed, she felt he was "too impressionable in general, that even his reading had too much influence over his writing."[11] She had shipped two trunks full of quaint art objects from Mexico City, and she filled the house with them now: painted vases, little clay animals, pieces of colorful woven fabric, ceremonial masks used by the Indians. (One night when the moon was full Steinbeck slipped out of bed and donned one of these masks and leaped about the house naked, frightening Carol and the dog. She begged him never to do that again, fearing that he would provoke some ancient Indian deity.

Steinbeck felt happy in his new study, and he got up at dawn each morning to work. As he approached the end of most books, he would grow impatient and excited, pressing to the finish and sleeping in the same room as the manuscript. Without the distraction of Ed Ricketts and his friends at Pacific Biologicals, he worked dawn to dusk. It was, for the moment, "all work and no play," as he told his agent. In a ledger that he kept that summer, he wrote: "For the moment the financial burdens have been removed. But it is not permanent. I was not made for success."[12] When he got down to discussing his short novel, he was no more sanguine about its quality. "It is an experiment and I don't know how successful. It is two-thirds done. There are problems in it, difficult of resolution. But the biggest problem is a resolution of will. The *rewards* of work are so sickening to me that I do more with the greatest reluctance. The mind and will must concentrate again and to a purpose."

Every morning he settled at his oak desk in his small workroom with a view of the canyon, the manuscript spread out before him, always fighting to "find the beauty to put into it." He had a strong sense of experimentation. This story was something new for him: a simple human tale, very bold in outline. He was no longer concerned so much with the phalanx. This tale of two lost souls, George and Lennie, was daringly simple. Too simple? he wondered. "The idea of building too carefully for an event seems to me to be doing that old human trick of reducing everything to its simplest design. Now the designs of lives are not so simple."

It was a "long, slow summer" in which the marriage seemed to be going well. Steinbeck was utterly absorbed as he moved through various drafts of the novel, and Carol seemed content to write poems and garden and work on the new house, which still needed a lot of attention. They were "practically camping" that summer, she said. The hope was that, by fall, the house would be fixed up as she wanted it. Steinbeck's pleasure in the house is apparent in a letter to George Albee:

> I have a little tiny room to work in. Just big enough for a bed and a desk and a gun rack and a little book case. I like to sleep in the room I work in. Just at present there is hammering going on. We are building on a guest room. We had none and really need one. It will have big glass doors and screens so that it will really be an outside porch when we want to open the doors. Dr. McDoughal of Carnegie was up the other day and told us we have six varieties of oaks on the place besides manzanata, madrone and toyon. We're in a forest, you know.[13]

Steinbeck was happy there, savoring the seclusion. His relationship with Carol had become less strained, and this seemed to him another byproduct of the move from Pacific Grove. The fact that his novel was going well only enhanced his good feelings toward the place.

As noted in Chapter 2, the story had its origins in the author's own experience of hoboes—"bindlestiffs"—and migrant workers. Conscious of Carol's accusation that he did not "borrow" as subtly from other writers as he might, Steinbeck became more conscious of his influences. In fact, the relationship between tradition and the individual talent is a complex one, and no decent writer is unaware of the literature that stands behind his or her present text. It would be naïve to call Steinbeck a plagiarist, as some critics have, simply because he often absorbed ideas or, even, whole scenes from other novels. Literature is a living tissue of allusions, and texts feed on and breed texts. Writers may suffer, in Harold Bloom's famous phrase, "the anxiety of influence." More often they simply take what they need and, in so doing, transform the material of their precursors into something of their own. Scott Fitzgerald, no mean plagiarist himself, thought that Steinbeck had gone too far in *Of Mice and Men*. He wrote to Edmund Wilson about Steinbeck's dependence on Frank Norris:

> I'd like to put you on to something about Steinbeck. He is a rather cagey cribber. Most of us begin as imitators but it is something else for a man of his years and reputation to steal a whole scene as he did in "Mice and Men." I'm sending you a marked copy of Norris' "McTeague" to show you what I mean. His debt to "The Octopus" is also enormous and his balls, when he uses them, are usually clipped from Lawrence's "Kangaroo."[14]

In *McTeague* (1899) there is a woman named Maria Macapa who has a relationship with a junk dealer named Zerkow; Maria dreams of escaping from the hideous poverty of her surroundings much like Lennie; like Lennie, she is often encouraged to recite her dream of the good life (although Zerkow torments her with this, whereas George has Lennie go through his litany of expectations just to make him feel better). The rhythms of their dialogue are, as Fitzgerald noted, echoed in *Of Mice and Men*, but the similarities stop there. Steinbeck has digested his source and made something new from it.

The novel was finished by the second week in August and sent to Elizabeth Otis. Oddly enough, Steinbeck entertained little hope that he would benefit materially from the book, which he felt would have low sales. "I guess we'll have to pull in our horns financially," he had written to George Albee, "I don't expect the little book, *Of Mice and Men*, to make any money." The reaction at the publisher was, as usual, mixed—Steinbeck had never yet written a book that everybody thought was going to do well—but Pat Covici claimed to like it, and he said he would bring it out "early in the New Year." Steinbeck sensed no real enthusiasm from Covici, although he was grateful that his editor was willing to publish him.

Covici had in fact been standing firmly behind his new author, acquiring the rights to all of Steinbeck's earlier books (*Cup of Gold*, *The Pastures of Heaven*, and *To a God Unknown*) and relaunching them in new editions with prefaces. Thus far *Tortilla Flat* had been the most commercially viable of Steinbeck's books, and it continued to sell steadily through the summer of 1936. The hostile reaction of some critics to *In Dubious Battle* had, unquestionably, depressed its sales, but it was nonetheless considered by Covici "a moderate success." The fact that Steinbeck appeared to be so endlessly productive was heartening to Covici, who foresaw a long and continuing relationship between editor and author.

In mid-August, Steinbeck was visited by George West, a young editorial writer from the *San Francisco News* who had read and much admired *In Dubious Battle*. The bright-eyed young journalist appealed to Steinbeck to write for his paper; much to his surprise, the novelist eagerly accepted a commission to write a sequence of pieces about the situation of migrant farmers in California. The idea was that he should visit various regions of the state to witness firsthand the conditions under which these people lived and worked. West was especially interested in the success or failure of the camps set up by the federal government to aid the migrants, many of whom were undernourished and ill.

Steinbeck always liked moving on to another project, especially one that would offer him a new kind of experience. He rushed out and bought an old bakery truck—a "pie wagon" as he called it—and transformed it into a version of the modern camper; it was fitted out with a cot, an icebox, a chest for storing clothes, and a trunk full of pots and plates. On August 26 he headed into San Francisco for a meeting with West and his colleagues to make sure that he understood the assignment exactly. He also visited the office of the Resettlement Administration, where he got a briefing about the federal program in California to aid migrants; this was followed by a tour of the San Joaquin Valley led by the regional director of the organization, Eric H. Thomsen.

Thomsen drove Steinbeck down through the Central Valley, and they stopped at some of the camps along the way. Thomsen wanted the writer to see how different it was for families who had gotten help from the government and those who hadn't. The reality of the situation startled Steinbeck, who was unprepared for the starkness of what he saw: whole families lived in cardboard boxes or in large disused pipes; indeed, shelters were constructed from anything that came to hand: an old rug, some straw mats, pieces of driftwood. Food was scarce and expensive, and people in some areas were reduced to eating rats and dogs. Babies were dying from lack of adequate nutrition or proper medical services. This was the front line of poverty in America, and Steinbeck was saddened and outraged.

He proceeded on his own after a certain point, stopping at some of the camps Thomsen had recommended, and everywhere he was stunned by the magnitude of the problem. The simple numbers were staggering: hundreds of thousands of families had arrived in California from the so-called Dust Bowl states: Oklahoma, Arkansas, Texas, Nebraska, and Kansas. They were all called Okies or Texicanos by the Californians, whatever their actual state of origin, and they had all been rudely dispossessed, turned off the land their families had tilled for generations. In 1936 alone, almost ninety thousand Okies crossed the California border in search of jobs and a better life.

The Depression had combined with years of drought, land speculation, and various wrongheaded agricultural practices to make survival in the Dust Bowl states impossible; the impoverished farms were being repossessed by banks and landowners. Another aspect of the problem was the drift toward agribusiness, which had already begun in the twenties; farming techniques were employed to maximize production, and one consequence of these techniques was that unexpectedly harsh winds blew away the topsoil in what were once fertile regions. The already precarious situation of farmers and sharecroppers in the Southwest was miserably exacerbated.

The obvious place for migrants to go was California, with its extremely visible and successful agricultural industry, but they were sadly mistaken about their prospects. For a start, California's large-scale agriculture favored the corporate farm: less than one tenth of the farms in that state produced over half the total produce in 1935. Absentee ownership was common, which meant that hired "managers" ran the actual farming operations. For many years these large farms had been encouraging the migration of badly paid foreign laborers; Chinese, Filipino, Mexican, and Japanese workers were commonplace, although the bulk of them were from nearby Mexico—a migratory trend that began in the first decade of the century and continues to this day. It would therefore not be easy to filter a large new group of migrant workers into the system as it stood.

In *Factories in the Field*, an influential book published at the end of the thirties, Carey McWilliams described the situation: "In 1937 it became increasingly apparent that a basic change had taken place in the character of farm labor in California. Although the change had been taking place for some time, it was suddenly realized in 1937 that the bulk of the state's migratory workers were white Americans and that the foreign racial groups were no longer a dominant factor."[15] The change had begun about 1933, when the Depression had reached its lowest point. In 1925, only a small percentage of the agricultural laborers on large California farms were drawn from the native white population, but the Commission of Immigration and Housing estimated in 1934 that roughly fifty percent of the labor-camp population was native white American, with about one third being Mexican and the rest taken from the relatively small Filipino, Japanese, and Chinese communities. This demographic shift quite naturally created huge problems of adjustment.

One of the many consequences of this influx of white American citizens accustomed to the workings of democracy was that protests about low wages and poor working conditions were inevitable. As long as "foreigners" were being exploited, the press was not going to say a word, but when "regular" white Americans were being treated like dirt, herded into unsanitary camps, left to starve or work for starvation wages, a protest movement was bound to occur sooner or later. By 1935, Route 66, the major highway from Oklahoma to California's Central Valley, was clogged with jalopies, even though jobs were extremely scarce at the end of the journey. In his newspaper articles, Steinbeck describes in stark terms the mayhem that resulted:

> Thousands of them are crossing the borders in ancient rattling automobiles, destitute and hungry and homeless, ready to accept any pay so that they may eat and feed their children. And this is a new thing in migrant labor, for the foreign workers were usually imported without their children and everything that remains of their old life with them.
>
> They arrive in California usually having used up every resource to get here, even to the selling of the poor blankets and utensils and tools on the way to buy gasoline. They arrive bewildered and beaten and usually in a state of semi-starvation, with only one necessity to face immediately, and that is to find work at any wage in order that the family may eat.[16]

Most of the farms in the Central Valley were owned by corporations or wealthy farmers who operated multiple ranches, and their crops of fruits and vegetables had for many years been harvested by semiskilled Mexicans or poor locals who had no choice but to accept ludicrous wages. The sudden surplus of labor led inexorably to grotesque living conditions and, ultimately, violence, as tens of thousands of migrants prowled the valley in competition for a handful of jobs. The makeshift camps that arose on the outskirts of farms were filthy and overcrowded, and the migrants were hungry.

The local people reacted badly to this invasion, as Steinbeck explained: "The hatred of the stranger occurs in the whole range of human history, from the most primitive village farm to our own highly organized industrial farming. The migrants are hated for the following reasons: that they are ignorant and dirty people, that they are carriers of disease, that they increase the necessity for police and the tax bill for schooling in a community, and that if they are allowed to organize they can, simply by refusing to work, wipe out the season's crops."

Police attempted, without much luck, to turn back the migrants at the California border or, at least, to discourage them from continuing on. It was therefore miserable for the Okies, who were mainly self-respecting citizens from the Bible Belt who did not appreciate being called lazy and immoral. In addition to simple verbal abuse, they were preyed on by local vigilante groups and harassed by the police. That a war of sorts should break out was inevitable, although Americans beyond the California borders were not fully aware of the extent of the trouble: another reason why Steinbeck found his assignment from the *San Francisco News* well worth the effort. Like so many writers of this era, he considered it part of a writer's responsibility to bear witness, to address a social crisis with the hope of effecting some kind of change.

The only relief for migrants came in the form of government camps, which were the brainchild of Paul S. Taylor, who worked for the California Department of Rural Rehabilitation. Beginning in 1935, these "sanitary camps," as they were called, spread slowly along the Central Valley. Unfortunately, there was considerable opposition in Washington to this program (tax revenues were obviously insufficient to meet the demand for services, and the original idea of creating twenty-five "demonstration" camps was reduced to fifteen. There were three mobile camps as well: camps that could be moved around to deal with emergency situations.

David Wyatt has suggested that "Steinbeck's journalistic assignments drew him ever deeper into the fate of his culture, and especially toward those who had been discarded by it."[17] And there is no doubt that the author's eyes were opened even wider by his journey through the Central Valley in August of 1936. He went to the Gridley camp, which was just outside the state capital of Sacramento. The manager of that camp liked Steinbeck, and he told him to be careful as he proceeded south: his picture had been circulating—or so he was told. Traveling in the baker's van, Steinbeck proceeded slowly, dropping by Salinas to see how the situation had developed in the small migrant city that had grown up on the outskirts of his boyhood home. "It's a rotten and depressing situation here," he wrote to Toby Street. "This isn't the place I knew as a boy." He stopped at several camps along the San Joaquin Valley, always blending in with the migrants to interview them, attempting as best he could to find out for himself what was really going on.

The federally funded camps were meant as examples or blueprints that could be emulated by the owners of large farms, who were encouraged to set up similar facilities on their own land. Almost none of the farmers agreed to follow suit, so the program cannot be said to have served the purpose for which it was intended. On the other hand, the few camps that were funded did save many lives and gave the migrant workers and their families who were lucky enough to land in them a chance to make a new beginning. Even more crucially, the camps became first-aid centers for people in the midst of a massive health crisis.

One of the original camp managers was Tom Collins, who would become Steinbeck's good friend as well as a figure in his imagination. *The Grapes of Wrath* is partially dedicated "to Tom—who lived it." And Tom did. He was head of the Arvin Sanitary Camp, known by its denizens as Weedpatch. It was easily one of the most successful operations in the program, and Steinbeck was impressed by what he stumbled on. He later recalled his first meeting with Collins:

> The first time I saw Tom Collins it was evening, and it was raining. I drove into the migrant camp, the wheels of my car throwing muddy water. The lines of sodden, dripping tents stretched away from me in the darkness. The temporary office was crowded with damp men and women, just standing under a roof, and sitting at a littered table was Tom Collins, a little man in a damp, frayed, white suit. The crowding people looked at him all the time. Just stood and looked at him. He had a small moustache, his graying, black hair stood up on his head like the quills of a frightened porcupine, and his large, dark eyes, tired beyond sleepiness, the kind of tired that won't let you sleep even if you have time and a bed.[18]

Two thousand people crammed into this camp's temporary shelter, and many were suffering from such contagious diseases as measles and mumps, even pneumonia and tuberculosis. "You had children too weak to stand," recalls one survivor of this camp.[19] "They tried to put those with sickness in separate sheds, but it didn't work. There was influenza, typhoid, all kinds of things. Old people would just sit and stare, and a lot of them died more of sadness than anything else. The younger people were mostly full of anger. They were downright mad. Somebody had kicked them off their land back home, and here they were, with no work, nothing to look forward to. Riots broke out here and there, but they weren't so hard to squash because nobody felt good. You couldn't fight back if you didn't feel good. That was the secret the bosses and police had, and they knew they'd win."

Collins had been raised a strict Catholic, and had trained for the priesthood for a brief while. As one friend later recalled: "There was always about Tom something of the missionary. He had that predatory look in his eye, a way of smiling when you talked. You knew he had your better interests at heart."[20] Collins taught school in Alaska and Guam, then founded a school for juvenile delinquents in San Francisco. After moving to Los Angeles when his school failed, he took a job with the F.T.S. (Federal Transient Service), founded by the Roosevelt administration to deal with the homeless. In 1935 he moved to the Resettlement Administration and became the first manager of a sanitary camp, where his success was legendary and unique, largely because of his instincts for democratic organization. He gave the residents the authority to govern their own daily lives in the camp, refusing to adopt a paternalistic attitude that could have backfired on him; a committee of residents was formed at Weedpatch and put in charge of making rules for the camp and enforcing them. "There was a spirit in these camps," says one former resident of Weedpatch.[21] "It was people looking after people."

Steinbeck spent a week in Weedpatch, following Collins around on his daily chores, interviewing residents, watching and listening, mingling. He took sheaves of notes each night in his pie wagon. Sherm Eastom was head of the governing committee at Weedpatch, and his family (according to Dewey Russell, who succeeded Collins as camp manager) was often said to have provided a model for the Joads in *The Grapes of Wrath*. One must, however, be wary of saying definitely that any single person was a source for a given character. Characters in fiction are often composites.

Steinbeck left Weedpatch in his bakery truck with a briefcase stuffed full of reports given to him by Collins. These reports, which Collins sent to headquarters in Washington twice a month, bristled with wry observations about camp life, with invaluable statistics, personal histories (including health records) of camp residents, and other kinds of information that would be of use to Steinbeck in writing his articles for the *News* and, later, in composing *The Grapes of Wrath*. A born ethnographer, Collins also recorded camp songs and observations on migrant dialects that quite naturally fascinated Steinbeck.[22] The reports were a gold mine for a writer, and he knew it. He drove home toward Los Gatos excited and resolved to do something to help the migrants and their cause.

On the way home he stopped again in Salinas and was horrified by the deterioration in the situation. The lettuce strike had led to violent behavior from both sides: Even the local burghers, the sort of people his father and mother had known well and identified with, had become hostile, and some of them formed vigilante groups to attack the "Red revolutionaries" who they believed were exciting these otherwise docile migrant workers to violence. One resident of Salinas remembers that "a group of maybe two dozen men, local merchants and members of the Rotary, went marching out there to the camp outside town with clubs and rifle butts. They wanted to bash some heads in. Everybody was so mad. But they did solve the problem. The troublemakers were put in a barn under armed guard, and the kingpins were sent away. Nobody was allowed to walk the streets after dark for over a month. The police just stayed out of it."[23]

Steinbeck wrote immediately to Collins when he finally got home: "I want to thank you for one of the very fine experiences of a life. But I think you know exactly how I feel about it. I hope I can be of some kind of help. On the other hand I don't want to be presumptuous. In the articles I shall be very careful to try to do some good and no harm."[24] A check accompanied the letter, and Steinbeck suggested that the money be used by the migrants for raising livestock. He also promised to get in touch with some people who might send books that could be used by the camp's children, whose education was being seriously neglected in these hideous circumstances.

Huddled in his small study overlooking the woods, Steinbeck wrote in short order a general piece on the migrant situation for the *Nation* (September 12, 1936) called "Dubious Battle in California" and completed the articles commissioned by the *San Francisco News*. The seven parts of the series (which as a whole were called "The Harvest Gypsies") took up in turn different aspects of the crisis: the origin of the problem, the contrast between California's older breed of migrant workers and the Dust Bowl migrants, the living conditions as he found them in squatters' camps, and so forth. His approach was judicious and balanced, although a polemical tone underlies it. Steinbeck's compassion was obvious throughout, and he made no bones about demanding justice. At the same time he began editing some of the camp reports, hoping to make a book of them. "I'm working hard on another book that isn't mine at all," he explained to George Albee. "I'm only editing it, but it is a fine thing. A complete social study made of the weekly reports from a migrant camp."[25] This was another of those projects that, for one reason or another, came to nothing.

Steinbeck returned to Weedpatch at the end of September, stopping in Salinas on the way back to track the progress of the crisis in his home town. He wrote to Elizabeth Otis: "I just returned yesterday from the strike area of Saunas, and from my migrants in Bakersfield. This thing is dangerous. Maybe it will be patched up for a while, but I look for the lid to blow off in a few weeks."[26] It was very painful to him to witness the destruction, he said, of "that dear little town where I was born."

The publication of the "little book," as he often called *Of Mice and Men*, was scheduled for winter 1937. As usual, there were mixed reactions before publication. Herman Shumlin, the producer who had optioned *In Dubious Battle*, disliked it and refused to consider the possibility of a play adaptation. Several of Pat Covici's colleagues shared these reservations about the book, although Covici himself remained loyal. The tide turned with some good news in January: the Book-of-the-Month Club had chosen *Of Mice and Men* as a Main Selection, thus guaranteeing a large audience and, of course, substantial sales. Steinbeck told Elizabeth Otis that he found the news "gratifying but also . . . frightening."[27]

The Steinbecks took advantage of their new financial ease, adding some good pieces of furniture to their new house. This included a homemade gramophone, which Toby Street helped Steinbeck to assemble. Although isolated, the house in Los Gatos became a magnet for interesting people. As usual, Toby Street, Carl Wilhelmson, and A. Grove Day could be counted on as visitors. George Albee turned up for a weekend with his wife. The reviewer Joseph Henry Jackson came by several times that winter, as did Tom Collins. Ed Ricketts stopped by on many occasions, as did Steinbeck's younger sister, Mary, who never liked to go for too long without seeing her brother. New friends entered the picture too, including Martin and Elsie Ray, who owned a local winery.

Judson Gregory was a local potter, and he went to several parties in the Steinbeck house off Greenwood Lane. He recalls that "everybody drank a lot, mostly cheap local wine. John was the ringmaster, dominating the conversation, which was usually about politics. He thought the country was coming apart, and that if something wasn't done fast a revolution would break out. He didn't want that. He was no communist, like all the papers said. He supported Roosevelt. His wife, Carol, disagreed with him on a lot of things, and some cold currents went back and forth between them. Sometimes John got out of line and raised his voice or slapped the wall with his hand, and you could see that Carol hated it. I once left a party angry about something John had said and she followed me to the gate and said not to mind him, that he was upset about his book that was coming out. She protected him and kind of mocked him in public at the same time. It was peculiar."[28]

Of Mice and Men, the upsetting book in question, appeared in early February of 1937. The public response was swift and gratifying, taking even Steinbeck's publisher and the author himself by huge surprise. By the middle of February, the book had sold 117,000 copies. "That's a hell of a lot of books," Steinbeck wrote to Pat Covici on February 28, rubbing it in. He was justified in doing so: the book was flying out of the stores, and the press had begun to swarm around Steinbeck, desperate for interviews.

The reviews were mostly respectful, even complimentary, although *Time* sneered at the little novel, calling it a "fairy tale." Writing in *The Nation*, Mark Van Doren embodied the negative reaction to the book: "All but one of the persons in Mr. Steinbeck's extremely brief novel are subhuman if the range of the word human is understood to coincide with the range thus far established by fiction."[29] Ralph Thompson's review in the *New York Times* (February 27) was more typical, calling the book "completely disarming." Another critic, Harry Hansen, went so far as to call the novel "the finest bit of prose fiction of this decade."

Steinbeck's story of two wandering bindlestiffs, George and Lennie, has become a permanent fixture of American literature. The book's subject is the nature of innocence, and it is explored with compassion and skill. The semiretarded Lennie and his guardian, George Milton, are men with a fragile dream of owning land and settling down into an Edenic future. "Guys like us, that work on ranches, are the loneliest guys in the world. They got no family. They don't belong no place," George tells his friend, who can barely understand him. "With us it ain't like that. We got a future. We got somebody to talk to that gives a damn about us. . . . An' why? Because I got you to look after me, and you got me to look after you, and that's why."

Bound by their dream of settling down together on a piece of land they can call their own, George and Lennie walk together into their inevitably dim future. On the ranch where the story takes place, Steinbeck's odd couple meet Candy, an aging farmhand who grieves over his toothless, rheumatic dog, which is finally shot because it smells up the bunkhouse. They brush up against Curley, the evil son of the boss, and Curley's wife—the seductive but rather dim and insensitive woman who unwittingly tempts Lennie and gets herself killed by him. Steinbeck here takes a traditionally sexist view of the world, seeing the male environment of the bunkhouse as a kind of idyll that is interrupted by the evil woman who cannot help herself. She is a creature of her own whims; her physical passion for men and her need for their company. Eve once again ruins everything in the Garden of Eden.

Other memorable characters in the novella are Slim, a "jerkline skinner" who has "Godlike eyes" that fasten on to a man so firmly that he can't think of anything else, and Crooks, a proudly benevolent stable hand with a hunched back who, because of his black skin, is shunned by the rest. Steinbeck is able here to summon a vivid but minor character with a few bold strokes, and this enhances the tale immeasurably.

Ed Ricketts had told Steinbeck that he should not be waylaid by what "could" or "should" happen but by what "did." It is therefore interesting that Steinbeck originally called the book *Something That Happened*. (Ricketts, in fact, suggested the change in title.) The author remains detached throughout, blaming no one for the fact that, as Robert Burns said, "The best-laid schemes o' mice an' men / Gang aft a'gley." Antonia Seixas has noted that "the hardest task a writer can set himself is to tell a story of 'something that happened' without explaining 'why'—and make it convincing and moving."[30] This, indeed, is what Steinbeck accomplishes in this brief, compelling novella (or "novelette," as short novels were often called in the thirties).

We do, however, get something like moral reflection from Slim, the most intelligent character in the story. He is a man "whose ear heard more than was said to him," and he listens to George tell of the dream he shares with Lennie with rueful detachment; he alone realizes that this dream must necessarily fail; the economics of their situation will not allow for success. It is Slim, the "prince of the ranch," who tells George in the final poignant scene that he indeed must act directly in response to Lennie's killing of Curley's wife. "You hadda, George," he tells him in the end, after George has killed his best friend humanely to save him from being lynched. "You hadda." Slim's compassionate nature is signaled by his invitation to George: "Come on, George. Me an' you'll go in an' get a drink."

The novella showed a side of American life that most people had never experienced directly, and Steinbeck's plain style struck readers then, as it still does, as something true and memorable. As simple narrative, *Of Mice and Men* demonstrates once again the raw storytelling power Steinbeck could summon, and the final scene, which teeters on the brink of sentimentality, seems both inevitable and deeply tragic. One grieves, with George, for Lennie. But there are many other layers in this book. For a start, it can be read as sharp protest; the mere act of Steinbeck's describing so concretely the situation of bindlestiffs in California was a political gesture in the charged atmosphere of the late thirties. The author's urgency, his anger at the way men like George and Lennie were being treated, is felt on every page. One might also find various allegorical strands in the text: its mythlike simplicity invites this kind of interpretation. Finally, as the fruit of Steinbeck's inquiry into nonteleological thinking, *Of Mice and Men* may be considered an accomplished piece of speculative fiction, as Peter Lisca has pointed out.[31] That is, Steinbeck examines the consequences of Lennie's behavior dispassionately; the plot was "something that happened," with reference to moral agency. In a sense the story is made all the more poignant because of the author's detachment; he views George and Lennie, and their behavior, from above, nonjudgmentally; their specific human story becomes part of the swirl of human interaction, a swirl that is without a prescribed end. No divine interaction will change the lives of these characters for the better, and no redeeming grace may be found in their demise.

The fact that *Of Mice and Men* was conceived as a play in novella form made it easily convertible to the stage, and it was not long before George S. Kaufman, the famous Broadway playwright and director, approached Steinbeck about making the conversion. (Sam H. Harris, who was much revered on Broadway, was enlisted as producer, thus ensuring a first-class production.) Kaufman wrote to encourage Steinbeck, telling him that his novel "drops almost naturally into play form and no one knows that better than you."[32] He added: "It is only the second act that seems to me to need fresh invention. You have the two natural scenes for it—bunkhouse and the negro's room, but I think the girl should come into both these scenes, and that the fight between Lennie and Curley, which will climax Act 2, must be over the girl. I think the girl should have a scene with Lennie *before* the scene in which he kills her. The girl, I think, should be drawn more fully: she is the motivating force of the whole thing and should loom larger." The fact that she was never even given a name shows that Steinbeck did not intend for her to play a large part in the story. As Kaufman wished, her role was considerably expanded for the play and, later, for the film.

Meanwhile, *Of Mice and Men* leaped onto the bestseller lists. Letters to Steinbeck poured in from strangers and friends alike, as did requests for interviews, readings, public appearances, and autographs. To his chagrin, Steinbeck was often forced to travel several miles to the nearest telephone to respond to urgent requests of one kind or another, most of which proved mere annoyances. Once, a tourist turned up at his front gate with her little daughter in tow, and when she saw Steinbeck she cried: "Dance for the man, darling! Dance!" To Elizabeth Otis, the frustrated Steinbeck wrote: "This ballyhoo is driving me nuts."[33]

For some time the Steinbecks had been hoping to visit Europe, and now they had both the money and a good reason to get out of the country. On March 23 they took a freighter called *The Sagebrush* from San Francisco to the East Coast via the Panama Canal, thus replicating the journey Steinbeck had made more than a decade before. The ship docked in Philadelphia, and the Steinbecks took a train into New York's Pennsylvania Station, where they were met by Pat Covici, eager to waylay his newly famous author for a couple of weeks.

Against his wishes, Steinbeck attended a dinner that very night in honor of Thomas Mann, by now a famous refugee from the Nazis. He had protested to Covici that he didn't have a suit or necktie, but these worries were brushed aside by his eager editor. "I can get you a suit," he said. The banquet was held at a large New York hotel, and Steinbeck suffered through most of it. Near the end, he rushed out into the hotel bar, where he ordered a double brandy and soda. When Covici came to retrieve him, he muttered into his drink, "I can't believe grown men will stand up and say such ridiculous things in public."

He found himself in a bind that would become only too familiar. His growing reputation had turned him, suddenly, into a public person, but his shyness and his essential disbelief in publicity and "society" tugged him in the opposite direction. "He was never happy at parties," Elaine Steinbeck says. "Never in his life. And he always detested public events. He would much rather stay home and read, or write, or talk to friends. Publicity always depressed him." Covici, alas, insisted that Steinbeck give a press conference before he left for Europe, and he reluctantly consented. Reporters and photographers swarmed the offices of Covici-Friede, and the shy author was pictured in the national press the next day (in a photograph that became widely known) sitting behind a desk with a bottle of brandy beside him. Given the emphasis on alcohol in *Tortilla Flat*, it's not surprising that soon the public began to associate Steinbeck and drinking: an association he would never quite shake.

A lot of carousing took place during that two and a half weeks in New York. Steinbeck, when drunk, became sullen, and he withdrew from Carol, who responded badly to this rejection. She became "mad" in a way reminiscent of Zelda Fitzgerald, doing crazy things that embarrassed and angered her husband, thus driving a wedge further between them. One night she stormed out of the hotel after a drunken fight, and Steinbeck went stumbling after her, furious. He lost her in the crowd and returned sullenly to the hotel room. When she didn't return by well after midnight, he grew frantic and began to search hospitals and police stations, aware that New York City was no place for a drunken woman to roam by herself in the middle of the night, especially if she was unfamiliar with the city and its dangers. Not finding her, he called Covici and others, who joined the nightlong search. Carol was nowhere to be found.

When she eventually turned up the next morning, disheveled but unhurt, Steinbeck was beside himself with rage. This incident became yet another in a mounting collection of grievances against Carol that Steinbeck harbored. He was extremely conventional in many ways (a true son of John Ernst and Olive Steinbeck), and he did not like the idea that his wife was running around the city drunk; perhaps even worse, he could not tolerate any public embarrassment. "That unpredictable side of Carol," his sister says, "was too much for John. I think she frightened him. He never knew what she might do next." It must also be said, in Carol's defense, that Steinbeck was insensitive to her needs and, perhaps, even drove her to this behavior by his withdrawal of intimacy. A vicious circle was set in motion whereby Carol's petulance provoked her husband's anger, which in turn drove him inward; the gulf between them widened, further exaggerating their differences. Feeling alone in the world, Carol behaved in a wild or "mad" way that brought the cycle around once more.

Exhausted, the Steinbecks boarded the S.S. *Drottningholm* in late May, bound for Sweden. On the first night at sea, they began to talk about what had happened in New York more openly, and their relationship temporarily became more intimate and satisfactory to them both. Their cabin, however, was uncomfortable: located at the bottom of the ship, it had no windows, and the lighting was dreadful; it seemed "cramped and musty," and they could hear the engine clanging nearby. But the prospect of a long sea voyage and a European vacation was appealing to them both just now. Carol was eager to see her marriage move in a positive direction, and Steinbeck wanted to get as far away from the public din as possible. "This escape ought to be good for us," he wrote aboard ship to Pat Covici." I need to get away from being John Steinbeck for a little while."

Notes

1. Maxwell Geismar, *Writers in Crisis: The American Novel Between Two World Wars* (Boston: Houghton Mifflin, 1942), p. 250.

2. May Ann McCarthy, "Minority Report," *The Nation* (March 5, 1936), pp. 226–27.

3. Contemporary newspaper accounts such as this one were a primary source for Steinbeck. Cf. William Howarth, "The Mother of Literature: Journalism and *The Grapes of Wrath*," in *New Essays on The Grapes of Wrath*, ed. David Wyatt (Cambridge: Cambridge University Press, 1990), pp. 71–99.

4. Interview with Willard Stevens, August 1992.

5. Warren French, *John Steinbeck* (Boston: Twayne, 1975), p. 62.

6. Julian N. Hartt, *The Lost Image of Man* (Baton Rouge, La.: Louisiana State University Press, 1964), pp. 74–76.

7. For a particularly useful discussion of the politics of *In Dubious Battle* see John H. Timmerman, *John Steinbeck's Fiction* (Norman, Okla.: University of Oklahoma Press, 1986); see also Howard Levant, *The Novels of John Steinbeck: A Critical Study* (Columbia, Mo.: University of Missouri Press, 1974).

8. *Steinbeck: A Life in Letters*, ed. Elaine Steinbeck and Robert Wallsten (New York: Viking, 1975), p. 123.

9. Interview with Webster Street. On tape at Stanford University's Steinbeck archive.

10. Jackson J. Benson, *The True Adventures of John Steinbeck, Writer* (New York: Viking, 1984), p. 327.

11. Interview with Allen Simmons, August 22, 1992.

12. Benson, p. 330.

13. Steinbeck and Wallsten, p. 133.

14. F. Scott Fitzgerald, *Correspondence of F. Scott Fitzgerald*, ed. Matthew J. Bruccoli and Margaret M. Duggan (New York: Random House, 1980), p. 612.

15. Carey McWilliams, *Factories in the Field* (Boston: Little, Brown, 1939), p. 305.

16. The articles were reprinted in a pamphlet by Steinbeck called "Their Blood Is Strong" (San Francisco: Simon J. Lubin Society, 1938).

17. David Wyatt, *New Essays on "The Grapes of Wrath"* (Cambridge: Cambridge University Press, 1990), p. 12.

18. From John Steinbeck's "Foreword" to an unpublished novel manuscript by Thomas A. Collins. The piece was eventually published in *Journal of Modern Literature* (April 1976): 211–13.

19. Interview with Eleanor Wheeler, September 12, 1991.

20. Interview with George Sterns, June 1991.

21. Ibid.

22. For a detailed account of Steinbeck's interest in the folk songs of the period, see H. R. Stoneback, "Tough People Are the Best Singers: Woody Guthrie, John Steinbeck, and Folksong," in *The Steinbeck Question: New Essays in Criticism*, ed. Donald R. Noble (Troy, N.Y.: Whitston, 1993), pp. 143–70.

23. Interview with Edward Kastor, September 11, 1991.

24. Benson, p. 347.

25. Steinbeck and Wallsten, p. 132.

26. Benson, p. 348.

27. Steinbeck and Wallsten, p. 134.

28. Interview with Judson Gregory, December 1992.

29. Mark Van Doren, "Wrong Number," *The Nation* (March 6, 1937), p. 42.

30. Antonia Seixas, "John Steinbeck and the Non-teleological Bus," in *Steinbeck and His Critics*, ed. E. W. Tedlock Jr. and C. V. Wicker (Albuquerque, N. Mex.: University of New Mexico Press, 1957), p. 277.

31. Peter Lisca, *The Wide World of John Steinbeck* (New Brunswick, N.J.: Rutgers University Press, 1958), pp. 138–39.

32. Steinbeck and Wallsten, p. 136.

33. Ibid., p. 137.

ROBERT DeMOTT

"Working at the Impossible": The Presence of Moby-Dick in East of Eden

"A good writer always works at the impossible. There is another kind who pulls in his horizons, drops his mind as one lowers rifle sights. And giving up the impossible he gives up writing. Whether fortunate or unfortunate, this has not happened to me."

—John Steinbeck, *Journal of a Novel* (1969)

"The writer who writes within ... the modern romance tradition may not be writing novels which in all respects partake of novelistic orthodoxy; but as long as those works have vitality, as long as they present something that is alive, however eccentric its life may seem to the general reader, then they have to be dealt with; and they have to be dealt with on their own terms."

—Flannery O'Connor, *Mystery and Manners* (1961)

1

"No one is his own sire."

—Herman Melville to Evert Duyckinck (1849)

The following event is such an intriguing example of serendipity that it might as well have been invented. On 23 January 1857, John Steinbeck's

From *Steinbeck's Typewriter: Essays on His Art*, pp. 75–106. © 1996 by Robert DeMott.

patrilineal great-grandfather, Walter Dickson, and his wife, Sarah Eldredge
Dickson, two Massachusetts Seventh-Day Baptists who had undertaken
agricultural and missionary work in the Middle East, entertained Herman
Melville during the writer's extended recuperative journey through the Holy
Land (Melville's travel cure proved nearly as tiresome as his ailment). "I
walked out to see Mr. Dickson's place. About an hour from Joppa Gate. . . .
At the house we were . . . introduced to Mrs. D. a respectable looking elderly
woman. . . . They have two daughters married here to Germans, & living
near, fated to beget a progeny of hybrid vagabonds.—Old Dickson seems
a man of Puritanic energy, and being inoculated with this preposterous Jew
mania, is resolved to carry his Quixotism through to the end. . . . The whole
thing is half melancholy, half farcical—like all the rest of the world," Melville
confided that day.[1]

It takes a Quixote to know one: in sketching Deacon Dickson,
world-weary Melville, who believed he might have written the "Gospels"
in his century (most recently *The Confidence-Man*, his bitter vision of
human gullibility), projected some of his own obsessiveness, morbidity,
and frustration into the portrait. Beyond that, he unintentionally penned
the earliest notice of the future author of *The Grapes of Wrath* and *East of
Eden*, because though Steinbeck rarely spoke publicly of his paternal line,
he clearly inherited the Dicksons' puritanic energy and evangelistic mania
(Walter Dickson contributed fanatical letters to the Seventh-Day Baptists'
organ, the *Sabbath Recorder*), if not for preposterous tasks like farming the
desert and reaping wayward souls before the millennium, then surely for the
equally arduous work—"the ancient commission"—of writing books with
which to reach minds and hearts: "Man himself has become our greatest
hazard and our only hope. So that today, Saint John the Apostle may well
be paraphrased: In the end is the word, and the word is *man*, and the word
is *with* man," Steinbeck testified in his Nobel Prize Acceptance Speech in
Stockholm on 10 December 1962.[2]

In what must surely be among the most unusual of American literary
visitations, Melville's words, it might be said, touched Steinbeck from before
the cradle as well as from beyond the grave. Although Steinbeck was aware
of his family's tragedies and misfortunes in the Holy Land as early as 1945
(*SLL*, 278), it was two decades later before news of Melville's visit to his
ancestors reached him. In Haifa in 1966, on a tour through the Holy Land,
Steinbeck was presented with the journal entry which had been published
eleven years earlier in a scholarly edition of Melville's *Journal of a Visit to
Europe and the Levant* (*TAJS*, 979). Steinbeck immediately wrote to his
agent, Elizabeth Otis: "Oh! there are lovely things in the Melville account
of the Dicksons. I wonder why we have never found it before."[3] And yet
the implications of Melville's visit had started converging at least a decade

and a half earlier, for Steinbeck had long been aware of the "lovely things" to be found in Melville's prose—particularly *Moby-Dick* (1851), "one of his favorite novels" (*TAJS*, 667)—which Steinbeck discovered with full force a year or so before its centenary, when a spate of Melville biographies, critical studies, and editions of *Moby-Dick* attracted public attention between 1949 and 1950.[4]

While at first glance—compared, say, to his contemporaries, Thomas Wolfe and William Faulkner—John Steinbeck might seem an unlikely benefactor of Melville's expressive romantic strain, the fact is that Steinbeck became passionately attracted to *Moby-Dick* and carried on a conversation with it until his death, so that this chapter can be considered a trope of that referentiality, a doubloon reflecting various facets of belated engagement and literary inheritance. Steinbeck's reading of Melville's great book was more than simply a coincidence, an expediency, or a vicarious exercise, but another instance of something profound that "happened" to him like a gifted presence he could not refuse that entered the environment of his awareness, "the warp and woof of . . . consciousness" (*EE*, 413). "The older text," Robert Alter claims, "is not just something the poet reads but something that *possesses* him, and the recreation of the old work in the new is an effort to make sense of that experience of possession, to explain what cultural memory means."[5] Though far different in many respects, *East of Eden* is, like *Moby-Dick*, a searching, questioning, speculative fiction (*TAJS*, 667–68) which points up the difficulties of positing a coherent ideology about the mass American experience. Melville's ship of state (presented through his inflating rhetoric of democratic tragedy) and Steinbeck's garden of Eden (presented through its conflating language of sexual pathos) function as powerful tropes precisely because they are rendered in ironic ways, and in ways that fit in their authors' politics and the shifting aesthetic tempers of their respective eras.[6]

Besides interrogating the deepest psychological implications of malevolence in the universe, as well as exploitation, anger, misogyny, and silence, both novels enact drastic statements on the abuse of power and the nature—and limits—of parental and literary authority. And yet beneath—or in spite of—the overarching mythology of corrupt national and personal identities (expansionism and capitalism, tyranny and dynastic destiny) that imbues both books, Melville and Steinbeck arrive at a humanistic (and hermeneutical) consensus. Just values, they suggest, reside in finely balanced personal gestures of sacramental or imaginative communication that acknowledges Otherness: Ishmael narrating his story that honors language and blesses whales, even as it accommodates their essential slipperiness and unknowableness; Steinbeck's narrator culminating his tale with Adam Trask's deathbed blessing that honors individual integrity even as it underscores the communal burden of complicity. To arrive at these moments, Melville and

Steinbeck produced unconventional "hybrid" fictions—self-reflexive but not necessarily solipsistic—with which to address the meaning of meaning and to lay bare the truth-making process.[7] Indeed, once tentatively completed, that process begins again: Ishmael revisions (and in chapter 54, "The Town-Ho's Story," rehearses) his own drama before telling it; Cal Trask appears at the threshold of revising the sinful tales of his parents. The trajectory of each narrative at once decenters meaning and defers closure in a constant process of reinventing itself.

Keeping in mind that an inevitable distortion occurs in cases of creative inheritance and appropriation arrived at through reading, this essay focuses primarily on *East of Eden* as a work which receives and reinscribes some key Melvillean echoes, resonances, parallels, and strategies. In seeking out these textual affinities and intertextual entanglements with Melville's central book, and in proposing ways in which these realities endure in a modulated way in Steinbeck's work, my purpose here is interpretative and descriptive rather than traditionally evaluative, and is holistic and ecological rather than patently critical. Regarding these avenues of inheritance, I do not think that the scene of Steinbeck's writing was situated in a murderous field of Oedipal warfare, as Harold Bloom has so dramatically proposed, but in a middle ground of transference, an arena of debate between Steinbeck's unmediated dream of originality (which he never realized) and the local restraints of his own imaginative (re)sources (which were always apparent to him.)[8] Of course, *East of Eden* became the site of a certain amount of inevitable struggle, not just between precursor Melville and latter-day Steinbeck, but also between Steinbeck's nostalgia for being nurtured by the past and his desire to transform it. Steinbeck's insistence on reclaiming the operation of free will (never fully attainable but never fully abdicated either) can be considered a metonym for his newly engendered authorial self, which paradoxically wanted to stretch its artistic limits at the same time it sought to accommodate (and disguise) constraints imposed by Melville's text, the boundaries of literary tradition, and of course Steinbeck's own writerly abilities: "My god this can be a good book if I can only write it as I can hear it in my mind" (*JN*, 42).

2

"Great writing has been a staff to lean on, a mother to consult. . . ."
                                        —John Steinbeck, *Journal of a Novel*

When, in January 1951, after several years of gestation and false starts, John Steinbeck sat down to begin concentrated work on the book he had been preparing for all his life, he was at a crucial artistic moment. Steinbeck realized the necessity for a thorough transformation in his writing style, narrative technique, and subject matter. Besides the influence of Cold War politics, personal upheavals occurred in 1948 to propel Steinbeck toward his revolution—he grieved for his closest friend and former collaborator, Edward F. Ricketts, who died in a May train wreck, and he was devastated that summer (and for a long time to come) by a bitter divorce from his second wife Gwyn, mother of his two children (*TAJS*, 614–22). This collision of events turned him inside out: his emotional and psychological wounds figured in his treatment of Samuel Hamilton's death and in his searing portrayal of Cathy Ames Trask's womanhood. A novelist most famous for the objective documentary style, phalanx (group-man) theory, nonteleological philosophy, and proletarian bent of his late 1930s fiction, Steinbeck took a headlong dive into uncharted waters by consciously abandoning the dictates of prevailing literary realism that had marked his most successful earlier novels. He deliberately turned away from the "squeemish" [sic] mimetic mode, "the modern fashionable method" (*JN*, 43) that emphasized tightly controlled movement, circumscribed characterization, seamless omniscient narration, and fidelity to the aesthetic illusion of social realism.

Instead, like Melville leaving behind the mannered successes of *Redburn* and *White-Jacket* and launching into the treacherous philosophical depths of *Moby-Dick*, at a similarly conflicted moment of personal and national crisis, Steinbeck gave up his secure routine and embraced a comparatively naked presentation of self in looser, grander, more expressive mode of fiction.[9] In this crisis of authority, this moment "of profound readjustments" (*SLL*, 359), he realized there was much on the line: "The craft or art of writing is the clumsy attempt to find symbols for the wordlessness. In utter loneliness a writer tries to explain the inexplicable. And sometimes if he is very fortunate and if the time is right, a very little of what he is trying to do trickles through—not ever much. And if he is a writer wise enough to know it can't be done, then he is not a writer at all. A good writer always works at the impossible" (*JN*, 4). *East of Eden* was meant to embody Steinbeck's deepest beliefs in the sanctity of individual dignity, the "glittering instrument" of the human soul, and his advocacy toward the power of language to effect communication if not outright transformation. For Steinbeck as well as for *Eden*'s characters, such changes began in utter loneliness and ended in spiritual humility where language might "establish a relationship of meaning, of feeling, of observing" (*SLL*, 523).

East of Eden is Steinbeck's partly historical, partly fictional epic tale, based on the Cain–Abel story, of several generations of fictional Connecticut Trasks (Steinbeck took their name from "a friend of my father's—a whaling master named Captain Trask" whose family lived near Paso Robles) and quasi-real-life Hamiltons (Steinbeck's matrilinear family) whose lives run parallel, then contiguously, in a sixty-year period from 1862 to 1918, mostly in California. (Each successive generation of Trasks is fated to repeat the sins of its fathers.) At one pole of this counterpoised novel Steinbeck has situated his semifictional, larger-than-life grandfather, Samuel Hamilton, who stands, like Ishmael, for everything potentially sacramental in the fallen world. Against this pragmatic yeoman savant (William James is his favorite philosopher)—and against everyone else in the novel for that matter—Steinbeck sets up Adam Trask's wife, Cathy Ames Trask, the mother of their two children, Caleb and Aron (whom she abandons after she shoots Adam and leaves him for dead). Kate, as she comes to be known, is a seducer, a murderer, the vicious madame of a Salinas brothel, and a moral "monster" of the first order who dominates the book. Adam Trask is ranged between Samuel and Kate. This patently American Adam (conceived several years before R. W. B. Lewis gave the literary type a name) is naïve, guileless in the ways of heterosexual love, and fatally determined to create a dynastic farm on his land. If Kate is the axle of the novel, Adam is its hub. He fails the edenic ideals of his quest, but he becomes the instrument through which emphasis on free will—a conditional situation symbolized by the word *timshel* (meaning "Thou mayest")—permits human beings (his wayward son Caleb first and foremost) to gain the potential to triumph over sin and to return to the wellsprings of their integrity.

This quick plot sketch, however, does little to capture Steinbeck's initial enterprise. In its original form, *East of Eden* boldly departed from tradition. In fact it was a startlingly innovative, double-voice, cross-referential work. On the lefthand page of a large (10 3/4 x 14 inch) lined ledger book Steinbeck wrote daily warm-up letters. This became a kind of running workshop journal addressed to Pascal Covici, his esteemed Viking Press editor, who had, in a sense, filled in for the deceased Ed Ricketts as Steinbeck's latter-day compatriot. These entries formed an informal, personal commentary on Steinbeck's daily artistic processes and his intentions for the novel. Across from the journal, on the right-hand page of the ledger book, Steinbeck composed the chapters of his novel, which was initially addressed specifically to his sons, Thom and John, aged six and four: "I am choosing to write this book to my sons. . . . They have no background in the world of literature, they don't know the great stories of the world as we do. And so I will tell them one of the greatest, perhaps the greatest story of all—the story of good and evil, of strength and weakness, of love and hate, of beauty and ugliness. I shall try to demonstrate to them how these doubles are inseparable—how neither can exist without the other and how out of their groupings creativeness is born" (*JN*, 4). The novel's essential dualism was not only thematic, then, but formal as well.

Unfortunately, the published novel represents a truncated version of Steinbeck's "inseparable" conception. All of the journal entries were dropped (later to be published posthumously in 1969 as *Journal of a Novel*) and many of the direct homilies to his children were dropped as well, so *East of Eden* is a good deal tamer and leaner than Steinbeck planned.[10] Nevertheless, the published version along with the integrally linked journal (it too was slightly edited for publication) retains enough traces of Steinbeck's initial informing vision and spirit to show that he was working at a level of discourse far different from his previous fiction. "In considering this book and in planning for it I have thought of many great and interesting tricks. I have made new languages, new symbols, a new kind of writing: and now that the book is ready to go, I am throwing them all away and starting from scratch" (*JN*, 6). In the process of reexamining the ontological ground of his past work, Steinbeck worked hard to achieve a perspectival position with *East of Eden*, which, he felt, combined "all forms, all methods, all approaches" into a unique order. "I am not going to put artificial structures on this book," he said. "The real structures are enough. I mean the discipline imposed by realities and certain universal writers" (*JN*, 118), of whom Melville—with his deep sense of Manicheism, his abiding awareness of philosophical and aesthetic dualism, and his use of alternating narrative and cetological chapters in *Moby-Dick*—was surely one.

Throughout 1951, as Steinbeck worked at his "impossible" task of finding "symbols for the wordlessness," Melville's masterpiece was a model type and forerunner of his bold experiment: "The admired books now were by no means the admired books of their day. I believe that Moby Dick, so much admired now, did not sell its small first edition in ten years. And it will be worse than that with this book" (*JN*, 29).[11] *Moby-Dick* exemplified the nonlinear narrative and dramatic "pace" (*JN*, 29) Steinbeck sought to revive in contemporary form. Steinbeck's newly adapted technique would allow him to develop his characters not only through the contemporary means of dialogue and exposition but through the older method of personal analysis as well (*JN*, 43). The technique also would allow the writer to slip in and out of his triple role as an implied narrator, editorial speaker, and actor in his own novel. "For many years I did not occur in my own writing. . . . But in this book I am in it and I don't for a moment pretend not to be," he said (*JN*, 24). Steinbeck's eclectic method—"neither new nor old fashioned" (*JN*, 43)—drew inspiration from Melville's phenomenological version of the American romance, with its go-for-broke style, exemplified by mythopoesis, philosophical dualism, self-referential artifice, processive narration, multiple authorial roles/voices, and symbolism.[12]

In this breach *Moby-Dick* became an empowering book for Steinbeck because, while it could not set him utterly free, it represented the fully orchestrated symphony of effects, the encyclopedic canvas, and the atmosphere of mystery and probability that Steinbeck set out to resuscitate in 1951, the hundredth anniversary of *Moby-Dick*'s publication. Thom Steinbeck, the novelist's eldest son, recalled his father first introducing him to *Moby-Dick* that centennial year by reading it aloud in hopes of firing his eldest son's appreciation for reading. He pointed specifically to his father's continued enthusiasm for the novel's "elegant form"—its dazzling layered construction, and its bold, rhythmic, energetic language, and its abundant symbolic technique, characterization, and setting. Steinbeck considered *Moby-Dick* to be a "sacred" text, an exemplary story of human conduct—at once an enduring American culture myth, a profoundly magical journey, and a moving drama of redemption. The tragic story of unrepentant Captain Ahab's doomed, vengeful quest aboard the *Pequod* to slay the white whale, narrated in the alternatingly chatty, philosophical, comical, ironical, lyrical, scientific, literary, and theatrical voices of survivor Ishmael, is a supreme literary achievement, one of "the great stories of the world," the older Steinbeck claimed.[13]

Moby-Dick is also a testament to Quixotic obsessiveness on at least three levels—Ahab's monomaniacal hunt for the beast, Ishmael's countering sacramental desire to poeticize the living whale, and of course, beyond that, the driven Melville's need to create a capacious fictive structure—part epic, part stage drama, part anatomy, part lyric poem—that would incorporate these antagonistic, extreme modes of perception, cognition, and being without trivializing any one of them: "To produce a mighty book, you must choose a mighty theme," Ishmael announces (*MD*, 456). Mighty *Moby-Dick* is a cosmogony, an entire world within the covers of a single work. That world was panoramic, comprehensive, epic, and encyclopedic in its reach and in its sweep and depth of knowledge. *Moby-Dick* attempts to explain ("Let me explain," Ishmael says over and over) the deepest wonders of the human and natural world to Melville's audience: "life—the cosmos and everything in it taken as a microcosm—confronts man as a compelling but insoluble mystery."[14] Steinbeck's obsessive intention in *East of Eden* was similar: he began the novel to explain the world's Manichean bipolarity and sexual mysteries to his two young sons and to introduce them to their roots via his recollection of their ancestors. In his imaginative reconstruction of California's Salinas Valley, Steinbeck chronicled the evolution of his personal cosmogony as surely as the *Pequod* portrayed Melville's on the *Acushnet*.[15] In anatomizing that world—in attending to details about individual characters, geography and setting, as well as the large motions of historical and social forces—Steinbeck too exhibited his own brand of encyclopedic knowledge:

"The kind of book I am writing should contain everything that seems to me to be true" (*JN*, 24).

3

"It is with fiction as with religion: it should present another world, and
yet one to which we feel the tie."
—Herman Melville, *The Confidence-Man* (1857)

While *East of Eden* can be considered a "poetic answering" of *Moby-Dick*, obviously they do not fit like hand and glove; the latter is not a slavish knock-off of the former, and it is simply not true that *Moby-Dick* is referred to repeatedly in the *East of Eden* letters."[16] There is actually only one direct reference in *Journal of a Novel* and, more often than not, Melville's book is latent in *East of Eden*, lurking in the shadows behind and below Steinbeck's private and public texts, which is to say at the informing edges of his consciousness, where it waits to be transformed, revised, reinvested. Its proximity is enough, however, to color a great deal of Steinbeck's novel on everything from the pursuit of artistic form to the achievement of enabling beliefs, as I hope the following section will illuminate.

Both writers were so inflamed by their topics that their enthusiasm cascaded into private realms. Perhaps because they were aware that their respective manuscripts were extremely unorthodox (despite their nominal subjects, both books are as much "about" creativity and the resources of language as anything else), both men seemed to require a specific, trusted audience to explain their efforts. In 1850 and 1851 from his venues in New York City, then in Pittsfield, Massachusetts, Melville provided an inside narrative of his intentions by penning some of his most brilliant letters, first to Evert Duyckinck, but then especially to his Lenox neighbor, soul mate, and confidant, Nathaniel Hawthorne. Melville's letters have a sweep and energy characteristic of his restless, questioning mind; they manifest an air of impassioned self-rehearsal as he ranges from news of domestic particulars to talk of "ontological heroics" (*C*, 196). Melville dedicated *Moby-Dick* to the older Hawthorne, "In token of my admiration for his genius." When the novel was published, Hawthorne's reaction (his letter unfortunately is not extant) overjoyed Melville: "A sense of unspeakable security is in me this moment," he exclaimed in November 1851, "on account of your having understood the book" (*C*, 212).

Steinbeck built his self-confidence and focused his attention by journalizing; his daily letters to Covici, also full of explanatory fervor, ranged in subject from such quotidian tidbits as his preference in pencils to arcane philosophical disquisitions. Through it all he addressed the elder Covici as a mentor and confidant. Steinbeck too wrote his novel in New York and in Massachusetts, where, during the summer of 1951, he also crafted by hand for Covici a special mahogany box to hold the autograph manuscript of his novel. *East of Eden*, of course, is lavishly dedicated to Covici in "gratitude and love." (In his spare time Steinbeck amused himself by fishing and boating with his boys, whittling wooden sperm whales, and visiting the Nantucket Whaling Museum.)

Both books enact a retrospective view of the historical, personal, and literary past. *Moby-Dick* and *East of Eden* rise primarily from autobiographical ground, from acutely felt personal awarenesses and closely observed experiences. Filtered through the symbolic distance created by memory, those experiences are further augmented, if not in fact shaped, by research. Melville reprised his *Acushnet* whaling experience of a decade past; Steinbeck recreated his native California from Manhattan and Nantucket, two eastern islands a continent away from the main geographical setting of his book. Additionally, the opening chapters of *East of Eden* function like Melville's "Loomings" because they evoke through memory Steinbeck's generative past. As with the conflicting "wild conceits that floated" into Ishmael's "inmost soul" (*MD*, 7), Steinbeck's "rich" past looms both beautiful and terrible and becomes an ominous introduction to the book's bittersweet action. Steinbeck's incantatory refrain—"I remember"—announces on *East of Eden*'s first page as surely as *Moby-Dick*'s catchy opening—"Call me Ishmael"—a journey into a world of imaginative proportions vivified by the shape-shifting teller of the tale (who defies narrational propriety); it is a magical world signaled by the most basic and inviting of narrative licenses: "Once upon a time. . . ." In this vein, for Melville "true places" are never "down in any map" (*MD*, 55), while for Steinbeck, the storyteller "must name a thing before you can note it on your hand-drawn map" (*EE*, 6).

If these intensely felt books embody the primal energy and turbulence of geographical space, they also are enriched by literary artifice and allusions. Both Melville and Steinbeck read to write, to use Charles Olson's phrase, so that each book reflects its author's literary researches and preferences. Melville ransacked more extensively than Steinbeck but probably no more shamelessly. Melville's inspired transformation of his literary, historical, and cetological sources is but one example of Ishmael's contention that he "swam through libraries" (*MD*, 136).[17] Steinbeck's borrowings—his quoted and inset texts—were similarly functional and aesthetic. *East of Eden*—his "culling of all books plus my own invention" (*JN*, 31)—draws upon works by Herodotus, Plutarch, Marcus Aurelius, Dr. John Gunn, Lewis Carroll, William James, and Erich Fromm (*SR*, xxxii–xliii). Both novels center on and exploit embedded biblical texts for their own ends—the typological Old Testament parables of Jonah (*Moby-Dick*) and of Cain and Abel (*East of*

Eden) are central to plot, theme, and characterization in each. Plurality—what Melville playfully termed a "higgledy-piggledy" quality (*MD*, xvii)—is further encoded in the many literary styles and discourses; although Melville resorts far more frequently than Steinbeck to puns, jokes, and extravagant metaphors, both writers mix graphic realism with soaring philosophical flights and discursive exposition with rapturous, lyrical passages.

Both writers also create plots which strain plausibility and therefore require our willing suspension of disbelief. This is especially true of characterization as well. In Ahab, Queequeg, and Fedallah, as well as in Sam Hamilton, Cathy Trask, and Lee, Melville and Steinbeck invented characters who are more often allegorical or exotic than physically or socially normative. Many characters have crippled or missing body parts (Ahab's leg, Moby Dick's deformed lower jaw, Captain Boomer's arm, Cyrus Trask's leg, Kate's hand, "wrinkled as a pale monkey's paw" [*EE*, 324]), or they are scarred in significant, emblematic ways (Ahab's lightning scar, Queequeg's tattoos, Charles Trask's and Kate's Cain-marked foreheads), underscoring their links to the nether world of grotesque experience—the "speechlessly quick chaotic bundling of a man into Eternity" (*MD*, 37) and the interminable hell of the Trask family's conflicted relationships.

Kate is Steinbeck's most diabolical example. She is a demented isolato, a female tyrant, who sometimes out-Ahabs Ahab in her cold-heartedness, selfish pursuit of power, and calculating disregard for the sanctity of human life. The similarities between these two sensational gothic characters seem more than coincidental, as Warren French noted thirty-five years ago.[18] Ahab's inordinate pride, his overbearing hubris, and the "sultanism" of his brain (*MD*, 147)—"I'd strike the sun if it insulted me. . . . Who's over me?" (*MD*, 164)—is echoed in Steinbeck's portrayal of Kate—"I'm smarter than humans. Nobody can hurt me,'" she says (*EE*, 323). Both Ahab and Kate are driven by fate; Ahab's soul, grooved to run on iron rails, has its equivalent in Steinbeck's statement that "Whatever she had done, she had been driven to do" (*EE*, 552). Both are reclusive and isolated; bear-like Ahab in his "caved" cabin "sucking his own paws" (*MD*, 153) is echoed by cat-like Kate in the "cave" lean-to of her brothel feeding on her own enmity, anger, and silence (*EE*, 474). Furthermore, both dissemble to advance their secret agendas and both necessarily employ Ahab's "external arts and entrenchments" (*MD*, 148) to consolidate their power over underlings. In addition, both debase the process they are in charge of fostering. Ahab selfishly undermines the economic purpose of the *Pequod*'s owners. In the world of Steinbeck's novel, where "the church and the whorehouse arrived in the Far West" at the same time (*EE*, 217), prostitution purportedly provides some redeeming social value, except at Kate's brothel, where bondage, sadomasochism, and blackmail make it a dirty commercial venture, fit only for revenge and extortion. Ahab's dream of revenge—to get even with Moby Dick for dismasting him—is reflected in Kate's admission to Adam that her deepest purpose is to get even with Mr. Edwards, the New England whoremaster who had once disfigured her and left her for dead (*EE*, 323).

Just as Ahab, who, like some twisted latter-day Prometheus, vows to "spit his last breath" (*MD*, 572) at Moby Dick for mankind's sake, Kate too is totally consumed by hatred—ostensibly for Adam but also for the human race in general, which, in an equally perverse way, she hopes to disabuse of hypocrisy. At key points before their demise (to be discussed in section 4), Kate and Ahab both perform litanies that reaffirm the source of their demonism: Ahab's address to the "clear spirit of clear fire" in chapter 119 ("The Candles")—"'To neither love nor reverence wilt thou be kind; and e'en for hate thou canst but kill'" (*MD*, 507)—finds its cunning duplicate in Kate's gleeful assertion that only hatred, evil, and folly exist in the world (*EE*, 321–26). Partly Ahab, partly Moby Dick, then, Kate's function is central to the dramatic and moral action of the book. Like Ahab's doubloon or Ishmael's metaphor of philosophical whiteness, the depth of each character's personality is judged by his or her reaction to Kate's bottomless, inscrutable evil. But confrontation can lead to spiritual or psychological redemption: just as Ishmael was saved from his nightmare vision of complicity in "The Try-Works," first Adam is reborn from his "nightmare dream" vision and escapes Kate's cruelty, then their son Cal is redeemed as a whole person by knowledge of his mother's tainted nature and by his father's deathbed blessing (*EE*, 602).

Indeed, just as both books mingle mythic, psychological, or moral wellsprings of human motivation and conduct, aspects of characterization and setting overlap and blend into each other. In *East of Eden*, Lee, the Trask family's Chinese servant, is wise, gentle, and nurturing with both adults and children (Adam Trask acts like both at times). Far from being a stereotypical oriental character, Lee plays a variety of increasingly complex roles in the novel. And Lee is also Steinbeck's androgynous man, his feminized man who, in the tradition of Ishmael's "marriage" to Queequeg, remains committed to constancy in human relationships, not in an exotic world elsewhere but in the new frontier of human endeavor, the family of man, the place Ishmael himself prophesied as the sphere of "attainable felicity" (*MD*, 416). In his scholarly investigations into the meaning of *timshel*, Lee replicates the task of Melville's "sub-sub librarian" (*MD*, xvii) by providing the etymology of the book's central symbol word. Like Queequeg's hieroglyphic coffin, *timshel* can save lives by preserving free choice and moral duty and restoring love and integrity. Steinbeck's linguistic symbol empowers select characters to challenge sin by entering the full sacrament of their imperfect humanness, their mutual "joint stock company," to use Melville's apt phrase. Lee has some of Queequeg in him as well—paradoxically, though they are both non-western, they are the most Christian-like people in their novels—generous, forgiving, compassionate, and understanding.

Moreover, both works employ settings which reinforce symbolic aspects of characterization. Indeed, Thom Steinbeck singled out setting as one of *Moby-Dick*'s chief attractions to his father.[19] By this he meant that Melville had made the unfamiliar cosmos of the globe-circling *Pequod* "real" at the very same time he invested it with mystery, wonder, and terror. By setting *East of Eden* in California's agriculturally rich Salinas Valley, Steinbeck privileged its small-town past and sought to make real a world unfamiliar to an increasingly sophisticated and urban audience and to locate qualities of wonder and evil, sacredness and profanity, within its civic boundaries.

Both Melville and Steinbeck believed that their capacity to uncover life's deepest truths was necessarily limited in an indeterminate world, but artistic duty and personal curiosity demanded they try. Melville's operative belief that, "in this world of lies, Truth is forced to fly like a scared white doe . . . and only by cunning glimpses will she reveal herself" ("Mosses," 244) has its parallel in Steinbeck's statement that only "a little" of what the artist tries to do "trickles through" (*JN*, 4). Their narrators' pronouncements are often marked by honest self-doubt, demurral, or denial. Ishmael frequently stops short of the full disclosures warranted in his narrative office by admitting that some truths "would be to dive deeper than Ishmael can go" (*MD*, 187). "Dissect him how I may, then," he confesses of his attempts to capture the whale in prose, "I but go skin deep; I know him not, and never will" (*MD*, 379).

Where Ishmael must "explain" the compelling and indefinite "phenomenon of whiteness" otherwise all his "chapters might be naught" (*MD*, 188), Steinbeck's narrator seeks to plumb the equally mysterious phenomenon of sexuality, the heart of mortal inscrutability: "What freedom men and women could have, were they not constantly tricked and trapped and enslaved and tortured by their sexuality!" (*EE*, 75). Feline Kate becomes the focus of the narrator's didactic expositions—and increasingly indeterminate resolutions—on public and private evil, human fate, and the haunting spectre of genetic determinism. As much as Steinbeck wanted to be positive, getting at the truth "secreted in the glands of a million historians" (*EE*, 130) remains a puzzling and elusive task. Regarding his main character, Steinbeck literally deconstructs his intention by reversing direction in chapter 17: "When I said Cathy was a monster it seemed that it was so. Now I have bent close with a glass over the small print of her and reread the footnotes, and I wonder if it is true" (*EE*, 184). In this self-immolating fiction, even the vaunted certitude of the author's role is undercut.

This kind of disruptive flip-flopping appalled early critics of both novels who seemed unable to recognize that the novelists shared a propensity to improvise and were less concerned with the consistent ordering of a well-made fiction than the immediate compulsions of their creative consciousness. This was especially relevant for Melville's wandering act of composition. According to a letter written to his British publisher Richard Bentley on 27 June 1850, Melville first conceived of *Moby-Dick* as "a romance of adventure, founded upon certain wild legends in the Southern Sperm Whale fisheries" (*C*, 163), and while the exact chronology of the evolution and composition of his masterpiece is not known, it is true that the book grew substantially—even drastically—through at least three distinct periods, and that during those phases from August 1850 through the following summer, Melville was constantly adding, elaborating, and revising his text in a sometimes frenzied and haphazard way.[20] To take the most obvious of instances, Melville changed his initial whaling journey (still evident in the "shore narrative" section of the opening twenty-two chapters) into an epic tragedy as Ahab's role exerted more and more pressure on his imagination and his fresh reading of Shakespeare influenced his newly discovered tragic and philosophical bent.

Steinbeck did not build in quite such an obvious helter-skelter manner, but he too continually modified his novel.[21] Steinbeck was a writer who characteristically "thought out" his books repeatedly in his head before he wrote them (a process which sometimes lasted for years) or who in certain cases knew exactly where he was going before he started (for example, writing toward the scene of Rose of Sharon breast-feeding a starving man on the last page of *The Grapes of Wrath*). But in this instance Steinbeck found himself giving way to autochthonic impulses, especially in regard to characterization (his Cain/Abel paradigm did not hold up in all the ways he envisioned) and plot (his alternate Trask/Hamilton story lines became blurred and the Hamilton plot attenuated). "Dam it, this book gets longer, not shorter. Everything has pups. I never saw anything like the way it grows" (*JN*, 79). His working titles reflect the vicissitudes of his method. The book was called "Salinas Valley," then "My Valley," then "Cain Sign" (each title valorized a different fictive aspect). After he fully realized the psychological significance of the first sixteen verses of Genesis, Steinbeck found his permanent title, *East of Eden*: "my discovery of yesterday is sure burning in me . . . I think I know about the story finally after all this time," he noted on 12 June 1951 (*JN*, 104).

Both novels exist simultaneously on multiple levels of engagement, so that it is impossible to separate the layers of narrational and dramatic strands. Both books resist what Steinbeck called the easy formulations of plot; rather, they are themselves, which is to say they are unique architectural, spatial constructions, even if rough-hewn, unsymmetrical, and seemingly unfinished. From his upstairs study at Arrowhead, his

Pittsfield home, Melville told Hawthorne on 29 June 1851, "I have been building some shanties of houses . . . and likewise some shanties of chapters and essays" (*C*, 195). Steinbeck too imagined that houses and books grew in similar ways (*JN*, 20), and he too characteristically found it difficult to write at all without first inhabiting a suitably comfortable and isolated workplace. Even their distrust of a perfectly finished product was similar: "God keep me from completing anything," Melville writes. "This whole book is but a draught—nay, but the draught of a draught" (*MD*, 145). And Steinbeck claimed flatly at one point, "I do not ever intend to finish it" (*JN*, 14). Melville's embrace of the organic method—"Out of the trunk, the branches grow; out of them, the twigs. So, in productive subjects, grow the chapters" (*MD*, 289)—is subtly paralleled in Steinbeck's narrative position not as an objective recording consciousness but as a convincing fabricator of characters and events from competing "hearsay," "stories told," and "memories" (*EE*, 8). Tracing out the "growth and flowering" of such sources takes the narrator in a variety of unpredictable directions surprising both to himself and, he guesses, to his audience (*JN*, 39, 116).

Clearly, *Moby-Dick* gave Steinbeck the courage to experiment with form, structure, and point of view. I use the word *experiment* with special emphasis because even though *Moby-Dick* was written midway in the nineteenth century it was also the first full-scale experimental novel in American fiction: it displayed a number of daring technical features which have only recently—in the past thirty years or so—become assimilated into postmodernist contemporary fiction. In updating Melville's organic form, artful digressions, and self-reflexivity (which includes frequent commentary on the process of making a book, especially important for the original version), Steinbeck was attempting to forge a fabular, metafictional novel.[22] *East of Eden* belonged not so much to the past or even to his own time but to the future of the children for whom he was writing the book in the first place. I don't think it is too much to claim that, because they turn so often on the hermeneutical implications of the metaphor of reading (Leviathan as text, Queequeg as a puzzling hieroglyphic volume, Father Mapple's sermon on Jonah; Samuel and Lee's central act of interpreting Genesis, and the narrator's own attempt to decode the "indecipherable" language of Kate's life), both *Moby-Dick* and *East of Eden* first challenged, then taught, their respective audiences to relearn the act of reading and therefore not only participate in "the drama of literary performance" but also perform a public function.[23] In the sense that they encourage readers to become not simply consumers of information, but participants in the construction of meaning as well, both are prophetic, perhaps even subversive, texts that have required the passage of time for audiences to catch up with them and to consider them more than "hideous and intolerable" allegories.

In *Moby-Dick*, Ishmael's conversion narrative (which reaches its psychological climax in chapter 96) and his ongoing cetological divagations cannot be subordinated to the dramatic trajectory of Ahab's quest for revenge against the white whale because they are all part of the same "warp and woof" (*MD*, 215) of consciousness, to be treated with "equal eye" (*MD*, 374). Likewise, in *East of Eden* Steinbeck himself showed that the story of his country and the story of himself were so deeply intertwined that they were one and the same. Just as Herman Melville repeatedly crossed into the persona of fictive Ishmael, for instance in dating the composition of chapter 85 (at "fifteen and a quarter minutes past one o'clock P.M. of this sixteenth day of December, A.D. 1850" [*MD*, 370]), so Steinbeck did not curb his desire to break through to the other side of the artist's mirror. How else can we willingly accept that the fictional Adam Trask actually visits the real-life John Steinbeck at his parents' home on 132 Central Avenue in Salinas (*EE*, 385)? Whether we call such effects magical realism or poststructural ludism, Steinbeck and Melville were both ahead of their times.

In this jarring, metarealistic sense, both books are *scriptible* or *writerly* texts (to use Roland Barthes's terms) because they disrupt the normally passive posture of their audiences by employing self-conscious technique and interrupted literary form.[24] "There are some enterprises," Ishmael apologizes in chapter 82, "The Honor and Glory of Whaling," "in which a careful disorderliness is the best method" (*MD*, 361). Steinbeck's method, too, loops back and forth from the novel's traditional dramatic plot to a series of literary apologies or thematic advocacies of its subject matter. Chapter 13, ostensibly about Adam Trask's purchase of the Sanchez farm from its current owner, Bodoni, begins with the narrator's justification of the honor and glory of the human mind, "the preciousness" in "the lonely mind of man," which in turn becomes a reflexive commentary on the process of the novel itself and the necessity of embodying "the freedom of the mind to take any direction it wishes, undirected" (*EE*, 132). To fill in the metaphoric silences and subtextual spaces calls for a suitably imaginative reader with an aggressively acrobatic attitude.

In their zigzag tack toward an ever-receding horizon of truth, both Melville and Steinbeck expressed their experiences in candid, brutal, and often shockingly irreverent terms. In September 1851, Melville warned his genteel Pittsfield neighbor, Sarah Huyler Morewood, not to read *Moby-Dick* because "Polar wind blows through it, & birds of prey hover over it" (*C*, 206); the merging diabolism in Cathy Trask prompted Steinbeck to claim that she would "worry a lot of children and a lot of parents" (*JN*, 46). It should come as no surprise that the former believed *Moby-Dick*, whose motto was "*Ego non baptiso te in nomine patris, sed in nomine diaboli*" (*MD*, 489), to be a "wicked book" (*C*, 212), while the latter felt *East of*

Eden was "a terrible book" (*JN*, 156) which reflected the "shocking bad taste" Steinbeck associated with the greatest literature (*SLL*, 436). When their labors were done both writers felt similar reactions: each doubted the efficacy of his work, each admitted an enormous sense of relief, and, despite the sheer emotional commitment of living so long with their demanding offspring, each spoke of a follow-up—restless Melville "Kraken" (*C*, 213), which turned out to be *Pierre* (1852), and Steinbeck's unwritten sequel, intended to cover the period from World War I to the Korean War. "In my book just finished I have put all the things I have wanted to write all my life," he told Bo Beskow on 16 November 1951. "This is 'the book.' If it is not good I have fooled myself all the time. I don't mean I will stop but this is a definite milestone and I feel released. Having done this I can do anything I want. Always I had this book wanting to be written. . . . There will be another one equally long. This one runs from 1863 to 1918. The next will take the time from 1918 to the present" (*SLL*, 431).

4

"The Pequod's sea wings, beating landward, fall / Headlong . . . / Off 'Sconset. . . ."
—Robert Lowell, "The Quaker Graveyard in Nantucket" (1944)

I began with a little-known historical event; now I'd like to conclude with a quasi-fictive sequel, a fantasy of sorts. It requires "plenty" of Melville's ample "sea-room" ("Mosses," 246), as well as portions of Steinbeck's impossible horizons and undirected directions. My fantasy circles back on an event that I am not positive ever happened but certainly could have. It is an event which can't necessarily be proven by external facts or recorded history but seems nonetheless plausible, given the circumstances and the results.

On the afternoon of Wednesday, 15 August 1951, I imagine John Steinbeck could easily have traveled the six miles or so from "Footlight" (the Steinbecks' rented cottage on Baxter Road next door to the Coast Guard's Sankaty Point Light in Siasconset) to the Unitarian Church in Nantucket for the Historical Association's "Melville Memorial" Observance marking the one-hundredth anniversary of the publication of *Moby-Dick*. It was another "muggy and thick and foggy" day (*SLL*, 428), as it had been for over a week, and Steinbeck was playing hooky from the manuscript of *East of Eden*, which he had daily been composing since February, first in New York City, then from 18 June onward, in 'Sconset, where he was summering with his wife Elaine and sons Thom and John.

In true Melvillean style, Steinbeck had become a "fast fish," deeply hooked by his manuscript, as much pursuing it as he was pursued by it.

Since his arrival on the island he had worked obsessively in the cottage's small upstairs back study. The window of his writing room faced inland, away from the distracting panorama of the ocean (the front of the cottage was no more than thirty feet from the high-flown edge of 'Sconset Bluffs). Steinbeck worked on his "big" novel right into the previous weekend, that is, through Sunday, 12 August. Then he took a few days off—"the longest layoff since I started the book" (*JN*, 145)—to prepare the Japanese lanterns and the twenty-one-gun salute from his new Abercrombie and Fitch marine cannon, as well as some other surprises for his wife's birthday party on Tuesday the 14th (*TAJS*, 689–90). The birthday celebration was clearly a success: "The birthday was fine," he noted on Thursday, 16 August (*JN*, 145). And to his agent, Elizabeth Otis, he boasted in a letter that same day that the party "was a humdinger and I think Elaine was happy with it" (*SLL*, 427).

That Thursday also, Steinbeck made a fairly long entry in his working journal in which he assessed his own mood and state of mind and indicated his plan of attack for the final section of the novel (emphasizing the realistic development of Cal Trask and Abra Bacon), though he did not actually write anything at all on the novel that day (*JN*, 145–46). In fact he took several more days off—that is, 17, 18, and 19 August—before launching into Book Four on Monday, 20 August (*JN*, 146). This much is known and recorded; meantime, mysteriously, Steinbeck said nothing at all about his whereabouts on Wednesday, 15 August.[25]

Now comes the speculative part of my tale, which concerns that lacuna, that conspicuous silence, upon which even his widow and his private diary could shed no light. On the 15th, I imagine, still a little tired from having completed Book Three of *East of Eden* on 12 August (that is, all the way through chapter 33, or more than two-thirds of the entire novel), Steinbeck treated himself to an extra day off; unmoored from his manuscript, but still in a celebratory mood, he took in—and I will qualify this by saying in thought if not in deed, spiritually, if not corporeally—the Historical Society's Melville Memorial Meeting which, as I said earlier, was convened to celebrate the centenary of *Moby-Dick*, and the ninety-ninth anniversary of Melville's first—and only—visit to Nantucket (Melville published *Moby-Dick*, with its eighty-eight references to Nantucket, before he had ever set foot on the island). Steinbeck too was already attuned to the significance of Nantucket as an historical, cultural, and literary site, for three months earlier he had written to Otis to discuss the feasibility of doing a "pet project—a set of informal but informative articles about the island of Nantuckett [sic]."[26] His requisite curiosity about the place and its cultural history was matched by his energetic sense of belonging: "This island is wonderful. I feel at home here. I wonder if it is my small amount (1/4) of my New England blood operating. . . . I never felt better about working" (*JN*, 107).

Steinbeck might have been aware of the Melville meeting since at least Saturday, 4 August, for the *Nantucket Inquirer and Mirror* ran this notice on its front page: "'Melville Memorial' To Be Held on Wednesday, Aug. 15th." And it might have been of interest to him that besides the main speaker, Wilson Heflin, two of Melville's granddaughters were slated to appear also—Mrs. Eleanor Melville Metcalf and Mrs. Frances T. Osborne. As it turned out, Melville's descendants were unable to attend (thereby scuttling an unimaginably spectacular ending to this essay), but the presentation by Professor Heflin on "Melville and Nantucket" went ahead as scheduled, as did historian Edouard Stackpole's introductory talk. The event was covered in the *Inquirer and Mirror* on Saturday, 18 August 1951 (p. 3); the report makes no mention of Steinbeck's being present, though he could have slipped in unnoticed. All in all, the celebration of Melville and his relations on the very island Steinbeck was then visiting, and especially the praise of Melville's most famous book—*Moby-Dick*—had a redoubled effect on Steinbeck.

If this fantasy about Steinbeck's "attendance" is so outrageous that it strains credulity, I am quick to counter that, in these revisionist times, his physical presence isn't the real point. For whatever reason, during that seven-day hiatus from his manuscript, Steinbeck dove back into his copy of *Moby-Dick* (Willard Thorp's edition, or maybe Leon Howard's), perhaps by reading passages to his sons and in other appropriate ways meditating about the life-and-death issues, the mysteries of iniquity, that Melville's novel raises but never quite answers. When Steinbeck resumed writing *East of Eden* again on Monday, 20 August, *Moby-Dick* manifested itself in the same way a submerged whale can suddenly breach and make its presence palpably known.

Chapter 34, one of Steinbeck's major discursive chapters, concerns the world's central story, the battle of good and evil, which is also one of *Moby-Dick*'s main themes. There is an interior signature at work that, if I read it properly, shows Steinbeck imitating Melvillean discourse in the penultimate paragraph of his newly penned chapter: "In uncertainty I am certain that underneath their topmost layers of frailty men want to be good and want to be loved" (*EE*, 414). That paradoxical diction—"uncertain certainty"—and that hierarchical valuation—"topmost layers"—are Melvillean syntactical constructions, signifying that Melville's text had merged into Steinbeck's present moment. Even Steinbeck's organizing strategy in chapter 34 simulates Melville's. In chapter 96, "The Try-Works," Ishmael's warning on the deadening effects of fire ("Look not too long in the face of fire, O man! Never dream with thy hand on the helm!"), is supported by his pointed reference to a classic text—Solomon *Ecclesiastes*—whose "fine hammered steel of woe" underscores the chapter's theme of human vanity and accountability (*MD*, 424).

These elements, substantially grounded and enriched by the sad tale of Perth, the *Pequod's* blacksmith (chapter 112), are paralleled in Steinbeck's literary allusions to Herodotus's story of Solon and Croesus in *The Histories*. This becomes a cautionary tale that concerns the apocryphal issue of human vanity and good fortune and which in turn mirrors Steinbeck's own proposition on universal accountability: "It seems to me that if you or I must choose between two courses of thought or action, we should remember our dying and try so to live that our death brings no pleasure in the world" (*EE*, 415). In Steinbeck's drive toward resolving these knotty issues, the final paragraph of chapter 34 corresponds to the final paragraph of Melville's chapter 105, "Does the Whale's Magnitude Diminish?—Will He Perish?" In Steinbeck's line—"And it occurs to me that evil must constantly respawn, while good, while virtue, is immortal" (*EE*, 415)—there are resonances of Melville's belief that "Wherefore, for all these things, we account the whale immortal in his species" (*MD*, 462). *Moby-Dick* and *East of Eden* are hymns to the persistence of beneficence in whatever form it is to be found.

Further, the outrageous vanity of Ahab's realization—"now I feel my topmost greatness lies in my topmost grief"—in chapter 135, "The Chase—The Third Day," is echoed in the hellbent personal attitudes of two other tyrannical captains of industry, Rockefeller and Hearst, whom Steinbeck pillories in chapter 34 as grasping, satanic men incapable of proper human love. Moreover, Ahab's final condition—"'Am I cut off from the last fond pride of meanest shipwrecked captains? Oh, lonely death on lonely life!'" (*MD*, 571)—presages the demise of Kate, who becomes repentant for her dastardly actions only by default, only minutes before her untoward suicide.

Here we read Steinbeck reading Melville, but with an inevitable twist, a meaningful and willed reinscription. Where Promethean Ahab perishes in his unmediated final effort to penetrate the whale's imprisoning "wall" of "inscrutable malice," to thrust through the pasteboard mask of reality (believing he can still insinuate the ultimate purpose of the universe, can revenge himself—and therefore mankind—against the evil symbolized by the White Whale's agency), Kate penetrates through her "wall" of self and finds a principle of vacancy on the nether side of consciousness; this enervating emptiness is so horrifying that it decenters and stalls all questions of moral purpose or ethical behavior. If Kate gains a modicum of sympathy in the way Melville, for example, had briefly raised Ahab's humanity in chapter 132, "The Symphony," it is quickly subverted by the ironic legacy of her will: her son Aron would live "all his life on the profits from a whorehouse" (*EE*, 583), a figuration ultimately no less ironic and far-reaching than Ishmael's being saved from drowning by Queequeg's coffin. In this bizarre moment of climax, Kate too remains as lonely and isolated in death as she had been in life: "She was cold and desolate, alone and desolate" (*EE*, 552). After harpooning Moby Dick, Ahab dies a terrible death—partly willed, partly fated (in a sense, he too commits suicide)—garroted by the very whale line he has just thrown; yanked from the small boat, he disappears "ere the crew knew he was gone" (*MD*, 572). First Ahab, then the *Pequod* dissolve into nothingness, pass "out of sight" into the spinning vortex of the ocean. In much the same way Kate shrinks in terror to nothingness, too: "The gray room darkened and the cone of light flowed and rippled like water . . . as she grew smaller and smaller and then disappeared—and she had never been" (*EE*, 554). Both Ahab and Kate seem in the end to have been consumed by divergent aspects of a similar kind of monomania; their overweening sense of the difference of their differences collapses in on them, so that in their lust for destruction both can be said to deconstruct their identities before our eyes.

From first to last, *East of Eden* reveals that Steinbeck was alive to the multiple implications of Melville's theme, style, technique, and characterization. In the wondrous geography of the storytellers' world, for which we are required (at least briefly when entering the terrain of romance) to suspend our capacity for disbelief, anything can happen in the net of narrative: characters can be utterly good or blatantly evil; a ghostly Parsee can prophesy the future and aged Chinese savants can undertake the study of Hebrew in order to interpret a single word; a man, grievously insulted by the universe, can find in all the oceans of the world the lone whale which caused his treachery, while another man, wounded by marital treachery for ten years, can find the courage to redeem himself and his son by granting the gift of free will (like Ahab, Adam lacks the "low, enjoying power" and, through most of Steinbeck's novel, is "damned in the midst of Paradise!"); and finally, authors can perform dazzling feats of narrative sleights-of-hand that astound, perplex, and delight us.

In our daylight hours we might cavil at the apparent inconsistencies and flaws in both books (they are full of anomalies, factual contradictions, and lapses), but at night, say, when we take up *Moby-Dick* or *East of Eden* as we once might have done when we were younger and our reading intentions were perhaps purer or more accommodating, these books strike us as being resolutely unsubordinated to real life. Their consistency—their narrative logic—is closer to the world of dreams, which is to say it is internal, metaphoric, and poetical, because it is born out of and sustained by a continuing human need to tell and to hear stories which are frighteningly moving and finally somehow mysterious: "A child may ask, 'What is the world's story about?' And a grown man or woman may wonder, 'What way will the world go?'" (*EE*, 413). Certainly in originally addressing his book to his sons, Steinbeck—as John Ditsky claimed two decades ago—"knew what he was doing."[27] *East of Eden*—like *Moby-Dick*—is a book that in the very best sense is intended first for the child in all of us, then the grown-up. If, to jaded adult readers, *East of Eden* fails to be completely convincing, it is nevertheless a magnificent undertaking because again, like *Moby-Dick*, it is a book whose scope of vision, risk-taking technique, and assault on the impossible are not only huge, compelling gestures but are their own reasons for being. To read either of these scriptural texts in the right spirit of faith requires that we emulate "archangel" Hawthorne and look past "the imperfect body, and embrace the soul" (*C*, 213).

5

"He expands and deepens down, the more I contemplate him. . . ."
—Herman Melville, "Hawthorne and His Mosses" (1850)

In much the same way that Hawthorne's writings dropped "germinous seeds" into the "hot soil" of Melville's soul" ("Mosses," 250), so Melville's book continued to infiltrate Steinbeck's. And if Herman Melville penned the first review of the double-edged Steinbeckian character, Steinbeck himself continued to return the favor a century later. Besides his involvement in Sag Harbor's Old Whalers Festival and his help in founding the International Whaleboat Competition in which contestants attempted to harpoon "Mobile Dick" each year (*TAJS*, 953), Steinbeck never paid homage to Melville with more spritely gamesomeness than in his last novel, *The Winter of Our Discontent*, which is set in New Baytown, Long Island, a former East Coast whaling center modeled on Sag Harbor. Steinbeck's protagonist, Ethan Allen Hawley, descendent of whaling captains, tells Red Baker, an Irish setter: "Read *Moby-Dick*, dog. That's my advice to you."[28] Hawley's playful words echo this challenge in chapter 79, "The Prairie": "Read it if you can," Ishmael says as he meditates on the "wrinkled hieroglyphics" of the sperm whale's "sublime" brow (*MD*, 347).

As book and cultural icon, sublime *Moby-Dick* exerted more than mere literary influence on Steinbeck. It became a spiritual forerunner, a fountain of right knowledge, an enabling text, and a continuing reference point for Steinbeck's own headaches with the authority of critical valuation. Wounded by Arthur Mizener's front-page attack in the 9 December 1962 edition of the *New York Times Book Review*—"Does a Moral Vision of the Thirties Deserve a Nobel Prize?"—Steinbeck composed a ruminative, defensive letter to Pascal Covici invoking an analogy with Melville's reception: "You can almost hear . . . Mizener's guffaws of rage if a book should come out called Moby Dick." Twentieth-century reviews "would do just what the critics did when it was published," Steinbeck asserted facetiously (*S&C*, 230). Steinbeck's conception of *Moby-Dick*'s American reception (in Britain, *The Whale* fared far better) was in the main quite accurate, especially when one considers the myopic and fault-finding reaction of Melville's friend, Evert Duyckinck, editor of the taste-making *Literary World* (Melville canceled his subscription and satirized the journal and its editor in his next book, *Pierre*).

That there was something conspiratorial in *Moby-Dick*'s commercial and critical failure became a fixed idea with Steinbeck in the 1960s; it offered added proof that certain writers—despite their innate worth or worldly acclaim—remain outside the walls of literature's holy citadel. If it increased Steinbeck's contempt for critics, it also increased his regard for fellow writers, Melville first and foremost. Steinbeck's defensive posture is apparent in his sketch of American literature that appears toward the end of the nonfictional *America and Americans*, his last book: "At the time when the Golden Age of classic writing was flourishing in the East Coast centers of learning, when the accepted were members of an establishment endowed with keys to the heaven of literary acceptance, at this very time Herman Melville was writing *Moby Dick*, the first edition of which did not sell out for forty years" (*A&A*, 134). Melville's realization in "Hawthorne and His Mosses"—that all portraiture is self-portrayal (249)—subtly infuses Steinbeck's summary passage, so that its meaning cuts both ways—toward the melancholic and farcical, toward the Quixotic and puritanical, toward the past and present, toward the quick and the dead, toward quotation and invention. Thus Steinbeck's signification—at once his "little lower layer" of homage and lament—was his way of completing the circuit of Melville's vested presence and fulfilling his long sojourn of "working at the impossible."

Notes

1. Herman Melville, "Journal 1856–57," in *Journals*, ed. Howard C. Horsford with Lynn Horth, vol. 15, *The Writings of Herman Melville*, ed. Harrison Hayford, Hershel Parker, and G. Thomas Tanselle (Evanston and Chicago: Northwestern University Press and Newberry Library, 1989), 93–94. All references to Melville's works in this essay will be to the following editions. *Moby-Dick or The Whale*, ed. Harrison Hayford, Hershel Parker, and G. Thomas Tanselle, vol. 6, *The Writings of Herman Melville* (Evanston and Chicago: Northwestern University Press and Newberry Library, 1988) (hereafter cited as *MD*). "Hawthorne and His Mosses," in *The Piazza Tales and Other Prose Pieces 1839–1860*, ed. Harrison Hayford, Alma A. MacDougall, and G. Thomas Tanselle, vol. 9, *The Writings of Herman Melville* (Evanston and Chicago: Northwestern University Press and Newberry Library, 1987) (hereafter cited as "Mosses"). *Correspondence*, ed. Lynn Horth, vol. 14, *The Writings of Herman Melville* (Evanston and Chicago: Northwestern University Press and Newberry Library, 1993) (hereafter cited as *C*).

2. John Steinbeck, *Speech Accepting the Nobel Prize for Literature* (New York: Viking Press, 1962), 10. Steinbeck speech is reprinted in *The Portable Steinbeck*, ed. Pascal Covici Jr. (New York: Viking Press, 1971), 690–92.

3. "John Steinbeck to Elizabeth Otis, 19 February 1966" (*SCSU*, 77). Steinbeck continued: "My grandmother certainly did marry a German and they did produce at least one hybrid vagabond, namely me." Although most of this account of the Melville–Dickson visit was available as early as 1951 in Jay Leyda's two-volume chronicle, *The Melville Log: A Documentary Life of Herman Melville* (New York: Harcourt, Brace, 1951), which Steinbeck owned but probably only browsed in (*SR*, 69), he did not learn of it until this moment in 1966, when a staff member at the American Embassy showed him a copy of Howard C. Horsford's edition of Melville's *Journal of a Visit to Europe and the Levant, October 11, 1856– May 6, 1857* (Princeton: Princeton University Press, 1955). As early as 1962 Steinbeck expressed interest in writing about the Dickson group's outrages in the Holy Land, where members of the family had been murdered and raped by marauding Bedouins, but the full saga never came to pass. See John Steinbeck, "Letters to Alicia," *Long Island Newsday* 12 February 1966, 3W, and his account in *America and Americans* (New York: Viking Press, 1966), 59, 65 (hereafter cited as *A&A*). For background on the Dicksons in Palestine and their significance—largely unremarked upon by biographers—see my "Steinbeck's Other Family: New Light on *East of Eden*?" *Steinbeck Newsletter* 7 (Winter 1994): 1–4.

4. Newton Arvin, *Herman Melville* (New York: William Sloane, 1950), Richard Chase, *Herman Melville: A Critical Study* (New York: Macmillan, 1949), and Geoffrey Stone, *Melville* (New York: Sheed and Ward, 1949) are biographies that all appeared in this brief period. Howard Vincent *The Trying-out of "Moby-Dick"* (Boston: Houghton Mifflin, 1949) was a full-fledged study of Melville's sources and his book's composition. Several editions of *Moby-Dick* were marketed too: by Maxwell Geismar (New York: Pocket Books, 1949); Sherman Paul (New York: Dutton [Everyman's Library], 1950); and Leon Howard (New York: Modern Library, 1950). It is not possible to tell precisely when Steinbeck first encountered *Moby-Dick*. It might have been prior to 1949 or 1950, but I have found no documentary evidence to support that contention. My surmise is that Steinbeck's introduction to Melville's book occurred as a result of the publicity preceding and surrounding the centenary of *Moby-Dick*'s publication in 1951. Around that time or a little afterwards, Steinbeck acquired Willard Thorp edition of *Moby-Dick* (New York: Oxford University Press, 1947), Leyda *The Melville Log*, and Leon Howard *Herman Melville: A Biography* (Berkeley: University of California Press, 1951) (*SR*, 79).

5. Robert Alter, *The Pleasures of Reading in an Ideological Age* (New York: Touchstone Books, 1990), 134. "We are as much informed of a writer's genius by what he selects as by what he originates," Ralph Waldo Emerson proposed in an 1859 essay. See "Quotation and Originality," in *Letters and Social Aims*, vol. 8 of the Centenary Edition of *The Complete Works of Ralph Waldo Emerson*, ed. Edward Waldo Emerson (Boston: Houghton Mifflin, 1904), 194.

6. Ironically, *Moby-Dick*'s triumph as a work of art and the wholesale embrace of Herman Melville as a great writer belong more to our century than to his own. Melville's surge to fame as an American literary genius, the canonization of his formally innovative *Moby-Dick* as a central American text, and the growing critical acceptance of the romance as an indigenous and potentially hegemenous American literary form (because of, among other things, its antisociety values), were all occurring in the late forties. It seems reasonable to suggest that Steinbeck's 1949 decision to abandon the patently communitarian thrust of his early fiction in favor of the importance of creative individuality was not only occasioned by his own experiences in the Soviet Union in 1947 (documented in *A Russian Journal*, published by Viking Press in 1948) but also by the critical dynamics of the post–World War II era, including efforts to promote American exceptionalism and a "new liberalism" encoded, for instance, in critic/biographer Richard Chase's 1949 study of Melville (especially

his preface). During the Cold War, then, phalanx organization and totalitarianism were out; individuality, free will, moral choice, native experience, and direct personal statements were in: "And this I believe: that the free, exploring mind of the individual human is the most valuable thing in the world.... And this I must fight against: any idea, religion, or government which limits or destroys the individual" (*EE*, 32). Not surprisingly, Ishmael and Samuel Hamilton represent models of antiauthoritarian individuation; tyrannical Ahab and Kate go down to defeat. See Donald E. Pease's suggestive discussion of Melville and the Cold War, "Melville and Cultural Persuasion," chap. 7 of his *Visionary Compacts: American Renaissance Writings in Cultural Contexts* (Madison: University of Wisconsin Press, 1987), 235–75. Although he mentions Steinbeck only in passing, Thomas Hill Schaub's *American Fiction in the Cold War* (Madison: University of Wisconsin Press, 1991) presents a theoretical way of situating *East of Eden* in the era's quest for a "new liberalism" (vii). For an instructive critique of the romance tradition's privileged position at mid-century, see William Ellis, *The Theory of the American Romance: An Ideology in American Intellectual History* (Ann Arbor, MI: UMI Research Press, 1989), and especially William V. Spanos, *The Errant Art of "Moby-Dick:" The Canon, the Cold War, and the Struggle for American Studies* (Durham, NC: Duke University Press, 1995), 12–36.

7. Joseph N. Riddel, *Purloined Letters: Originality and Repetition in American Literature*, ed. Mark Bauerlein (Baton Rouge: Louisiana State University Press, 1995), 79. The introduction by Joseph G. Kronik and Mark Bauerlein states: "reflexivity remains a critical component of the [American] work, but totalization and closure are dismissed . . . as a fundamental misconception of writing" (15). Robert Alter notes such works consistently convey "a sense of the fictional world as an authorial construct set up against a background of literary tradition and convention." See his *Partial Magic: The Novel as a Self-Conscious Genre* (Berkeley: University of California Press, 1975), xi. For an ambitious reading of reflexivity in *Moby-Dick*, see A. Robert Lee, "*Moby-Dick*: The Tale and the Telling," in *New Perspectives on Melville*, ed. Faith Pullin (Kent, OH: Kent State University Press, 1978), 86–127; and on similar aspects in *East of Eden*, consult Louis Owens, "The Mirror and the Vamp: Invention, Reflection, and Bad, Bad Cathy Trask in *East of Eden*," in *Writing the American Classics*, eds. James Barbour and Tom Quirk (Chapel Hill: University of North Carolina Press, 1990), 235–57. On the issue of Melville's self-condoned narrative authority and the propensity among democratic writers for rhetorical structures, see Kenneth Dauber, who states in *The Idea of Authorship in America: Democratic Poetics from Franklin to Melville* (Madison: University of Wisconsin Press, 1990), 209, that "in *Moby-Dick* . . . Melville readdresses himself to the question of what authorizes an American book." The same could be said of Steinbeck's project in *East of Eden*.

8. Not all of Harold Bloom's work is thoroughly committed to inter-textual and inter-writer warfare. In *A Map of Misreading* (New York: Oxford University Press, 1975), 3, Bloom claims somewhat ethereally that "Influence . . . means that there are no texts but only relationships between texts. These relationships depend upon a critical act, a misreading or misprision, that one poet performs upon another. . . . The influence-relation governs reading as it governs writing, and the reading is therefore a miswriting just as writing is a misreading." Juggling similar issues of contestation and relatedness from a different perspective in *Purloined Letters*, the late Joseph Riddel has written: "If every quotation tropes, it does not necessarily vanquish or displace, or even sublate. . . . It renders, translates, transposes. And no law of genre can rule quotation; it is fabulous, fabulating, carrying things away into their other" (29).

9. On Melville at this crucial juncture, see Michael Paul Rogin, *Subversive Genealogy: The Politics and Art of Herman Melville* (New York: Knopf, 1983), 102–28; on Steinbeck,

see John H. Timmerman, *John Steinbeck's Fiction: The Aesthetics of the Road Taken* (Norman: University of Oklahoma Press, 1986), 210–18.

10. Mark W. Govoni, "'Symbols for the Wordlessness': The Original Manuscript of *East of Eden*," *Steinbeck Quarterly 14* (Winter–Spring 1981): 15.

11. *East of Eden*'s initial print run was more than 112,000 copies; the novel has never been out of print. Though *Eden* fared spectacularly, Steinbeck was intuitively correct in calling up *Moby-Dick* as a model for his "huge" unprecedented efforts. According to G. Thomas Tanselle, in *A Checklist of Editions of "Moby-Dick," 1851–1976* (Evanston and Chicago: Northwestern University Press and Newberry Library, 1976), 7, the first print run of the British edition of *The Whale* (published in London in three volumes by Richard Bentley in October, 1851, without, among other abridgements, the all-important "Epilogue" chapter) was 500 copies, and of *Moby-Dick*'s American edition, published in a single volume the following month in New York by Harpers Brothers, 2,915 copies. Overall, *Moby-Dick* sold about 3,700 copies in both editions between 1851 and Melville's death in 1891 (it was out of print during his last four years) and earned its author a little over $1,200. (See also "Historical Note," *MD*, 686–89.) Steinbeck's comments about *Moby-Dick*'s publishing history (he always spelled the title without a hyphen) are thematically similar to the introduction to Leon Howard edition of *Moby Dick* (1950).

12. There are as many variations on the definition of romance as there are critics who have written about it. Despite inherent problems in fixing this highly contested term and in spite of Steinbeck's protestation that *Eden* would not be a "romanza" (*JN*, 63), or light fantasy, what attractions Steinbeck may have found alluring in Melville's more weighty version of the form can be verified in studies by Richard Chase, *The American Novel and Its Tradition* (1957; reprint Baltimore: Johns Hopkins University Press, 1980); by Paul Brodtkorb Jr., *Ishmael's White World: A Phenomenological Reading of "Moby-Dick"* (New Haven: Yale University Press, 1965); and by Richard H. Brodhead, *Hawthorne, Melville, and the Novel* (Chicago: University of Chicago Press, 1976), 9–25. Steinbeck, who mixed critical skepticism and mythic poesis, retained some elements of the form in *East of Eden* and dispensed altogether with others.

13. Thom Steinbeck, telephone interview by author, 3 October 1985.

14. Harrison Hayford, "'Loomings': Yarns and Figures in the Fabric," in *Artful Thunder. Versions of the Romantic Tradition in American Literature in Honor of Howard P. Vincent*, eds. Robert DeMott and Sanford Marovitz (Kent, OH: Kent State University Press, 1975), 122.

15. See Warren French's treatment of Steinbeck cosmogony, "*East of Eden*—California and the Cosmic California," chap. 10 in the revised edition of *John Steinbeck* (Boston: Twayne, 1975), 143. French uses John Milton and William Blake as touchstones for considering the cosmogonal realm of Steinbeck's novel. I have extended his implications to include parallels with Melville. In a similar vein, see Lawrence Buell's essay, "*Moby-Dick* as Sacred Text," in *New Essays on "Moby-Dick*," ed. Richard H. Brodhead (New York: Cambridge University Press, 1986), 53–72; and Jay Parini's *John Steinbeck: A Biography* (New York: Henry Holt, 1995), 351, which claims "*East of Eden* is an exercise in secular scripture."

16. The dynamics of "poetic answering" are explored in John Hollander, *Melodious Guile: Fictive Patterns in Poetic Language* (New Haven: Yale University Press, 1988), 56. See Louis Owens, "The Mirror and the Vamp," 240, for his comment about *Moby-Dick* references.

17. In his elliptical *Call Me Ishmael: A Study of Melville* (New York: Reynal and Hitchcock, 1947, reprint London: Jonathan Cape, 1967), 37, Charles Olson called Melville a "skald," who "knew how to appropriate the work of others. He read to write." Recently

Susan Howe, borrowing Coleridge's term, dubbed Melville a "library cormorant." See her *The Birth-mark: Unsettling the Wilderness in American Literary History* (Middletown, CT: Wesleyan University Press, 1993), 5. The range of Melville's borrowings is dazzlingly deep and wide ("Historical Note," *MD*, 635–47). Besides Vincent's classic study of Melville's use of whaling documents, *The Trying-Out of "Moby-Dick,"* consult also Mary K. Bercaw, *Melville's Sources* (Evanston, IL: Northwestern University Press, 1987), and Merton Sealts, *Melville's Reading* (Columbia: University of South Carolina Press, 1988). Sealts's earlier version, *Melville's Reading: A Check-List of Books Owned and Borrowed* (Madison: University of Wisconsin Press, 1966) served as inspiration and model for my *Steinbeck's Reading: A Catalogue of Books Owned and Borrowed*.

18. Warren French, "Patchwork Leviathan," in chap. 13 of his *John Steinbeck* (Boston: Twayne, 1961), 153. Both novels, French asserts, "concern the self-destruction of a monomaniac." After that, however, he notes that the similarity ends, "for the focussing upon a monomaniac that crystallized Melville's vision seems to have dissipated Steinbeck's."

19. Thom Steinbeck, interview by author, 8 December 1985, Carmel, CA.

20. Scholarship on the convoluted composition of *Moby-Dick* is itself detailed, conflicting, and complex ("Historical Note," *MD*, 648–49). The most persuasive account of the book's three stages of development is by James Barbour, "'All My Books Are Botches': Melville's Struggle with The Whale," in *Writing the American Classics*, 25–52.

21. Roy S. Simmonds, "'And Still the Box is Not Full': Steinbeck's *East of Eden*," *San Jose Studies* 18 (Fall 1992): 60–63.

22. See David Wyatt's introduction to Penguin's Twentieth-Century Classics edition (*EE*, xvi), and especially Steven Mulder, "The Reader's Story: *East of Eden* as Postmodernist Metafiction," *Steinbeck Quarterly* 25 (Summer–Fall 1992): 109–118. For a consideration of the link between nineteenth-century romance and contemporary metafiction, see Edgar A. Dryden, *The Form of American Romance* (Baltimore: Johns Hopkins University Press, 1988), 169–210. Dryden furthermore proposes to show "that the act of reading generates the enabling energy of American romance . . . the curious and troubling moment where the act of reading appears to mark and disturb the American novelist's passage from life to writing and to entangle experience with an intertextual system of relationships" (xi).

23. See Stephen Railton, *Authorship and Audience: Literary Performance in the American Renaissance* (Princeton: Princeton University Press, 1991), 7.

24. Roland Barthes, *S/Z*, trans. Richard Miller (New York: Hill and Wang, 1974), 4–5. See also Steven Mailloux, *Interpretive Conventions: The Reader in the Study of American Fiction* (Ithaca, NY: Cornell University Press, 1982), 48 and 69, for more on the implications of disrupting reader passivity.

25. In an interview with me on 14 May 1992 at the "Steinbeck and the Environment Conference" held in Nantucket, Elaine Steinbeck was understandably unable to recall her husband's specific activities that day forty years earlier. Another source proved futile as well. *The Standard Diary for 1951*, one of Steinbeck's recently unsealed personal ledger books (housed at the Pierpont Morgan Library, New York City), contains 209 pages of handwritten entries by Steinbeck but is almost entirely blank for the month of August 1951. "I have not kept day book because days too full," he noted on 6 August, with "all the million things of the summer." For more on Steinbeck's unpublished diaries, see "'One Book to a Man': Charting a Bibliographical Preface to *East of Eden*" later in *Steinbeck's Typewriter*.

26. "John Steinbeck to Elizabeth Otis, 21 May 1951" (*SCSU*, 49).

27. John Ditsky, *Essays on "East of Eden,"* Steinbeck Monograph Series, no. 7 (Muncie, IN: John Steinbeck Society of America/Ball State University, 1977), ix. Howard Levant, in *The Novels of John Steinbeck* (Columbia: University of Missouri Press, 1974), 258, calls *East*

of Eden "an admirably massive, essentially flawed narrative. . . . Steinbeck's great effort lies between these two poles, and there a critical judgment must take its abode if it is to be at all accurate." A less positive assessment is recorded by Louis Owens, who states that in *East of Eden*, Steinbeck ventured resolutely into the forests of Hawthorne and Melville's great ocean, and he lost his way." See his *John Steinbeck's Re-Vision of America* (Athens: University of Georgia Press, 1985), 155. Again, see "'One Book to a Man" for an overview of *Eden's* critical reception.

28. John Steinbeck, *The Winter of Our Discontent* (New York: Viking Press, 1961; reprint, New York: Bantam Books, 1970), 6.

CLIFFORD ERIC GLADSTEIN AND
MIMI REISEL GLADSTEIN

Revisiting the Sea of Cortez with a "Green" Perspective

This essay places *Sea of Cortez: A Leisurely Journal of Travel and Research* in the context of nineteenth- and twentieth-century "philosophical streams" of American environmental thought and compares Steinbeck's ecological reasoning to that of 1990s "ecowarriors." With one or two exceptions, *Sea of Cortez* proves to be a work ahead of its time, with a holistic view of nature approaching the Gaia hypothesis. Both prescient and prophetic, *Sea of Cortez* is especially notable for its early recognition that the ocean's resources are finite and cannot withstand for long the pressures of wasteful and destructive fishing practices.

Modern environmentalism was presaged by several philosophical streams whose headwaters can be traced in the conservationist, preservationist, and transcendentalist movements of the nineteenth and early twentieth centuries. On the one hand, thinkers such as John Wesley Powell and Gifford Pinchot viewed nature as a finite resource that had to be managed effectively to bring about more efficient development and to conserve it as a source for human profit.[1] In a related but different evolution, preservationist and transcendentalist thinkers such as William Cullen Bryant, Ralph Waldo Emerson, and Henry David Thoreau romanticized the natural environment,

From *Steinbeck and the Environment: Interdisciplinary Approaches*, pp. 161–175. © 1997 by the University of Alabama Press.

believing it to be a source of refuge, rejuvenation, and purification for the human spirit oppressed by a "world that is too much with us." John Muir, who founded the Sierra Club more than one hundred years ago, sought to conserve wilderness in its natural state, not necessarily for the use of humanity, but as a reserve from people's corrupting influence,[2] These were the forebears who contributed to the course of much that is the contemporary environmental movement.[3]

Still, what we define as contemporary environmentalism has characteristics that distinguish it from what came before. The preservationist, transcendentalist, and conservationist movements were at least a century old before they merged, in the years following World War II, in the writings of Rachel Carson and the activism of David Brower to become the collection of ecological ideologies subsumed under the umbrella of today's environmentalism.[4] The sages of the present movement integrated the ideas of their predecessors with new knowledge from the postwar world of plastics, pesticides, and profligate consumption into a more comprehensive ideology, recognizing not only the challenge of preserving natural resources, but also the threat created by industrial society's exploding use of unnatural substances. In doing so, contemporary environmentalism moved forward from its fountainhead philosophies. The ethic of Pinchot and Powell focused on the productive value that could be sustained from conserving natural resources, while the ideology that is the mainstream of the contemporary environmental movement stresses the interconnectedness of all things. Whereas Muir and his acolytes resolved to preserve patches of nature and set them apart to prevent abuse by people, contemporary ecology emphasizes that humans are a part of nature, not apart from it.

Contemporary environmentalism differs from its roots in that it recognizes nature as a finite resource and seeks to address the complex natural relationships upon which humanity depends for survival. It moves beyond the notions of conservation for more efficient use or preservation in order to maintain intrinsic value. As environmental historian Samuel Hays explains: "The conservation movement was an effort on the part of leaders in science, technology, and government to bring about a more efficient development of physical resources. The environmental movement, on the other hand . . . stressed the quality of the human experience and hence of the human environment" (13). Modern environmentalism is further distinguished from its predecessors, in the words of John McCormick, by "a broader conception of the place of man in the biosphere, a more sophisticated understanding of that relationship and a note of crisis that was greater . . . than it had been in the earlier conservation movement" (48).

Literary works often precede and foretell the articulation of philosophical concepts. And lovers of the natural world have been among the most devoted readers of John Steinbeck. Maybe it is because they see in his works strong identification with and respect for tillers of the soil and harvesters of the sea as well as an abiding reverence for the earth in its pristine state. Maybe it is because Steinbeck's appreciation for nature and his concern regarding humanity's relationship with it is more complex than a simple awe for the power and beauty of creation. Although Steinbeck wrote in a period of transition between the era of conservationism and the evolution of modern environmentalism, his ideas, as articulated in *Sea of Cortez*, reflect both the influence of the past and a vision of the future. A generation before such ideas were popularized, Steinbeck exhibited an ecological understanding and environmental sophistication both rare and unusual.

The pivotal role of the natural environment in the fictional writings of John Steinbeck is well established. From the pantheistic premises of *To a God Unknown*, complete with human sacrifice as a propitiation to the rain gods, to the Edenic function of the thicket in *Of Mice and Men*, where the safety and peace of the "fresh and green" pool and trees are juxtaposed with the rough, unpainted, and whitewashed bunkhouse, where the society of other human beings promises problems and the destruction of dreams, Steinbeck has presented Nature as touchstone and theme. Echoes of Thoreau are evident not only in Tom Joad's "maybe . . . a fella ain't got a soul of his own, but on'y a piece of a big one" but also in the Walden-like refuges his characters seek but seldom retain. Still, whereas any uses he makes of the natural environment in his fictional works are subject to the interpretations of readers, in *Sea of Cortez* Steinbeck blends the colorful and image-filled language of the creative writer with the observations of a scientist to make a clear and direct statement about his attitudes toward the natural world. And it is in this narrative that Steinbeck's writing augurs the philosophy that would not be popularly articulated for another generation.[5]

To the environmental activist of the 1990s, the most striking thing about Steinbeck's account of the Sea of Cortez expedition is what Richard Astro calls his "holistic" vision, a clear manifestation of an understanding of the systemic nature of the environment. This earth-embracing philosophy, although clearly influenced by his relationship with marine biologist Ed Ricketts, is also very much Steinbeck's own. Astro points out that "there are a half dozen statements about the holistic approach to life in the published narrative for every one in Ricketts's journal" (1973, 30), underlining its importance to Steinbeck. For his day, the author exhibited a surprising level of appreciation and respect for the notion that the activities of humanity, benign and/or exploitative, have a significant impact on the world we inhabit.

This worldview is evident throughout the narrative of the trip and first surfaces in the introduction, when Steinbeck reminds the reader that, once the expedition arrives at the Sea of Cortez, it will "become forever a part of it; that our rubber boots slogging through a flat of eelgrass, that the rocks we turn over in a tide pool, make us truly and permanently a factor in the ecology of the region" (*SOC* 3). Toward the end of the narrative he articulates what he identifies as the "Einsteinian relativity" of both the inanimate and the animate world, explaining: "One merges into another, groups melt into ecological groups until the time when what we know as life meets and enters what we think of as non-life: barnacle and rock, rock and earth, earth and tree, tree and rain and air. And the units nestle into the whole and are inseparable from it" (*SOC* 216). Here Steinbeck's observations of the tide pool echo a perception that did not become part of public culture until after his death. It would be not until over a generation later, in *The Closing Circle* (1971), that Barry Commoner, one of contemporary environmentalism's best-known champions, enunciated a similar message about this interconnectedness. For him it is the first law of ecology: "Everything is connected to everything else."

Steinbeck's clear understanding of the interconnectedness of the most minute and the largest components of the world is illustrated by his example of the limitations individuals bring to their visions of reality. As he explains, when one "has strength and energy of mind the tide pool stretches both ways, digs back to electrons and leaps space into the universe and fights out of the moment into non-conceptual time." He sums up his vision of the "wide and colored and beautiful" picture of both tide pool and universal observation, with the categorical statement that "ecology has a synonym which is ALL" (*SOC* 85).

What's more, Steinbeck's observations about the hazy boundaries between the animate and inanimate anticipate one of the more lively and provocative debates in the contemporary environmental movement, that surrounding the Gaia hypothesis. Proponents of Gaia, in the same way that Steinbeck connects rock and earth, earth and tree, "have observed that the boundary line between life and the inanimate environment that most of us assume to be resolutely engraved somewhere cannot be clearly drawn. Just as matter and energy are radically different yet ultimately interchangeable phenomena, so too are the environment and living organisms ultimately functions of one another" (Joseph 53). Like Steinbeck, J. E. Lovelock, the originator of the Gaia hypothesis, understood the natural wisdom of people untouched by the complexities of urban society. Explaining his choice of the name Gaia, after the Greek Earth Goddess, he muses about the difficulty urban dwellers and institutional scientists have with the theory that the planet is a living entity while "country people still living close to the earth often seem puzzled that anyone should need to make a formal proposition of anything as obvious as the Gaia hypothesis. For them it is true and always has been" (Lovelock 1979, 10–11). In *Sea of Cortez*, Steinbeck compares the "Our Lady of Loreto" statue in the church of the small village with "the Virgin Mother of the world," or the Magna Mater (*SOC* 175), seeing in the figure the archetypal concept of the earth as a living female being.

Steinbeck's recognition of the interconnectedness of humanity and its environment and the possibility of irrevocable change was not in keeping with the prevalent ecophilosophies of his day. Conservation was the dominant concept in the period prior to World War II. The New Deal policies of Franklin Roosevelt reflected the president's belief that the land and its treasures needed to be husbanded for human use. The programs conceived and implemented by Roosevelt and his lieutenants sought to harness nature for human good. Their form of environmental concern was well grounded in the Pinchot tradition of harnessing nature to improve the human condition. The Civilian Conservation Corps used the legions of unemployed to plant trees, dig reservoirs, build dams, and prevent soil erosion. The interconnectedness of nature was set aside in the 1930s in order to lift a depressed nation out of the worst of economic times.

Necessary to a holistic view of the world, a view predicated on the interconnectedness of the living and nonliving entities on this planet, is the concept of human beings as a species, subject to the same kinds of categorization and description as other species. Steinbeck understands the average persons inability to conceive of human beings in that way. In his contemplation of the issue, he characterizes human blindness: "We have looked into the tide pools and seen the little animals feeding and reproducing and killing for food. . . . We completely ignore the record of our own species" (*SOC* 16–17). This, he explains, is because "we do not objectively observe our own species as a species" (*SOC* 17).

Steinbeck's ruminations about the parallels between the human species and other species lead him to speculate about the genesis of humanity's bent for destructive behavior. He identifies the foundation of this behavior as a tendency peculiar to *Homo sapiens*. It is Steinbeck's observation that "man is the only animal whose interest and whose drive are outside of himself" (*SOC* 87). For him, the human desire for "property, houses, money, and power" is evidence of that external drive. All other species need only that which is necessary to survive: shelter, nourishment, and the opportunity to procreate. According to Steinbeck, though they may burrow in the ground, weave nests, or spin webs, create their habitat out of the "fluids or processes of their own bodies," other species leave "little impression on the world" (*SOC* 87). Humanity, on the other hand, is a species that injures the natural order and has "furrowed and cut, torn and blasted" the world. Human beings level mountains and litter the world with the debris of living. Once again, the images Steinbeck's text calls forth are amazingly contemporary. From the deck of the *Western Flyer*, over half a century ago, Steinbeck critiqued the modern "whole man," whose existence required the material paraphernalia created by runaway technical ability (*SOC* 87).

Steinbeck sees the results of this externalization as evidence of harmful mutation. Whereas other species experience mutation in self, our species, with its strong drive for possession and domination, exhibits its mutation in the direction of its drive. Hypothesizing in *Sea of Cortez* that both the Industrial Revolution and collectivization were mutations, Steinbeck worries about the future of humanity. His syllogism develops from a major premise of paleontology, that ornamentation and complication precede extinction, and from the minor premise that the human species' assembly lines, collective farms, and mechanized armies are the equivalents of the thickening armor of the great reptiles. He is thus led to the conclusion that the human mutations he has observed will eventually lead to extinction.

A half century later, the Sea of Cortez stimulated similar thoughts in naturalist John Janovy. Explaining that "paleontologists tell us that our planet has experienced several massive extinctions; in each the diversity of life was greatly diminished" (150), Janovy speculates that the world is experiencing its third major reduction in global diversity even as the reader peruses his words. The tropical rain-forests that are being cleared contain about 70 percent of the genetic information that, according to Janovy, spell "life on earth" (150). Nor did Steinbeck hold out much hope that the destructive tendencies or mutations would be stemmed. In his opinion, "conscious thought seems to have little effect on the action or direction of our species" (*SOC* 88).

Steinbeck's experience with environmental conflicts in 1940 is eerily prescient of an ecological tragedy that continues to be played out in contemporary ocean waters. The *Western Flyer*'s encounter with the Japanese shrimpers off of Guaymas is the subject of a graphically poignant chapter. Steinbeck describes the Mexican fishermen complaining bitterly about "the Japanese shrimpers who were destroying the shrimp fisheries" (*SOC* 246). Curious about this situation, the men of the expedition decide to pay the Japanese a visit. Steinbeck observes the operations of their fleet, commenting that "they were doing a very systematic job, not only taking every shrimp from the bottom, but every other living thing as well" (*SOC* 247). This practice, through which "the sea bottom must have been scraped completely clean," brought onto the decks of the Japanese dredge boats, not only their quarry, the bottom-dwelling shrimp, but tons of other mortally wounded sea creatures as well, which the usually frugal Japanese simply threw overboard. Steinbeck found the "waste of this good food appalling" and predicted that unless limits were imposed which maintained balance between catch and supply, "a very short time will see the end of the shrimp industry in Mexico" (*SOC* 248).

Steinbeck's dire prediction may have been forestalled by an event that his narrative could not anticipate. Late in the year that *Sea of Cortez* was published, the Japanese bombed Pearl Harbor, and the ensuing war kept Japanese draggers out of the area for the better part of a decade. Shrimping in the northern Sea of Cortez continues to be the single largest fishery of the entire Mexican economy. Many of the problems that Steinbeck encountered continue, however. Like the villagers who complained to Ricketts and Steinbeck, the fishermen of the small coastal communities remain concerned about the activities of large commercial vessels. Though studies show that the large boats are not energy-efficient, requiring twelve times the energy to harvest the same amount of shrimp as the small boats, their large catches and the necessities of a world market ensure their continued prevalence in the area. Furthermore, the wasteful by-catch policies of the large boats make their presence in the Sea of Cortez a concern for environmentalists. The Delegación Federal de Pesca en Sonora estimated that the by-catch (everything pulled up with the shrimp) is often twice the weight of the shrimp, and most of it dies before it can be returned to the gulf. The same is not true in the small boats, where much of the by-catch finds its way into the local economy.[6] The practices Steinbeck deplored continue, as he predicted, to the detriment of marine life and the local economy.

Steinbeck's book is full of expressions of admiration for the people he encountered in the small coastal villages of the Sea of Cortez. Though he tries hard not to sentimentalize them, his descriptions leave the reader with a strong sense that Steinbeck found their way of life markedly saner than that of industrialized countries. He fabricates the thoughts of an Indian of the gulf: "It would be nice to have new Ford cars and running water, but not at the cost of insanity" (*SOC* 242). He writes of their kindness, their calm, and the "invasion" of "good roads and high-tension wire" (*SOC* 244). Steinbeck was concerned about the impact of such invasions on the lives of the kind people he met, and in the chapter about the Japanese draggers, he categorically states that "catch limits should be imposed, and it should not be permitted that the region be so intensely combed" (*SOC* 249).

Steinbeck suggests that a study be made to ensure that "there might be shrimps available indefinitely" (*SOC* 249–50). Obviously, his advice was not heeded. As recently as the fall of 1991, University of Texas at El Paso researchers reported local shrimpers' complaints about the depletion of the shrimp beds. Present-day vessels drag the shrimp grounds an average of seven times per year. Steinbeck's prophecy that dragging would bring an end to the shrimp industry seems to be coming to pass. Fewer locals are able to make a living from the sea. Puerto Penasco, once a shrimping village, now sees tourism as its chief economic prospect. Shrimpers, who in the past could make enough in fishing season to survive for the whole year, now must seek other work to make a living. Not only are the shrimp being depleted, but large birds, such as pelicans, who depend on marine life, are also dying off. Indiscriminate collecting continues and pollutants are poisoning the upper gulf.[7]

Steinbeck does not want to brand the Japanese fishermen or Mexican officials who permitted the dragging as criminals. Yet while calling them "good men," he is quick to extrapolate the universal from the particular. Steinbeck saw that what was happening to one group of fishermen could happen worldwide. He proved prophetic. Today, the debate over fishing practices employing these and similar methods still rages. The world's fisheries have been severely depleted by technologically advanced techniques of capturing and processing marine resources into commodities for human consumption. The use of driftnets that, when strung between two ships sailing as much as forty miles apart, can literally sweep the ocean clean of all living things is a practice much disputed by nations and abhorred by environmentalists. Reacting to the practice much as Steinbeck reacted to what he saw a half century earlier, Charles Bowden, a 1990s ecowarrior, writes: "Think of it, 35,000 miles of nets go down each night, the nets 40 miles long, 30 feet deep, the weave invisible monofilament, the death by entanglement and suffocation. Nothing gets through; the technique is perfect. Curtains of death" (41). The state of California recently banned the use of these nets within its waters, as have the states of Washington and Oregon. Again, it is the Japanese "with their industry and efficiency" (249) who are most insistent on their use of these ecologically unsound methods. Steinbeck's concerns for the future of the Mexican shrimp industry fifty years ago are now voiced for all the world's fisheries.

Ironically, his ominous observations regarding the Mexican shrimp supply came to pass about a marine industry closer to home. During the early 1940s Ed Ricketts began work analyzing the shrinking supply of sardines in Monterey Bay. In 1936, the sardine catch brought to the Monterey canneries peaked at a billion and a half pounds, making it the largest fishery in the United States. The catch declined progressively from that point until the entire industry was destroyed by 1960. Astro's biography of Ricketts indicates that among the biologist's unpublished material and notebooks was information for a project to be titled "The California Sardine: An Ecological Picture" (1976, 37). Although Ricketts attributed only part of the shrinking sardine catch to overfishing, he did believe that a rational conservation program "based upon sound scientific knowledge of the ecology of the marine environment" would have stabilized the sardine production at about 400,000 pounds per year and established a "smaller but streamlined cannery row" (Astro 1976, 37). The conservation program that he envisioned was never put into effect. A lesson may have been learned from the Monterey Bay disaster; in April 1992, the federal government forbade the annual salmon catch for northern California and central Oregon fisheries because of the serious depletion of that resource.

In Monterey today, Ed Ricketts, John Steinbeck, and an aquarium are the principal resources for the economic viability of an area that once housed great sardine canneries. Tourism is the chief industry. A similar fate may await the Sea of Cortez. As the abundance of the fisheries is depleted, a factor no less dangerous to the environment has come into play. The quiet and deserted beaches that Steinbeck and Ricketts admired are now lined with condos. Tourism and developers may complete what the draggers and driftnets began.

While the environmentalists of today read much of Steinbeck's narrative with admiration for the modernity of his ecological thought, there are also instances where the reader is brought up short at his descriptions of behavior paradoxical in terms of his stated philosophy and/or disturbing in terms of present-day ecological mores. Perhaps the most troubling images, especially for those who dive, are the descriptions of many of the collecting trips. The section that portrays gathering specimens at the Pulmo coral reef is illustrative. Steinbeck notes that El Pulmo is the "only coral reef" found on the entire expedition (*SOC* 78). Certainly, anyone who knows about coral knows how much time is involved in the development of a reef. Novice divers are instructed not to touch coral, as a touch may kill it, and breaking off pieces of coral is taboo. Even though Steinbeck expresses wonder at the complexity of life's pattern on the reef, recording that "every piece broken skittered and pulsed with life" (*SOC* 76), he is seemingly untroubled by his destruction of that life, although some of his language does suggest sensitivity to the carelessness of the collectors. He writes of feet put down "injudiciously" (*SOC* 77), of a large fleshy gorgonian, or sea fan, the only one of this type found in the area, in fact on the whole trip, "pulled" up, and of the "rush of collecting" that makes the party "indiscriminate" (*SOC* 78).

Perhaps Steinbeck does not express overt reservations about this behavior because the injudiciousness often results, when going over the pieces of coral and rubble, in the discovery of "animals we had not known were there" (*SOC* 78). He complains that a lack of diving equipment prevented the collection of "concealed hazy wonders" on the undercut shoreward side of the reef, and as he describes diving "again and again for perfect knobs of coral" (*SOC* 79), contemporary diver/readers can only feel relief that the expedition lacked the requisite equipment.[8]

Still another disquieting impression is left by some of the anecdotes about Tiny's harpooning of large sea creatures. Initially one is relieved, when following the gruesome mutilation of the tortoise-shell turtle, Tiny decides never again to harpoon one: "In his mind they joined the porpoises as protected animals" (*SOC* 46). This relief is short-lived, however, as Tiny then decides to hunt manta rays. Though they have "no proper equipment" for this enterprise, the lack does not deter the crew from tormenting the majestic creatures, described by Steinbeck as being "twelve feet between the 'wing' tips" (*SOC* 251). The ecologically sensitive reader is horrified as Tiny harpoons ray after ray, for no defensible reason. Steinbeck's narrative expresses concern mainly about the fact that the method of hunting was not working as each stricken ray fades to the bottom of the sea and eventually breaks the harpoon line. Even Tex is unable to devise a workable system, though his trident spear comes up with a "chunk of flesh on it" (*SOC* 252). In his description, Steinbeck's tone is one of amusement at Tiny's hysteria, at his being "heart-broken." When the crew, trying to soothe Tiny, points out that there is nothing worthwhile to do with a ray once it is caught, Tiny explains that he wants to have his picture taken with it.

Steinbeck's ideas are also not in line with present thought on the subject of the importance of rare species and biodiversity. Discussing wealthy amateur collectors who seek immortality by having their names attached to a newly discovered species, Steinbeck proclaims: "The rare animal may be of individual interest, but he is unlikely to be of much consequence in any ecological picture" (*SOC* 216). Although he understood that the disappearance of such a common species as plankton "would probably in a short time eliminate every living thing in the sea and change the whole of man's life," Steinbeck also concludes that the extinction of one of the rare animals "would probably go unnoticed in the cellular world" (*SOC* 216).

Today's researchers in the pathology of the "cellular world" are learning of the healing effects of some of the rarest of species. One example is the Rosy Periwinkle. A plant native to the island of Madagascar, it is the main source of a drug used to combat cancer. Jay D. Hair, president of the National Wildlife Federation, whose daughter was cured by this drug, bemoans the fact that the natural habitat of this plant, the forested area of Madagascar, is almost totally destroyed. Taxol, which is derived from the rare yew tree, is another natural source of the life-saving drugs used effectively in the cure of ovarian and breast cancer. The habitat of this species is also gravely threatened by the clear-cutting practices of the nation's northwest timber industry. These are but two examples of obscure species whose extinctions could have harmful effects on the rate of progress with which humanity conquers some of its most vexing and destructive health hazards.

Still, although a few items in Steinbeck's account of the Sea of Cortez expedition may give pause, given the historical context and the requirements for scientific collecting at the time, the overriding impression is of an avant-garde and enduring achievement. Just as most well-documented stories about the problems of migrant workers refer to *The Grapes of Wrath*, so all thorough studies of the bay of Baja California mention *Sea of Cortez*. For naturalists, the work has achieved mythic status. In the words of John Janovy, Jr., it is a "parable" that is "now a part of the scriptures of marine biology" (7). For him, a field trip to the area was a trip "to a place made sacred by a book published in 1941" (8).

In *The Grapes of Wrath*, Ma Joad, despite all the hardships her family endures, speaks optimistically about the future: "Why, we're the people," she proclaims, "we go on" (310). A few years later, in his own voice, Steinbeck made a less positive assessment: "We in the United States have done so much to destroy our own resources, our timber, our land, our fishes, that we should be taken as a horrible example and our methods avoided by any government and people enlightened enough to envision a continuing economy" (*SOC* 250). He was also aware of the mistakes being made by other countries and the reverberating implications of their acts. In his horror at what he saw in the Sea of Cortez, Steinbeck noted that the Mexican official, who permitted the ecologically unsound practices, and the Japanese captain who pursued them, were good men, but men who were committing a "true crime against nature and against the immediate welfare of Mexico and the eventual welfare of the whole human species" (*SOC* 250). Revisiting the Sea of Cortez a half century later with a "green" perspective, we are struck by both how prophetic and how contemporary an environmentalist Steinbeck was.

Notes

1. John Wesley Powell is best remembered for his surveys of the Colorado River basin and the Grand Canyon in the 1850s and 1870s and for his efforts to convince Congress and the American people that the deserts of the western United States could be tamed through planned development. His ideas, revolutionary at the time, sought orderly and thoughtful settlement of the arid regions of the country through government management. His 1878 *Report on the Lands of the Arid Region of the United States* is widely regarded as establishing the conceptual framework upon which so much of this country's land management philosophy is now based. Two sources for more information about Powell are Wallace Stegner, *Beyond the Hundredth Meridian: John Wesley Powell and the Second Opening of the West* (1954), and John U. Terrell, *The Man Who Rediscovered America: A Biography of John Wesley Powell* (1969). Gifford Pinchot is the founder of the Forest Service and is generally recognized as the first to incorporate successfully the concept of scientific management of natural resources into public policy making. He differed from some of his contemporaries, such as John Muir, in that he viewed the forests as resources to be developed rather than preserved for their own sakes. Although he favored public control of the nation's natural resources, he consistently opposed as wasteful the setting aside of land in wilderness areas or parks. For a good discussion of the differences between Pinchot and Muir, see Roderick Nash, *Wilderness and the American Mind* (1982).

2. John Muir is regarded as the founder of the modern preservation movement. His lectures, writing, and activism around the turn of the century are credited with creating modern environmentalism, the idea that nature should be preserved and protected because

of its intrinsic beauty and value for recreation. He sought the development of wilderness areas where land would be set aside and left untouched by grazing or logging. His books, *The Mountains of California* (1894) and *The Yosemite* (1912), were the most widely read books on nature and the environment of their day.

3. Two helpful sources for information about these nineteenth-century conservationalists are Stephen Fox, *The American Conservation Movement: John Muir and His Legacy* (1981), and Douglas H. Strong, *Dreamers and Defenders: American Conservationists* (1971).

4. Rachel Carson is the author of perhaps the most influential of all contemporary environmental treatises, *Silent Spring* (1962). In it, Carson warns of the insidious and pervasive adverse impact on the natural environment of insecticides, suggesting that if broadcast unchecked, chemical poisons can cause the extinction of whole species. She is credited with opening a new chapter in the history of understanding the consequences for the natural world of humanity's activities. A marine biologist by training, she wrote other books—*The Sea Around Us* (1951) and *The Edge of the Sea* (1955)—that became international bestsellers. David Brower was the first executive director of the Sierra Club (1952–1969) and transformed the group from a small, California-oriented hiking club to an influential national organization. Brower is credited with developing a modern environmental lobby that could compete with the resources of big business through the mobilization of millions of voters. After he left the Sierra Club, he founded Friends of the Earth and the Earth Island Institute; the former has become one of the world's largest environmental organizations. For more information see Stewart L. Udall, *The Quiet Crisis and the Next Generation* (1988), and David Brower, *Work in Progress* (1991).

5. We are aware that in writing the narrative portion of *Sea of Cortez*, Steinbeck was using Ed Ricketts's journal. Both Richard Astro, *John Steinbeck and Edward F. Ricketts: The Shaping of a Novelist* (1973), and Jackson J. Benson, *The True Adventures of John Steinbeck, Writer* (1984), demonstrate that the ideas reflected in Steinbeck's narrative were generally shared by both men. Benson explains that Steinbeck "wanted to make the account a true reflection of the joining of their two minds" and of the "ideas they shared and developed together" (1984, 481). Astro concludes that in situations where Steinbeck greatly amplifies Ricketts's notes, it is probably because Steinbeck had greater interest in, or belief in the validity of, the concept in question (1973, 30). We are not interested in which man originated which idea but will assume, for the purposes of this essay that, as the author of the narrative, Steinbeck held the views he articulated and published.

6. Information about the fishing industry in the present Sea of Cortez is contained in "Energy Analysis and Policy Perspectives for the Sea of Cortez, Mexico," prepared by Mark T. Brown, Stephen Tennenbaum, and H. T. Odum (1991). It is originally a report prepared for the Cousteau Society.

7. Interview with Dr. Lillian Mayberry and Dr. Jack Bristol, Department of Biology, University of Texas at El Paso, El Paso, Texas, 30 September 1991. Dr. Mayberry has been conducting research trips to Puerto Penasco for seven years. The bay there has the second highest tide differential in the world, making it an ideal location for tide pool research.

8. We want to reiterate our "green" perspective, complete with its 1990s sensibility. Steinbeck and Ricketts were following correct procedures for good marine biological collecting of the 1930s. They lacked the photographic, video, or SCUBA equipment for a more judicious collection behavior.

MARILYN CHANDLER McENTYRE

Natural Wisdom:
Steinbeck's Men of Nature
as Prophets and Peacemakers

Steinbeck's prophets, men of broad understanding and
acceptance, draw their vision from the natural world. Jim Casy,
a lapsed preacher and wise counselor to the Joad family, finds
new faith in love of nature and renewed purpose through his
involvement with the people of the earth. At the center of
Cannery Row is Doc, marine biologist, whose holistic vision
and compassionate attention to human needs are similarly
drawn from close observation of his environment and nature.
Through a nonteleological acceptance of what is, both the
rigorous scientist and the intuitive preacher recognize the
interconnectedness of creation.

Steinbeck's indebtedness to the American transcendentalists, particularly
Emerson and Whitman, has been noted frequently.[1] That relationship lies
partly in his way of looking upon the natural world as a source of knowledge,
a text to replace or expand upon Scripture, which teaches those who have eyes
to see and ears to hear. For Steinbeck, as for his predecessors, the wise man
was above all else defined by his discerning relationship to the natural world,
allowing it to inform his understanding of human relations and enterprises.

In several of Steinbeck's novels we encounter variations on the type of
the wise man—a character whose self-knowledge, compassion for human

From *Steinbeck and the Environment: Interdisciplinary Approaches*, pp. 113–124. © 1997 by the
University of Alabama Press.

frailty, and sharp intuitions come from close association with the natural world. Two of the most notable of these are Casy, the preacher in *The Grapes of Wrath*, and Doc in *Cannery Row*. Both are solitaries who take frequent "flights into the wilderness" but who live among people who rely upon them for guidance. Both understand themselves and others with an insight that at times seems prophetic, and indeed in the motley circles they frequent they are accorded special status as counselors and wise men. Both are more educated than those around them, but each in his way has rejected the institutional forms and frameworks that endowed him with professional credentials and lives as a maverick of sorts, moving easily among circles of people to none of which he belongs. Both are explicitly linked with images of Jesus, though neither is conventionally religious. Both are "nonteleological thinkers" in the sense in which Steinbeck claimed that he himself viewed the world: not in terms of defined purposes, but with what he called "is thinking"—acceptance without second-guessing of the divine plan.[2]

For each, the source of wisdom and virtue appears to lie in communion with nature. And each, communing with nature, assumes the status and role of prophet in his community. Indeed it might be said that in these characters Steinbeck is working out a definition of prophecy and the importance of the prophet in modern life, not as one who calls for specific acts of repentance and return to a covenantal tradition, but as one who sees into the heart of nature and speaks forth what lesson it teaches. In doing so he, in effect, issues a warning call to turn away from those forms of civilized life that remove us from what Robinson Jeffers, Steinbeck's contemporary and fellow Californian, called "the great humaneness at the heart of things." And like Jeffers, he writes as one who is himself a visionary trying to find a language for the ultimate interconnectedness of all creation as a means for understanding what as humans we must do.

Steinbeck's most explicit articulation of this vision is given in *Sea of Cortez*, where he describes "nonteleological thinking" as a way of understanding the natural and thence the social world independent of the causal relations and presumed purposes we so readily posit to satisfy our need for comprehensible meaning. Freeman Champney sums up nonteleological thinking as "a mixture of philosophical relativism, the rigorous refusal of the scientist to be dogmatic about hypotheses, and a sort of moral fatalism" (Robert Murray Davis 1972, 30). Steinbeck himself explains, "Nonteleological thinking concerns itself primarily not with what should be, or could be, or might be, but rather with what actually 'is'— attempting at most to answer the already sufficiently difficult questions *what* or *how*, instead of *why*" (*SOC* 135).

To think in such a way entails a kind of humility related to Jeffers's idea of "unhumanism"—a rejection of the myopic anthropocentrism that distorts our understanding of the functioning of whole systems, the large patterns of evolution, the nature of natural and human communities as organic wholes that transcend the life and purposes of any individual within them. This capacity for "whole sight," as well as what Champney sees as relativism, antidogmatism, and ultimate acceptance of what is, defines the prophet in Steinbeck's world. In *The Grapes of Wrath* it is Casy, the unpretentious fellow traveler in the Joads' pilgrim band and maverick Christian in self-imposed exile from institutional religion, who embodies the nonteleological or "is" thinker capable of prophesying and ultimately enacting a larger truth than those around him are able to grasp.

Casy, who was once a preacher, now makes it a point of honor to reject his status and its privileges, assuring the Joads, who receive him as a kind of family chaplain, that he doesn't pray any more. But the habit of prayer is as ingrained in him as the way of life he leaves behind on the road to California: "'Fella gets use' to a plate, it's hard to go,' said Casy. 'Fella gets use' to a way a thinkin', it's hard to leave. I ain't a preacher no more, but all the time I find I'm prayin', not even thinkin' what I'm doin'"" (54). His prayer is no longer a petition to an omnipotent God but a way of being and a largeness of awareness that comes to him in moments of solitude in the wilderness. He recognizes in himself a natural kinship with the Jesus who fled the crowds and went up into the high desert to pray:

> I been in the hills thinking, almost you might say like Jesus went into the wilderness to think his way out of a mess of troubles. I ain't sayin' I'm like Jesus, ... But I got tired like Him, an' I got mixed up like Him, an' I went into the wilderness like Him, without no campin' stuff. Nighttime I'd lay on my back and look up at the stars; morning I'd set and watch the sun come up; midday I'd look out from a hill at the rollin' dry country; evenin' I'd fuller the sun down. Sometimes I'd pray like I always done. On'y I couldn' figure what I was prayin' to or for. There was the hills, an' there was me, an' we wasn't separate no more. We was one thing. An' that one thing was holy. (88)

The idea of the holy has expanded for Casy since his rejection of the church. It springs from an awareness of nature honed and trained by his frequent retreats, his attitude of receptivity, and a habit of mind that links what he knows of the unconscious natural world to a deepening intuition about the ways of human nature. To be in the wilderness "without no campin' stuff" is to be in more direct sensual contact with the earth than those for whom the multilayered insulations of clothing and shelter dull the raw sensate experience of nature. Casy's reflection here also traces a line

of thinking that begins in Christian typology and ends in a rejection of that
tradition in favor of a universalistic mysticism removed from the claims of
any institution. Like Emerson, the transcendentalist who left his pulpit
and went out among the people, and like Thoreau, who turned eccentricity
to high purposes, Casy opens his heart to a wider calling than the pulpit
afforded—to return to the earth and live close to it and the people who till
the soil and to learn from them:

> I ain't gonna baptize. I'm gonna work in the fiel's, in the green
> fiel's, an' I'm gonna be near to folks. I ain't gonna try to teach 'em
> nothin'. I'm gonna try to learn. Gonna learn why the folks walks
> in the grass, gonna hear 'em talk, gonna hear 'em sing. . . . Gonna
> lay in the grass, open and honest with anybody that'll have me.
> Gonna cuss an' swear an' hear the poetry of folks talkin'. All that's
> holy, all that's what I didn' understand'. All them things is the
> good things. (101–2)

In both these speeches there are echoes of transcendentalism, Protestant
theology, and Whitmanian democracy. Frederick Carpenter points out the
rich soil and deep roots that underlie Casy's philosophical statements as he
"translates American philosophy into words of one syllable" (324–25).[3] And
Peter Lisca comments that in these same articulations, Casy moves "from
Bible-belt evangelism to social prophesy" (Robert Murray Davis 1972, 98).
As a social prophet, however, his task is to prophesy to a particular and
peculiar people. It is in his shared life with the Joad family that he works out
his destiny and mission, often in terms reduced to their own simpler way of
understanding what he is about.

Despite Casy's protestations, the Joads and others continue to take him
for a preacher. The title sticks, and in that assigned role Casy assumes a place
in but not of the Joad family, increasingly committed to a vision of things
and a version of action that might be described as natural Christianity. His
models for prayer and action come from Jesus, but his epistemology emerges
not from any organized doctrine but from observation of, trust in, and love
for the natural world and the people who live close to the earth.

"I can see it like a prophecy," Casy says, prognosticating about the fate
of the people when tractors have made work "so easy that the wonder goes
out of work, so efficient that the wonder goes out of the land and the working
of it, and with the wonder the deep understanding and the relation" (126).
Like his Old and New Testament prototypes he sees the broad connections
among things, understands the ominous signs of destruction of the natural
order, and longs to save "the people" from the legal and economic machinery
that is devouring their lives and driving them off their land. "If ya listen," he

says, "you'll hear a movin' an' a sneakin', an' a rustlin', an'—an' a restlessness. They's stuff goin' on that the folks doin' it don't know nothin' about—yet. They's gonna come somepin onto all these folks goin' wes'—outa all their farms lef' lonely. They's gonna come a thing that's gonna change the whole country" (190).

Casy knows these things because he watches and listens and understands signs and portents. He stays awake nights, watching the stars and listening to the sounds of animals in their burrows. He frequently speaks what he knows in parables drawn from nature:

> But they's somepin worse'n the devil got hold a the country, an' it ain't gonna let go till it's chopped loose. Ever see one a them Gila monsters take hold . . .? Grabs hold, an' you chop him in two an' his head hangs on. Chop him at the neck and his head hangs on. Got to take a screw driver an' pry his head apart to get him loose. An' while he's layin' there poison is drippin' an' drippin' into the hole he's made with his teeth. (139–40)

Casy's sense of the enormity of the evil coming upon the people is commensurate with his great reverence for creation. At Grampa Joad's funeral he quotes, "All that lives is holy" (157). He has little respect for the laws of man, returning repeatedly to simple expressions of natural law as the only reliable guide for human action: "Law changes," he says, "but 'got to's' go on. You got the right to do what you got to do" (153).

His understanding of human nature as well as his rudimentary awareness of the profound involvement of human emotions and desires and needs in the life of the physical body as well as the body politic make him a healer. When Grampa falls sick, Ma finds Casy and asks him simply, "You been aroun sick people. . . . Grampa's sick. Wont you go take a look at him?" (148). Significantly enough, he can't fix a car, though he can administer comfort, healing, and leadership. All he can do when the car breaks down is shine the light for Tom and Al to see by. His work is with matters of "the sperit."

As the awareness of evil grows on Casy, so does his sense of mission. "I hear the way folks are feelin'," he says. "Goin' on all the time. I hear 'em an feel 'em; an' they're beating their wings like a bird in an attic. Gonna bust their wings on a dusty winds tryin' to get out" (275). Casy eventually dies by the principle of natural law, leading a strike, telling his attackers, "You got no right to starve people," and then, "You don' know what you're a-doin" (433)—final words that powerfully recall Jesus' words, "Father, forgive them, for they know not what they do."

Casy's homegrown natural theology has been the subject of much critical comment, especially the Emersonian echoes in his much-cited insight that "maybe all men got one big soul ever'body's a part of" (24). It is from this essentially pantheistic vision that his politics derive. Ownership makes little sense to him beyond the natural claim to what one needs. The arbitrariness of man-made boundaries seems not simply to ignore but to violate natural laws of distribution and interdependence. Frederick Carpenter in his essay "The Philosophical Joads" sums up Casy's story in this way: "Unorthodox Jim Casy went into the Oklahoma wilderness to save his soul. And in the wilderness he experienced the religious feeling of identity with nature which has always been the heart of transcendental mysticism. . . . the corollary of this mystical philosophy is that man's self-seeking destroys the unity or 'holiness' of nature" (324–25).

Casy's cosmic perspective on human affairs, his involvement in the immediacies of human needs, and his deep attention to the natural world as a source of wisdom are all reiterated in a new key in the character of Doc, the wise man of *Cannery Row*. Robert Benton has pointed out that the "ecological" cast of Steinbeck's thinking is reflected in his characterization of Doc—a way of thinking that "causes him to see man as an organism related to a vast and complex ecosystem" (Astro and Hayashi 1971, 133). In chapter 2 of that book, the narrator pauses characteristically to take a step back from the canvas on which he is painting the colorful local scene and take a cosmic perspective. He sees Lee Chong the grocer and Mack and the boys "spinning in their orbits" (125). The short chapter ends with a prayer: "Our Father who art in nature, who has given the gift of survival to the coyote, the common brown rat, the English sparrow, the house fly and the moth, must have a great and overwhelming love for no-goods and blots-on-the-town and bums, and Mack and the boys. Virtues and graces and laziness and zest. Our Father who art in nature" (125).

In light of this presentation of natural religion as the ideological backdrop to the narrative, Doc's close and attentive knowledge of nature endows him with not only professional but also prophetic credibility. In subsequent chapters the virtues of a good naturalist, as attributes of Doc's character, are manifestations of virtue in a much larger sense; Doc's patience in observing and collecting specimens for study, his steady commitment to objectivity, and his curiosity itself are seen as forms of compassion. He answers Hazel's desultory questions with more seriousness than they deserve because "Doc had one mental habit he could not get over. When anyone asked a question, Doc thought he wanted to know the answer. That was the way with Doc. He never asked unless he wanted to know and he could not conceive of the brain that would ask without wanting to know" (143). The simplicity and straightforwardness of his scientific habit of mind appear as an almost childlike innocence, a quality of guilelessness that wins him universal trust among the ragged crowd who surround him.

At times Doc's steadiness of focus is broken by a kind of whimsy, itself related to wider spiritual vision. When Hazel, observing a crowd of stinkbugs on the ice plant, asks "What they got their asses up in the air for?" Doc's first answer is, "I looked them up recently—they're very common animals and one of the commonest things they do is put their tails up in the air. And in all the books there isn't one mention of the fact that they put their tails up in the air or why" (147). Pressed further with "Well, why do you think they do it?" Doc answers, "I think they're praying," and to Hazel's shocked response adds, "The remarkable thing . . . isn't that they put their tails up in the air— the really incredible thing is that we find it remarkable. We can only use ourselves as yardsticks. If we did something as inexplicable and strange we'd probably be praying—so maybe they're praying" (147–48). The exchange speaks volumes about the way Doc brings together observation, research, deductive and inductive reasoning, contemplation, and a gentle humor that seems to proceed out of a detachment from the entangled human perspective that few men achieve.

Steinbeck's narrators take whole chapters to give voice and color to the natural environments the characters inhabit, embedding in those descriptions much philosophy about the right relation between earth and its creatures. But it is in these small exchanges that draw attention to the minute designs of the natural world that the novels reveal how nature shapes vision and character, how a place known intimately—a farm, a field, a tidepool—can become, as Casy puts it, "a way of thinkin'."

Doc's general wisdom, like Casy's, spills over the boundaries of professional definition. At various times he has to remind petitioners that he is neither a medical doctor nor a veterinarian nor a psychiatrist. Like the Joads with their proprietary expectations of Casy as personal chaplain, Doc's cohorts expect him to be all of these things as well as spiritual counselor, confessor, and source of ready money:

> Now Doc of the Western Biological Laboratory had no right to practice medicine. It was not his fault that everyone in the Row came to him for medical advice. Before he knew it he found himself running from shanty to shanty taking temperatures, giving physics, borrowing and delivering blankets and even taking food from house to house where mothers looked at him with inflamed eyes from their beds, and thanked him and put the full responsibility for their children's recovery on him. When a case got really out of hand he phoned a local doctor and sometimes one came if it seemed to be an emergency. But to the families it was all emergency. Doc didn't get much sleep. He lived on beer and canned sardines. (207–8)

Doc maintains his own spiritual and mental health by means of frequent retreats into music, poetry, and nature. His scrupulously scientific habit of mind is a counterpart to Casy's broadly intuitive epistemology but expresses the same deep reverence for what can be learned from the natural world.

> Doc had to keep up his collecting. He tried to get to the good tides along the coast. The sea rocks and the beaches were his stock pile. He knew where every thing was when he wanted it. All the articles of his trade were filed away on the coast, sea cradles here, octopi here, tube worms in another place, sea pansies in another. He knew where to get them but he could not go for them exactly when he wanted. For Nature locked up the items and only released them occasionally. Doc had to know not only the tides but when a particular low tide was good in a particular place. When such a low tide occurred, he packed his collecting tools in his car, he packed his jars, his bottles, his plates and preservatives and he went to the beach or reef or rock ledge where the animals he needed were stored. (210–11)

Doc doesn't even need a clock but lives by a tidal pattern: "He could feel a tide change in his sleep" (218). His knowledge has penetrated to his very body and bones. This kind of knowledge depends on humility, attentiveness, and long fidelity to the habit of patient contemplation—qualities that are also the basis of Doc's legendary compassion. But committed as he is to scientific accuracy and truth-telling, he has also had to learn that "people didn't like you for telling the truth" (213). Once, he recalls, on a walking trip through the South, he repeatedly encountered people who asked him why he was walking through the country but were disturbed by his honest answer:

> Because he loved true things he tried to explain. He said he was nervous and besides he wanted to see the country, smell the ground and look at grass and birds and trees, to savor the country, and there was no other way to do it save on foot. And people didn't like him for telling the truth. They scowled, or shook and tapped their heads, they laughed as though they knew it was a lie and they appreciated a liar. And some, afraid for their daughters or their pigs, told him to move on, to get going, just not to stop near their place if he knew what was good for him.
>
> And so he stopped trying to tell the truth. He said he was doing it on a bet—that he stood to win a hundred dollars. Everyone liked him then and believed him. They asked him in to dinner and gave him a bed and they put lunches up for him and

> wished him good luck and thought he was a hell of a fine fellow.
> Doc still loved true things but he knew it was not a general love
> and it could be a very dangerous mistress. (214)

The recognition in this passage that the solitary poses a subtle but vividly felt threat to the community recalls some of well-known stories about the suspicions Thoreau encountered among his fellows in Concord or, more dramatically, the association of intimacy with nature with witchcraft and occultism. Hawthorne's Roger Chillingworth in *The Scarlet Letter* illustrates this latter point; an herbalist whose compendious knowledge of the healing powers of herbs derives from long association with Indians and a solitary life dedicated to this study appears as a practitioner of "dark arts." More benevolent images like that of "Johnny Appleseed" still mark as an eccentric the individual who forsakes community life and communes with nature.

Doc understands this common suspicion, and with a diplomacy that is the measure of his great charity he takes care to foster his own needs in a way that does not threaten or alienate him from the community that depends on him. His understanding of the natural order, like Casy's, informs his social behavior. Much of Doc's activity among his cohorts on Cannery Row is a kind of pastoral subterfuge. Like Casy he is a shrewd assessor of human nature and calculates his demands and concessions accordingly. He also serves as a hub that draws people together in a way that makes community possible. He understands, like Casy, the wide web of interdependency that binds the things of this world and makes a mockery of short-sighted ideas of ownership. His generosity has a character of matter-of-fact common sense to it; it is simply the way of nature.

We do get an occasional ironic comment on the effects of such natural sanctity on the more commercially minded: "Lee was indebted to Doc— deeply indebted. What Lee was having trouble comprehending was how his indebtedness to Doc made it necessary to give credit to Mack" (227). But Doc knows that somehow things even out, like water seeking its own level. He trusts some principle of natural distribution as a basis for all moral action: people do what they can do, they act on what they can understand, and as long as they act in harmony with their nature things even out and we learn from one another. Thus his admiration for Mack and the boys escapes condescension because he understands the necessity of their presence in a world that needs just such a corrective. "Look at them," he says:

> They are your true philosophers. I think ... that Mack and the
> boys know everything that has ever happened in the world and
> possibly everything that will happen. I think they survive in this
> particular world better than other people. In a time when people

tear themselves to pieces with ambition and nervousness and covetousness, they are relaxed. All of our so-called successful men are sick men, with bad stomachs and bad souls, but Mack and the boys are healthy and curiously clean. They can do what they want. They can satisfy their appetites without calling them something else. (251–52)

Chapter 31 of *Cannery Row*, which details the life and frustrated enterprises of a gopher, serves as a parable to describe Doc's solitary, industrious life in the face of the social changes and chances that defeat his human ambitions. The gopher, like him, is busy, solitary, in the prime of life. He burrows into rich soil "on a little eminence" where he could watch Mack and the boys (300). He prepares an elaborate place for a female to join him and raise a family, but no female appears. He goes out to court one but comes back bitten. Finally, "he had to move two blocks up the hill to the dahlia garden where they put out traps every night" (302). Doc is, finally, the gopher in the dahlia garden. He adapts to an environment diminished in natural richness, unsympathetic to his higher ends but livable. He is a prophet unhonored by a mechanized, commercialized, secular culture, quietly, stubbornly cherishing ideals that culture has begun to threaten.

In these two figures, Casy and Doc, Steinbeck incorporates a complex vision of wisdom derived from attentiveness to the natural world. The best of what we call human virtue—compassion, forgiveness, clarity, flexibility—comes from the habit of attention. And in characters like these he would seem to be suggesting that nature teaches us what we need to know—and that our best teachers are those who have learned her lessons.

Notes

1. See, for example, Shigeharu Yoshizu, "Emerson and Steinbeck: On the Oriental Concept of Being" (1974); Duane R. Carr, "John Steinbeck, Twentieth-Century Romantic: A Study of the Early Works" (1976); and J. Edward Shamberger, "Grapes of Gladness: A Misconception of *Walden*" (1972).

2. For an explanation of Steinbeck's idea of "nonteleological thinking," see also Robert Murray Davis's introduction to *Steinbeck: A Collection of Critical Essays* (1972).

3. See also Floyd Stovall in *American Idealism* (1943), 164, for comment on Casy's Emersonian character.

DAVID WYATT

Steinbeck's Light

"You've made my life bright," John Steinbeck said, to his wife Elaine, on his deathbed. He liked the word "bright," perhaps because it rhymed with "light," a word that was, for Steinbeck, the much more important one. Light shines out everywhere in his work ("There is a shining," Joe Saul says at the end of *Burning Bright*); if we look for a structure of imagery in Steinbeck, as we were privileged to do before the fall of the New Criticism deprived us of such pleasures, we continually come up against the force that fights the dark. Steinbeck recurred to this structure in his most important public utterance, his 1962 Nobel Prize acceptance speech. There he describes the ancient commission of the writer as "dredging up to the light our dark and dangerous dreams."

The first letter in *A Life in Letters*, a book edited by Elaine, begins like this:

> Do you know, one of the things that made me come here, was, as you guessed, that I am frightfully afraid of being alone. The fear of the dark is only part of it. I wanted to break that fear in the middle, because I am afraid much of my existence is going to be more or less alone, and I might as well go into training for it.

From *The Southern Review,* Spring 2002, vol. 38, no. 2, pp. 399–412. © 2002 by David Wyatt.

Confessing at the start to a fear of the dark was a pretty farsighted thing to do. (The letter was written from Lake Tahoe in the winter of 1926, to a friend at Stanford.) Steinbeck here locates a problem that he will redefine as a theme. Fears are things one "goes into," just as writing involves, in part, a process of working through. It is one of his most Hemingwayesque passages—the writer is someone who sets out into the dark and tries to break rather than be broken by his fears. Over the years this sense of the writer as hero or agonist would give way to a sense of the writer as laborer or journeyman. Writing finally became, for Steinbeck, just another form of hard, honest work. But the obsession with light persisted—it is there on the last page of the last novel—and so can give to the career the status of a long and carefully structured poem.

"At last it was evening": *In Dubious Battle* begins with this sentence, which signals an access of power that makes the novel, along with *The Grapes of Wrath*, Steinbeck's greatest achievement. Many readers who praise the novel describe it as a triumph of rhythm, of the power generated by the continuous sensation, as Mac says, of "looking ahead." There is a tension created and maintained from the opening sentence that is unique in Steinbeck's work. "I wanted to get over unrest and irritation and slow sullen movement breaking out now and then in fierce eruptions. And so I have used a jerky method. I ended the book in the middle of a sentence."

To focus on image rather than pace, as I mean to do, may be, then, to turn away from the novel's most distinctive quality, its reluctant yet headlong inevitability. It risks a focus on mere decor. But Steinbeck thinks through his images and does so with a care that makes him a prime exponent of what Hart Crane calls "the logic of metaphor." Details that may appear to function as simple description serve to advance, in the novel, a complex theory of knowledge.

"At last it was evening." It's a promising beginning, one a little like that of Hemingway's "Indian Camp": "At the lake shore there was another rowboat drawn up." The reader arrives late, at the end of a period of waiting. Some kind of pressure has built up, and is now being released. An action is also about to start—or to end—we cannot be sure. And whatever is going on has to do with what Steinbeck calls, in *Travels with Charley*, a "quality of light." The paragraph continues:

> The lights in the street outside came on, and the Neon restaurant sign on the corner jerked on and off, exploding its hard red light in the air. Into Jim Nolan's room the sign threw a soft red light. For two hours Jim had been sitting in a small, hard rocking-chair, his feet up on the white bedspread. Now that it was quite dark, he brought his feet down to the floor and slapped the sleeping

legs. For a moment he sat quietly while waves of itching rolled up and down his calves; then he stood up and reached for the unshaded light.

We begin with a man in the early dark. He lets the light fade, then turns on a lamp. He seems to have some control over this sequence; we don't yet know that the action will trace both his growing political and emotional illumination along with the final darkening of his hopes. How much control Jim has over this process becomes a big question, one of the biggest in Steinbeck's work. Who—or what—commands the sources of the light? And what is the true experience of enlightenment, both its process and its price?

One thing that has to go is the past. "Everything in the past is gone," Jim says a few pages into the novel. He is speaking to Harry Nilson, the Communist organizer he has sought out in order to begin his new life. Old Dan may indulge in "the light of reminiscence," but Jim allows himself only one detailed memory. It has to do with his sister, May, and he recalls it for Harry in the form of a very short story, one of the most brilliant Steinbeck was ever to write. It's a story worth going through slowly, since it's the first piece of writing, except for the short stories Steinbeck wrote in the early 1930s, in which he fuses image, rhythm, and theme without bombast, mystification, or sentimentality.

Jim has been looking out Harry Nilson's window at some boys playing handball. He mentions playing and fighting when he was a kid, and wonders if kids fight as much as they used to. Harry allows that they do, and then Jim remembers May, who was the best marble shot he had ever seen and who could lick nearly everybody in the lot. Harry looks up.

> "I didn't know you had a sister. What happened to her?"
> "I don't know," said Jim.
> "You don't know?"
> "No. It was funny—I don't mean funny. It was one of those things that happen."

"Well, I can tell you about it," Jim says, in response to Harry's "What do you mean, you don't know what happened to her?" Telling here is opposed to knowing. It is an act one can perform in the face of a felt ignorance. The distinction between telling and knowing is captured in the two uses of the word "happen." Jim's "things that happen" refers to a brute sequence of events that cannot be anticipated, controlled, or perhaps even understood. Harry's "What happened?" expresses the wish for an explanation; it's a question that presumes the possibility of an answer. "What happened?" is, of course, a question a listener puts to a teller, and Jim answers Harry as a mere teller. He does not offer his story as explanation or consolation but as a simple rehearsal of the facts. And yet Jim's narrative is so beautifully structured by Steinbeck's control of pace, tone, and figurative language as to become an exemplum of the ways in which fiction can embody emotional and political truth.

The story Jim tells fills fewer than two printed pages. He and his sister sleep in the kitchen. When May is about fourteen, she hangs a sheet across the corner to dress and undress behind. One evening Jim comes home from playing ball and his mother asks, "Did you see May down on the steps?" Jim's old man comes home from work and also asks, "Where's May?"

They wait dinner for a while. Then the old man gets mad—"May's getting too smart"—and they eat.

In the paragraph that follows, Jim recalls his mother's "light blue eyes. I remember they looked like white stones. Well, after dinner my old man sat in his chair by the stove. And he got madder and madder. My mother sat beside him. I went to bed. I could see my mother turn her head from my father and move her lips. . . . About eleven o'clock both of 'em went into the bedroom, but they left the light burning in the kitchen. I could hear them talking for a long time. Two or three times in the night I woke up and saw my mother looking out from the bedroom. Her eyes looked just like white stones."

When Jim wakes up, the light is still burning. "It gives you a funny, lonely feeling to see a light burning in the daytime." His mother gets up and lights a fire. "Her eyes didn't move much." Jim's father comes out. "He acted just as though he'd been hit between the eyes."

At school, the girls say they haven't "seen May at all." The father stops by the police station, where "They said they'd keep their eyes peeled." Jim's tale goes on:

> That night was just like the one before. My old man and my mother sitting side by side, only my father didn't do any talking that second night. They left the light on all night again . . . [T]he cops sent a dick to question the kids on the block, and a cop came and talked to my mother. Finally they said they'd keep their eyes open. And that was all. We never heard of her again, ever.

There are a few more paragraphs—about how his mother's "eyes got a kind of dead look" and about how his father was sent to jail for assault—but Jim's story effectively ends with the word "ever."

This is one of the great American short stories. It does its work through Jim's profound unawareness of its power. As Steinbeck writes in *Tortilla Flat*, "The good story lay in half-told things which must be filled in out of the hearer's own experience." The story provides an example of what Richard Onorato calls the Truest Memory of Early Child hood—the unforgettable spot of time that, for each of us, sticks in the mind precisely because it defies understanding.

Jim's scarcely seems a story at all—a girl disappears, a family falls apart. Jim doesn't know what happened; all he can do is "tell . . . about it." Steinbeck will later make much of the virtue of not knowing, of accepting life as a sequence of "things that happen." By the time Casy voices this point of view, it has begun to harden into dogma: "There ain't no sin and there ain't no virtue. There's just stuff people do." Casy is persuasive enough, but Jim's story more powerfully makes the point. To begin with the words "I don't know," and to make the not knowing have to do with a lost sister—and a sister lost to the sexual dark—well, this is to endow Steinbeck's offhanded negative capability (neither he nor Casy will search after facts and reasons) with all the poignancy and chagrin of daughter- and sister-loss, of the endemic inability to protect what the culture assigns the brother and the father and the mother as their most valuable and dependent charge.

So why is this the one piece of the past that Jim hangs on to and gets to narrate? To boil it down to a portable meaning would be to say that in this story, Jim—by way of Steinbeck's art, an art that bespeaks him—offers a parable about the fate of love under capitalism. Mid-twentieth-century agribusiness is, after all, the particular target of Steinbeck's anger here, and he is acute in forecasting that America's battle over the rights of migrant labor would be most decisively fought in California's orchards and fields. What spirits the daughter away is surely her burgeoning sexuality, which some man chooses to exploit. But her disappearance is made possible by the profound isolation of these characters from one another—it is a home literally bereft of speech—and by the larger failure of community and absence of solidarity (the novel's last words are "He didn't want nothing for himself—," whereas capitalism is about wanting something only for the self) that makes the young and the innocent and the nascently sexual so casually vulnerable.

Now none of this is original—the lost daughter as a figure for unresolved cultural contradictions is the open secret of Western literature, from Persephone to Beloved. What makes it powerful is the compression and the imagery of this many-times-told tale. The story's brevity frustrates our desire for empathy; Jim tells it so quickly, and in so flat a tone, as to give us small chance to feel, let alone grieve. So little time, so huge a loss: the logic of length here argues that this is a story the significance of which Jim's world chooses to repress.

Steinbeck holds the story together by repeating versions of the verbs "know," "tell," "see," and "hear." All of these mark human capacities, actions people perform to find things out. Yet these capacities scarcely belong to the characters in the story—they belong, rather, to the texture of Steinbeck's prose and, by extension, to any strong reader of it. Jim's telling of a story he does not "know" the meaning of is simply the crucial instance of the alienation of these characters from the very powers that Steinbeck's writing at once displays and calls forth.

"See" is the core verb among these four, just as "eyes" is the key noun: "Did you see May" . . . "I could see my mother" . . . "I woke up and saw" . . . "They said they hadn't seen May" . . . "My mother had light blue eyes" . . . "her eyes didn't move much" . . . "He acted just as though he'd been hit between the eyes" . . . "They said they'd keep their eyes peeled" . . . "Her eyes got a kind of dead look."

Seeing is both a path toward and a conventional metaphor of the access of knowledge. As the sense most directly connected with the intellect, seeing usually brings with it all the lovely promises of distance, perspective, awareness, survey. Yet in Jim's story, eyesight does not produce insight. Instead, in the wonderful and repeated simile, the mother's eyes have become "like white stones." Jim can only register and marvel at this as he watches his mother go dead before the killing facts of life,

Imagery here conveys how one might feel about "things that happen," which are also things that cannot be helped. The image that does this most suggestively is the one Jim mentions three times, that of "a light burning in the daytime." Jim struggles with the notion that leaving the light on might mean something—to see such a thing gives him a "funny, lonely feeling." "Funny" is the word with which Jim has already twice summed up his sense of May's story, a word he takes back—"I don't mean funny"—in the very act of using it. The self-correction comes early and hints at Jim's intuition of all the ways his experience has impoverished not only his vocabulary but his ability to feel.

By drawing attention to the light in such a discreet yet obvious way— by repeating for a third time the pathetically inadequate and also strangely eloquent word "funny"—Steinbeck invites us to move from incomprehension to knowledge, to read the light burning as an image and to assign it a meaning Jim cannot. By leaving a light on in the daytime, May's parents persist in doing a thing when it is not needed and cannot help. What is this an image of but the bottomless pathos of human longing and especially the unending vulnerability of a parent's love, a longing that persists through all the inabilities to see or to know?

In chapter one of *In Dubious Battle*, and in the scene that immediately precedes the telling of May's story, Jim undergoes an interview in which he must answer the question "Why do you want to join?" The question leaves him in "perplexity." Steinbeck quickly moves to May's story because it provides the best explanation of Jim's life choice. The story also enacts in miniature what the entire novel so painfully brings home—that man can narrate truth, but not know it.

In *The Pastures of Heaven* (1932), Steinbeck allows one of his characters to muse about this paradox: "It's a strange thing, this *knowing*. It is nothing but an awareness of details." Precisely so. But what distinguishes Steinbeck from this character and from Jim Nolan is his further awareness that through the artist's arrangement of detail, a kind of enlightenment can take place. Steinbeck stands in relation to his novel as Jim does to the story of his sister: He narrates the details of an action the full meaning of which he cannot reason out. He answers his lack of knowledge with figuration—with all the formal and thematic devices that create the novel, the thing made. Even Plato, that sweet suspecter of poets and of the destabilizing power of make-believe, had to fall back on a complex metaphor to express, in his allegory of the cave, all that we cannot directly know.

In his first talk with Nilson, Jim recalls the books his father gave him when he was a boy. First on the list is Plato's *Republic*. This is the book, of course, that contains one of the West's most compelling fictions of how "our nature may be enlightened." Plato asks us to imagine ourselves as living in a cavernous chamber underground. We are chained by the leg and the neck so that we can see only what is in front of us; we cannot turn our heads. Behind us, a fire is burning. Between us and the fire, the "performers"—Plato does not specify who they might be—hold up puppets. What we see—and therefore what we take to be reality—are "the shadows thrown by the fire-light on the wall."

In chapter four of *In Dubious Battle*, Joe and Mac pay a visit to London's camp. "The trail came abruptly into a large clearing, flickeringly lighted by a little bonfire. Along the farther side were three dirty white tents; and in one of them a light burned and huge black figures moved on the canvas." Mac and Joe enter the tent, help deliver a baby, and seal the deal that makes the strike possible.

The image of the tent is as close as Steinbeck comes to an outright allusion to the allegory of the cave. But the allusion, nifty as it may be, is perhaps less important than the investment, shared with Plato, in the question of how we stand toward the light.

Caves abound in Steinbeck's work. They are sometimes a good place. In *The Winter of Our Discontent*, Ethan withdraws to a "little cave" by the sea, a place he uses for "taking stock." In *The Wayward Bus*, Mr. Pritchard shelters his neurotic wife in another "little cave," and it is there, after decades of frustration, that he breaks through the sexual impasse that his marriage has become, an event that leaves his wife free to dream of orchids. Tom Joad retreats to a cave to hide and heal after suffering the wound to his head. "It was lightless in the cave," Steinbeck writes. In the cave Tom gains his vision of human solidarity, one purchased by virtue of being compelled to develop an inner light.

Steinbeck's stories often focus, as Robert Murray Davis argues, on "men who consciously enter traps." The choice to do so can prove a good thing, an act that confers identity precisely because it also enforces limits against which the self can be tested, as it does for Ethan and for Tom. But the cave as a site of healing regression often modulates, in Steinbeck, into a place of self-enclosure. In *The Log from the Sea of Cortez*, Steinbeck identifies "an innate tendency to seek enclosing contact with a solid or rigid surface, as in a burrow." He calls this "Thigmotropism." What begins as a search for comfort and warmth too easily evolves, however, into a shutting out of stimuli, into willful depression, or ignorance, or holding off. At his death, in *Cup of Gold*, the pirate Henry Morgan feels himself "lying in an immeasurable dark grotto." It is a figure for the chests of treasure onto which he has displaced his desire, a chest like the one from his lost childhood in Wales that "sucked in the light." The dark bunkhouse in *Of Mice and Men*, Muley's "cave in the bank" near the abandoned Joad place, Mary Teller's "dusky" room in "The White Quail"—these are places where characters retreat in order to molder or to die. The life-denying logic of such withdrawals culminates in the story of Cathy Trask. "She doesn't want the light," Adam says to Sam Hamilton as Cathy lies in childbed. "It hurts her eyes." Once she gets her whorehouse, Cathy recoils even further, into a windowless room painted dark gray, one she has built for her special needs. "She believed," Steinbeck writes, "that the light pained her eyes, and also that the gray room was a cave to hide in, a dark burrow in the earth, a place where no eyes could stare at her."

"Nearly everyone has his box of secret pain"—so Steinbeck argues in *East of Eden*. Muley's and Mary's and Cathy's dark places may seem more about lessening pain than about avoiding knowledge. They express, perhaps, a simple desire to be alone. The imagery of light performs many functions in Steinbeck's work, and at its most basic it simply figures forth the possibility of life itself, a gift his characters can take or can leave.

It is in *In Dubious Battle* that Steinbeck most clearly links the ineluctable call into the dark with the difficult and life-giving work of knowing. On the day before he dies, Jim admits that he simply hasn't taken the time to look around, to get to know the world: "I never look at anything. I never take time to see anything. It's going to be over, and I won't know—even how an apple grows." Mac replies with impatience: "You can't see everything." The point is that the oppressive material conditions of Jim's youth and the unending activity of his brief political career have yielded no opportunity to acquire knowledge of anything more than grievance and hurt.

The Republic is a book about justice. But for Plato—and, it will turn out, for Steinbeck as well—epistemology trumps politics. If, as the allegory of the cave argues, knowledge is shadowy and indirect, the wise man refrains from revolutionary action and its passionate certainties. Steinbeck begins

Jim's story with a situation of felt and visible social injustice and works his way round to seeing it as not especially political. "I have used a small strike in an orchard valley," he wrote a friend, "as the symbol of man's eternal, bitter warfare with himself." Characters do not get far, in Steinbeck, having the right ideas; they have strong or "funny" feelings instead. Jim's beliefs about power in the world are vague and in any case go unarticulated. They serve largely as the pretext for a dramatic outgrowth of self.

This is to say that *In Dubious Battle* is a political novel of a peculiarly American sort, one that implies a possible redemption of the group by the transformation of an individual. Hemingway uses the same structure in *For Whom the Bell Tolls*; the promise of broader solidarity is affirmed by Robert Jordan's discovery of his ability to love Maria. Like *For Whom the Bell Tolls*, *In Dubious Battle* deals mainly with one man's education. We mark Jim's progress by the ways he opens up, especially with his eyes. And if we give weight to a letter Steinbeck wrote in 1950, Jim's search for self can be read as paralleling his author's: "The most precious thing in the world is your self—your individual, lonely self and that you can only find it after you have given it up. I won't say that I have found it but I have seen the signs and felt a little of the light."

"Without warning a blinding light cut out through the darkness and fell on the men's faces"—this is the light of property and power, and the hired men in overcoats use it to threaten Mac, Jim, and the strikers with expulsion from the valley. From the start, the strikers fight to repossess and control the light, and their struggle unfolds as an intermittent unblinding. "I got to have light," Mac says after he agrees to deliver the baby, and he gets some, but he more typically finds himself in a "damn half-light." When Anderson's place gets burned, he mistakes the fire for the light of the moon. "I can't see this path," Mac says, just before arriving at London's tent. Later, after setting up shop at Anderson's ranch, Mac and Jim walk out to talk with the men who have surrounded the camp. They end up with rifles at their backs. Here their blindness to risk is registered this way: "Under the orchard trees even the little light from the stars was shut off." Jim and Mac start to run, and Jim hides in the branches of an apple tree:

> He heard a scuffle and a grunt of pain. The flashlight darted about and then fell to the ground and aimlessly lighted a rotten apple. There came a rip of cloth, and then steady pounding of footsteps. A hand reached down and picked up the flashlight and switched it off.

What could better illustrate Plato's worldview than this overheard climax, where the sense of something going on comes by way of muffled, fragmentary sound and a darting, aimless light?

"I want to *see*," Doc Burton tells Mac. "I want to see the whole picture—as nearly as I can. I don't want to put on the blinders of 'good' and 'bad,' and limit my vision. . . . I want to be able to look at the whole thing." Doc speaks up for Steinbeck's favored way of seeing. It's an apolitical, quasi-scientific kind of looking—Doc's "senses" are all he has, he claims—that renounces faith or enthusiasm and reduces life to process, to what Doc calls "changing." Jim's father frames this view in another way: "He said he wanted to know things without believing them." All this fits with Steinbeck's commitment to non-teleological thinking and posits the hero as skeptical observer. But many of Steinbeck's appealing characters—among them Jody, Jim, Casy, and Tom—are passionate visionaries, and most are destroyed by what they see. They embody, against all of Steinbeck's habitual doubt, his equally strong yearning to break through to action and purpose.

This is why, when the crisis of Jim's novel finally comes, it comes as a transfiguration, a man riddled by light. As the owners close in and the men begin to lose heart, Jim springs up to tell them what a strike means: "'You're damn right I can do it. I'm near choking, but I can do it.' His face was transfigured. A furious light of energy seemed to shine from it." A boy runs into the tent; Doc has been shot. The men start running: "The night was almost complete." Jim runs toward his destiny the way Casy steps into his, in a calamity of light—"There was a roar, and two big holes of light." The world cannot accommodate the brilliance of Jim's vision; when Mac reaches down, the flashes from the guns still burn "on his retinas." He cries out and jerks his hand away, "for there was no face."

In *The Grapes of Wrath*, as in the 1936 short story "Breakfast," which inspired it, light acts less as a figure for transforming knowledge than as one for sustaining warmth. Very quickly after *In Dubious Battle*, Steinbeck seems to have come to agree with Miguel de Unamuno that "We die not from the darkness, but the cold." In order to change an unjust world you have to know things, things that cannot be known. So you are left with feeling, its suffering and its pleasures. "This thing fills me with pleasure," Steinbeck writes at the opening of "Breakfast." "I don't know why, I can see it in the smallest detail. I find myself recalling it again and again, each time bringing more detail out of sunken memory, remembering brings the curious warm pleasure."

The phrase "curious warm pleasure" directly links the speaker's sensation of remembering with Steinbeck's experience of writing. "Curious warm pleasure," he wrote his publisher in 1938, is what he feels when his writing goes well. Through the repetition of this phrase, author and character happily share an acceptance of not-knowing. For the unnamed speaker's "I don't know" shares little of the consequence of Jim Nolan's "I don't know." In "Breakfast," a man finds a kind of sister in the middle of the road; he does not mysteriously lose one. Author and character are also linked here in celebrating the power of remembered, artfully chosen "detail" to nourish and bring pleasure.

"Breakfast" continues:

> It was very early in the morning. The eastern mountains were black-blue, but behind them the light stood up faintly colored at the mountain rims with a washed red, growing colder, grayer and darker as it went up and overhead until, at a place near the west, it merged with pure night.
>
> And it was cold, not painfully so, but cold enough so that I rubbed my hands and shoved them deep into my pockets, and I hunched my shoulders up and scuffled my feet on the ground. Down in the valley where I was, the earth was that lavender gray of dawn. I walked along a country road and ahead of me I saw a tent that was only a little lighter gray than the ground. Beside the tent there was a flash of orange fire seeping out of the cracks of an old rusty iron stove. Gray smoke spurted up out of the stubby stovepipe, spurted up a long way before it spread out and dissipated.
>
> I saw a young woman beside the stove, really a girl.

She holds a baby in the crook of her arm. The wanderer approaches:

> I was close now and I could smell frying bacon and baking bread, the warmest, pleasantest odors I know. From the east the light grew swiftly. I came near to the stove and stretched my hands out to it and shivered all over when the warmth struck me.

He is welcomed like an old friend, yet no one knows or speaks any names:

> "Had your breakfast?"
> "No."
> "Well, sit down with us, then."

He eats and then "walk[s] away down the country road."

"Breakfast" ends with an epiphany of light:

> The two men faced the east and their faces were lighted by the dawn, and I looked up for a moment and saw the image of the mountain and the light coming over it reflected in the older man's eyes.

A man looking at men looking at the light: of what is this a figure except the writer himself? The tropism that prevails in Steinbeck is a kind of phototropism; like their author, his adaptive characters go and grow toward the light. In the speaker of "Breakfast," Steinbeck creates one of his most authentic self-characters, a man who is fully attentive and also utterly free. He has his vision, and then he moves on.

The Grapes of Wrath forgoes this lightness of being. Oklahoma light is the thing outside, a figure for our exposure in a world under the sun. Steinbeck's light movingly renders the pathos of our necessary submission to the rhythm of a day. Getting up and going to sleep engage us in a mortal drama, in what he calls in *East of Eden* "the birth and death of the day." *The Grapes of Wrath* begins with a desperate struggle to keep the sun in the sky: "The dawn came, but no day. In the grey sky a red sun appeared, a dim red circle that gave a little light." As Tom approaches home a "lonely dawn" creeps up, and Pa can barely see him against the rising light. Morning is the "good time" in Steinbeck, as Tom says, the moment of promise, but the day itself, with the sun that strikes at noon, or that disappears at nightfall like a "bloody rag," calls forth all our reserves of patience and endurance. As light strikes, warms, blinds, and disappears, it seems a force wholly beyond us, a figure for all the power we do not have.

Yet again, when the novel's crisis comes, it is a crisis of light, manmade light. Someone stands up among the "lanterns and torches," "Casy stared blindly at the light": In this heartbreaking scene, a good man is brought down in a confusion of human lights; a scene set up four hundred pages earlier by the "bar of cold white light" playing over an abandoned farm. Casy and Tom and Muley had then been "scairt to get in the light"; now the hero steps willingly into it. "He was jus' standin' there with the lights on' 'im," Tom tells Ma. It is Casy's political illumination ("It's need that makes all the trouble") that compels him into the "flashlight beams": The novel traces the steady growth of the human power to internalize and manipulate the light. Thus, when Ma visits Tom for a last time in his lightless cave, they are not cut off by any literal dark. "I wanta touch ya again, Tom. It's like I'm blin', it's so dark. I wanta remember, even if it's only my fingers that remember." She uses her hands to see his face; there is finally no need for further light. Tom then goes away, where he will be "all aroun' in the dark."

The next morning Ma gets up in the "lightless" boxcar. She shivers and rubs her hands together:

> She crept back and fumbled for the matches, beside the lantern. The shade screeched up. She lighted the wick, watched it burn blue for a moment and then put up its yellow, delicately carved ring of light. She carried the lantern to the stove and set

it down while she broke the brittle dry willow twigs into the fire box. In a moment the fire was roaring up the chimney.

This is the heart of Steinbeck's vision, and has become, by 1939, a figure not only for pleasure but for courage: a woman cooking breakfast. When Ma gets up and moves to the lantern and the stove, she measures how far she has and has not traveled, no farther perhaps than from the bedroom to the kitchen in that daily, anonymous ritual in which we get out of bed, rub our eyes, light up the world.

Twenty-two years later, in his last novel, Steinbeck has contracted his hopes. "It isn't true," Ethan Hawley broods, "that there's a community of light." The characters in *The Winter of Our Discontent* are comfortable—and miserable. They are tempted by nothing more than cheating on an essay contest or robbing a local bank. Ethan's son cheats; Ethan, finally, does not. Instead he withdraws to his cave at the sea's edge and thinks about putting an end to things, thinks of "a warm sea and a razor blade."

He has taken something with him, though, something he then forgets he has, and when he reaches for the razor blades, he feels "the lump" in his pocket: "Then in wonder I remembered the caressing, stroking hands of the light-bearer." It is his family talisman, a mound of translucent stone. The stone is "always warm to the touch," he has told us; it is "a continuity thing that inflames and comforts and inspires from generation to generation." When Ethan feels the stone, he thinks better of suicide. He clambers out of the cave, against the rising tide, and hurries home to give the stone to its rightful and new owner—his daughter, Ellen, the honest child, the one who tries to stop him when he bolts the house with the razors in his pockets, and the daughter that (unlike May) he has been able to nourish and protect.

This is the last scene in Steinbeck's last novel. He chooses to end his fiction-writing career by offering the reader a figure for figuration itself. "Carved on its surface," Ethan says of the stone, "was an endless interweaving shape that seemed to move and yet went no place." So the stone has pattern, but one that is open-ended and overdetermined, like the pattern of the best books. Like them, too, it embodies truth without knowing it. And finally, like them, it makes and sheds light: "[I]n my hand it gathered every bit of light there was." Steinbeck knows enough to know what he has given us, and he lets us know that he knows, right there, on the closing page.

MORRIS DICKSTEIN

Steinbeck and the Great Depression

M y encounters with John Steinbeck's work began, like most people's,
when I was quite young, with accessible short novels such as *The Pearl*, *The
Red Pony*, and *Cannery Row*. There was something elemental about them,
a rich, sensuous simplicity that also leads many readers to leave Steinbeck
behind as an enthusiasm to be outgrown. Luckily, I was never assigned one
of his novels to read in high school or college; his more ambitious books
were not ruined for me by bad teaching or premature exposure. But for me
Steinbeck remained little more than a strong regional writer who had created
an indelible impression of a small corner of California, especially the Salinas
Valley where he was born and the Monterey peninsula, with its canneries
and colorful paisanos, which had enchanted me as a young reader. But it
was only when I grew fascinated with the effects of the Great Depression
on American culture that another side of Steinbeck's work took hold of
me: the books of reportage and protest that earned him an indispensable
place in the social conscience of the Depression. Along with the work of
the photographers of the Farm Security Administration, such as Dorothea
Lange and Walker Evans, and documentary filmmakers like Pare Lorentz,
who inspired him and helped him see, Steinbeck became one of the key
witnesses to those years of social trauma and suffering. With the exception
of Harriet Beecher Stowe in *Uncle Tom's Cabin*, Upton Sinclair in *The Jungle*,

From the *South Atlantic Quarterly* 103:1, Winter 2004. © 2004 by Morris Dickstein.

and perhaps Richard Wright in *Native Son*, no protest writer had a greater influence on how Americans looked at their own country. The plight and migration of the Joads—as conceived by Steinbeck and filmed indelibly by John Ford—the Dust Bowl, the loss of a family home, the trek in search of work, the awful conditions for migrant farm labor, the struggle to keep the family together, became a metaphor for the Depression as a whole. This portrayal aroused sympathy and indignation that transcended literature and became part of our social history, as if Steinbeck had been reporting on a real family, which in a sense he was.

Unfortunately, his success as a protest writer undermined his literary standing, especially after the war, when such commitment came to be seen as limiting and simplistic. The Nobel Prize for Literature usually elicits a brief burst of national pride, but when Steinbeck received the award in 1962, the *New York Times Book Review* published a vigorous dissent by Arthur Mizener under the heading, "Does a Moral Vision of the Thirties Deserve a Nobel Prize?"—one of several attacks which, along with the prize itself, made it more difficult for him to write another work of fiction before he died in 1968. From the early critiques by Mary McCarthy, Edmund Wilson, and Alfred Kazin, Steinbeck had never been a favorite of the intellectuals or even of his fellow writers. It is no surprise that the *Times* attack was written by F. Scott Fitzgerald's first biographer, since Fitzgerald himself, though unfailingly generous toward most writers, was annoyed by Steinbeck's success, dismissing him in his letters as little more than a plagiarist who borrowed freely from his betters, including Frank Norris and D. H. Lawrence. Fitzgerald had his reasons: Steinbeck was the kind of socially committed writer who had displaced him in the 1930s and made his own work seem like a back number. Fitzgerald's uncharacteristic rage at Steinbeck was a lament for his own waning career.

Fitzgerald, in some personal despair, could hardly know that this current would one day flow in the opposite direction: the modernists, the more personal or more experimental writers of the thirties, whose work was then neglected in favor of social realism, would ultimately win out. The novels of Fitzgerald, Faulkner, Nathanael West, and Henry Roth would be canonized as American classics, while Steinbeck and Richard Wright would be the only social novelists of the thirties whose work would continue to be widely read. In Steinbeck's case this reversal would give rise to an enduring countermyth of the earthy storyteller disdained by the critics, taught only in high schools, and beloved by no one but ordinary readers, the People themselves, the collective entity that echoes through the pages of his most ambitious book. This was the burden of many articles published in 2002, the centennial of his birth, that made one feel that little had changed in forty years, except that the populism and protest that were belittled then could be celebrated today, without really accounting for what gives the writer his enduring power.

While there is little doubt that Steinbeck did his greatest work in the 1930s, most of what he published then had little connection to social protest, or even with the realism and naturalism to which his work has been too easily attached. Steinbeck first achieved some fame and readership not as a social critic but with his lighthearted evocation of the paisanos of Monterey in *Tortilla Flat* that echoes Malory's Arthurian legends. His first huge commercial success came with *Of Mice and Men*, the least political of his three novels about migrant farm workers, which went in rapid succession from Book-of-the-Month Club choice to Broadway play to Hollywood movie. In many ways this is less a social novel than a tissue of symbolic relationships; it fits in quite well with his short fiction of the early thirties, including *The Pastures of Heaven*, *Tortilla Flat*, and the stories in *The Long Valley*. To refute the received wisdom of Steinbeck as a protest writer, it would be tempting to locate the authentic Steinbeck in this prepolitical work, where I first discovered him. We could see these early books as his real imaginative center, even as his oblique response to the Depression (which scarcely figures in them at all), and argue that he was sidetracked into a social consciousness that was not at all natural to him.

By this reading, the core of Steinbeck's work would be his feeling for the land, his evocation of his native California as a natural paradise, his hatred of middle-class acquisitiveness and ambition, and his warm sympathy for outsiders who form a natural community built on impulse and fellow-feeling. Like nature itself, the instinctive anarchists of this community mock the values of commercial society by remaining oblivious to them. By emphasizing works with strong mythic underpinnings, such a reading would link Steinbeck not with proletarian writers or social realists, with whom he felt little affinity, but with the free-spirited explorers of low life like William Saroyan, Nelson Algren, and Henry Miller, whose heroes are anarchic individualists who live by their own code, by instinct, apart from the social values that constrain most other people. This kind of character is certainly close to the heart of Steinbeck's emotional life, the ground from which he starts out. There is a Rabelaisian strain in his work, an affection for hell-raisers and troublemakers who act out nature's mutiny against all social codes. It explains why he responded so strongly to writers as different as Frank Norris, Sherwood Anderson, and D. H. Lawrence.

One of the salutary features of Steinbeck's work that unsettles humanists and idealists is his insistence on the animal basis of human life, as seen in our fundamental need for food, shelter, physical expression, and, above all, tenderness and companionship. For better or worse, Steinbeck leaves humanity's more sublime aspirations to writers of cosmic or tragic ambition. In his letters he frequently sets aside such grand aims to stress the palpable and immediate. Asked by a friend in 1934 what he really wants out of life, he provocatively answers in strict biological and physical terms: "As an organism I am so simple that I want to be comfortable and comfort consists in—a place to sleep, dry and fairly soft, lack of hunger, almost any kind of food, occasional loss of semen in intercourse when it becomes troublesome, and a good deal of work. . . . I don't want to possess anything, nor to be anything. I have no ambition because on inspection the ends of ambition achieved seem tiresome" (*A Life in Letters* 92–93).

Steinbeck's modesty extends to his work, which also seems to belong to the biorhythms of his nervous system rather than any higher goals as an artist. In a 1933 letter, long before he was gripped by a social conscience, he writes: "I work because I know it gives me pleasure to work. It is as simple as that and I don't require any other reasons. I am losing a sense of self to a marked degree and that is a pleasant thing." This reminds us of Keats's famous notion of negative capability, the writer's loss of identity in his immersion in subjects outside himself. But where Keats attributes this chameleon quality above all to Shakespeare, Steinbeck goes on to disclaim being anything but a minor writer, a smooth, self-gratifying professional. "A couple of years ago I realized that I was not the material of which great artists are made and that I was rather glad I wasn't. And since then I have been happier simply to do the work and to take the reward at the end of every day that is given for a day of honest work. . . . I have a book to write. I think about it for a while and then I write it. There is nothing more. When it is done I have little interest in it. By the time one comes out I am usually tied up in another" (87).

These letters are typical. Steinbeck's description of himself as a physical animal, a simple organism, is consistent not only with his self-portrait as a writer but with the view of humanity that emerges in his early work. It also helps explain why those early books, all brief, episodic, and unambitious, were spun off with such facility. The writer himself was penniless and unknown, with no expectation of ever making money from his work. He was partly supported by his father, at some cost to his self-respect. He wrote *Tortilla Flat* as a refuge from the illness and constant care of his parents, who were both dying. "Its tone, I guess, is direct rebellion against all the sorrow of the house" (89–90). The success of the book would enable him to take on more ambitious projects, including *The Grapes of Wrath*, but his sudden popularity would complicate his life with a self-consciousness he had tried to avoid and could not bear. "I'm scared to death of popularity," he writes, soon after *Tortilla Flat* appeared. "It has ruined everyone I know" (111–12). It endangers a writer's honesty, besides making it more difficult to lose himself in his material. When he wins a prize for *Tortilla Flat*, he is loath to collect it in person. "The whole early part of my life was poisoned with egotism," he explains, "and then gradually I began to lose it." As a result, he claims, "in the last few books I have felt a curious richness as though my life had been multiplied through having become identified in a most real way with people who were not me." "If I become a trade mark," he fears, if he emerges from behind his work, "I shall lose the ability to do that" (119). Explaining his refusal to appear at book luncheons, give interviews, appear on radio programs, or even turn up to collect an award, he tells his agent, "I simply cannot write books if a consciousness of self is thrust on me. Must have some anonymity" (138).

The small fame and income that Steinbeck achieved after *Tortilla Flat* was nothing like the large fame and wealth thrust upon him four years later with the success (and notoriety) of *The Grapes of Wrath*, but these fears were prophetic of the terrible conflicts, the erosion of self-confidence he felt while writing that book and the sense of decline, of anticlimax, he felt after publishing it. "This book has become a misery to me because of my inadequacy," he wrote in his journal in 1938. By then it was his larger ambitions, his determination to do justice to a great subject, that brought him so much misery. To focus exclusively on the early books that preceded that fame would take him at his word as a minor professional writer who later happened to cause a sensation with some quasi-journalistic fiction that touched on burning social problems. It would beg the question of how those simpler, more casual works, which gave him such pleasure to write, set the stage for the larger books that, with all their flaws, brought him into angry collision with some of America's cherished values and with the forces that shaped society during the Depression.

For all his attraction to biological theory, which led him to use fiction to investigate notions like "group-man" and the "phalanx," Steinbeck was anything but a rigorous and systematic thinker. In gauging his response to the Depression, the subject for which he will surely be remembered, we must grapple with many seeming inconsistencies. How was the rich valley of *The Pastures of Heaven* of 1932 transformed into the ugly scene of labor conflict and exploitation of *In Dubious Battle* in 1936 and *The Grapes of Wrath* in 1939? How did the carefree poverty of the paisanos in *Tortilla Flat* of 1935 turn into the wretched, heartsick poverty of *The Grapes of Wrath*? How did the bohemian contempt for ownership, possessions, and steady work in *Tortilla Flat* give way to the Joads' desperation for work, or George and Lennie's poignant dream of self-sufficiency—of owning "a little piece a' lan'" and raising rabbits—which is at the emotional core of *Of Mice and Men*? And finally, how did Steinbeck's almost clinically objective sympathy for the strikers in *In Dubious Battle* and his mixed feelings about their calculating Communist organizers turn into his impassioned advocacy for the Joads in the epic and poetic pages of *The Grapes of Wrath*? Even in the natural paradise of the early books, his people are gifted at making themselves unhappy. But how did the snake of American capitalism, self-interest, and exploitation find its way into Steinbeck's California Eden, making it such a grim and miserable scene?

Steinbeck's initial vision of California as a fertile garden is the background against which his Depression drama is played out. *In Dubious Battle, Of Mice and Men,* and *The Grapes of Wrath* give us three versions of this story, supplemented by the bleak articles Steinbeck wrote about the conditions of migrant farm workers for the *San Francisco News* and *The Nation* in 1936, which mark his transformation from a detached observer who sees a strike as the crucible of a larger metaphysical conflict to an indignant muckraker and reformer exposing the abuses and human costs of the system. The fruit of American plenty on the California trees and vines is exactly the fruit that the beleaguered migrants cannot have, the dream that will never be realized. It hangs on the trees all around them, but they cannot enjoy it. The simple organic needs that John Steinbeck shares with the paisanos of Monterey are precisely the needs that loom so large for Lennie and George or for the Joads when they are thwarted by a selfish, competitive, manipulated system. "Ever'thing in California is owned," someone tells Tom Joad. "They ain't nothin' left. An' them people that owns it is gonna hang on to it if they got ta kill ever-body in the worl' to do it." Ownership turns people ugly. There are huge concentrations of agricultural wealth that need workers but also keep them close to starvation. This system deprives people of basic hope, human dignity, animal satisfaction, and even the means of survival, amid natural abundance. The seeming contradictions between Steinbeck's pastoral works and his protest novels are parts of a jigsaw puzzle that in the end fit perfectly together—though, as reviewers noted from the beginning, he never wrote two books that were exactly alike.

What kind of books were these? What use did Steinbeck make of the material that the Depression belatedly sent his way? Steinbeck did not seek out the subject of migrant labor because he was a committed reformer or because he saw it as the poisoned apple in his California garden. "He was always on the lookout for a story," says his biographer, Jackson Benson. In quick succession he had found and used one set of stories in *The Pastures of Heaven,* another in the cycle that became *Tortilla Flat,* yet others for the stories that would fill out *The Long Valley.* But this one was different. According to Benson, early in 1934 he met two fugitive union organizers and, with a nonfiction book initially in mind, arranged to buy the rights to their story. One of them, Cicil McKiddy, became a major source for *In Dubious Battle.* Steinbeck's strike in the Torgas Valley's apple orchards was loosely based on a prolonged and bitter 1933 cotton pickers' strike in which McKiddy was involved, as well as a peach pickers' strike that was won after four days. The modest, temporary gains achieved in these strikes incited the large fruit-growers to band together to shut out unions, harass and arrest organizers, and keep labor costs down to near-starvation levels. The cotton pickers were paid $1.50 for putting in a ten-hour day, and in Steinbeck's novel it is a five-cent cut to fifteen cents an hour that triggers the strike. The reduction could be enforced only because there was an oversupply of labor, including not only Dust Bowlers but Mexican and Filipino workers, though only the oppression and dreadful living conditions of *white* workers would eventually arouse the national conscience.

Oddly, Steinbeck makes his fictional strike more futile and tragic than the ones it was based on, just as he makes his organizers and strike leaders less heroic than their real-life models. Steinbeck was not thinking politically when he wrote this book. Instead, with the Miltonic echoes heard in the title, he portrays the strike as a struggle against overwhelming power and gives the whole story a flavor of fatality, reminiscent of some earlier works of literary naturalism. This dark, deterministic strain would carry over into the cruelly dashed hopes in *Of Mice and Men*, where the malevolent Curley, the boss's pugnacious son, and his lonely, seductive, unsatisfied wife trigger a catastrophe that seems inevitable from the first page. Yet there is never any doubt in *In Dubious Battle* that Steinbeck's sympathy is with the exploited men and their families, whom he never manages to individualize. These are the famous thirties "masses" who are victimized by their bosses, brutalized by callous authorities and vigilantes, and manipulated by their own selfless but unscrupulous leaders. Unlike *The Grapes of Wrath*, *In Dubious Battle* makes little effort to see the world from their point of view. Instead it is a study of group behavior, as articulated by the character of Doc Burton, the theorist of "group-man," and an exploration of the tactics of Communists who try to incite and direct the group, to manipulate the men for their own good.

Throughout the thirties, thanks to the rise of powerful mass movements like communism and fascism, writers and filmmakers grew entranced with problems of mass psychology and collective behavior. The conditions of the Depression were so overpowering that they brought traditional American individualism into question. Both *In Dubious Battle* and *The Grapes of Wrath*, in different ways, were experiments at seeing humanity in the collective terms that the Depression seemed to demand: first in biological terms, almost as a scientific experiment conceived by Steinbeck's marine biologist friend Ed Ricketts, then in an epic and biblical mode, as Steinbeck used one family to stand for a mass migration, and added sweeping interchapters that generalize this movement into a vast social phenomenon. Both of these literary approaches conflict with America's ingrained individualism, to say nothing of the traditional novel's need for distinct, well-defined characters who stand some chance of being agents of their own destiny. When Alfred

Kazin complained in 1942 that "Steinbeck's people are always on the verge of becoming human, but never do," he was pointing to a weakness that was also, on some level, a deliberate intention. Steinbeck touches on this point in *Working Days*, the journal he kept while writing *The Grapes of Wrath*: "Make the people live," he says to himself. "Make them live. But my people must be more than people. They must be an over-essence of people." For Steinbeck, realism had been more a commercial obligation than an article of faith. "I am writing many stories now," he said in a letter a few years earlier. "Because I should like to sell some of them, I am making my characters as nearly as I can in the likeness of men. The stream underneath and the meanings I am interested in can be ignored" (94). It was this symbolic or allegorical dimension, the story behind the story, that most engaged him.

When he wrote *In Dubious Battle*, Steinbeck did not yet feel that individualized characters were essential to his work. Instead he saw mass man as an ecosystem that lived and moved by different rules, especially under Depression conditions of want and powerlessness. A very perceptive admirer of this novel, André Gide, remarked in his journals that "the main character is the crowd." Steinbeck shows how weak and hopeless the workers are individually, how strong they can be when united by some common purpose. Yet in the novel's outbursts of violence, Steinbeck, like other observers of mass behavior, stresses the heavy, ominous quality of the crowd as well as its strength. His novel is remarkably ambivalent about the proletarian formulas it appropriates from other strike novels. These novels focus not only on industrial and working conditions but also on a process of initiation by which a veteran radical passes his savvy onto a young initiate, who comes to learn the value of struggle and to learn exactly how the system works. When the older man (like Preacher Casy in *The Grapes of Wrath*) becomes a martyr to the cause, his protégé is able to pick up the torch. Individual leaders and battles may be lost but the fight always goes on. With Mac and Jim, the two union organizers in *In Dubious Battle*, Steinbeck is less interested in individual workers than in how they can be molded and directed. He shows how the Reds keep their eye on long-term goals, shaping the men into an angry mass, a unified force, with little regard for their immediate human needs. Describing the book as "the best (psychological) portrayal that I know of Communism," Gide noted that everything in the book, "like the outcome of the struggle itself, remains dubious. Especially dubious the legitimacy of using treacherous means to bring about the triumph of even the most legitimate cause."

Nowhere in the book does Steinbeck show any theoretical or political interest in Communism. Despite his reportage on the conditions of migrant workers for *The Nation* and the *San Francisco News*, commissioned after this novel had made him appear as an expert on the subject, Steinbeck himself played no role in the ideological debates of the thirties. What interested him was not Communism but Communists as character types, not the kind of urban intellectuals who debate Marxist principles in dingy all-night cafeterias but the foot-soldiers in the field whose lives are as stripped down as the paisanos of Cannery Row. Mac and Jim are not strike "leaders," in Steinbeck's view, but men who have learned to tune in to the rhythms of group life, who become adept at using the material at hand, including their own human losses, as a means of playing on people and welding their anger into an iron fist. The intellectual Doc Burton, based on Steinbeck's friend Ed Ricketts, manages to be a skeptic and activist at the same time, dispassionate like Steinbeck himself, but the two Reds, Mac and Jim, have little patience with ideas. As purely practical men, organizers building a movement, they find Doc's intellectual detachment alien and disturbing.

As Mac educates Jim in his methods, we cannot avoid seeing how manipulative he is. First, he wins the trust of the men and their "natural leader," London, by delivering his daughter-in-law's baby, though we later learn that he knows nothing about obstetrics. In one of several scenes of graphic violence, he coolly breaks the nose of a young strikebreaker with surgical precision, to make him a walking lesson to others. "I want a billboard," he says, "not a corpse." Elsewhere, he says, "I can't take time to think about the feelings of one man. I'm too busy with big bunches of men." In Ralph Ellison's *Invisible Man*, which deals satirically with Communism during just this period, another veteran organizer warns the newcomer that "you mustn't waste your emotions on individuals, they don't count." "There's just one rule," Mac tells Jim early on. "Use whatever material you've got." He has little hope for this strike, but he's thinking ahead to other strikes and hardly cares who gets hurt along the way. His best bit of material is the fresh corpse of one of his own men, ironically named Joy, a scarred veteran of many labor battles, whose joyful martyrdom he turns to full advantage to sow indignation among the men. Ironically, his last bit of material is provided by his young acolyte Jim, over whose body he intones what is virtually the Communist motto in this book: "Comrades! He didn't want nothing for himself—." On this open-ended line the novel ends. By then, martyrdom is the only weapon the strikers have left.

This is where the human drama of *In Dubious Battle* unexpectedly slips in. In the growth of Mac's tender feelings for Jim, in his discomfort that Jim is learning his lessons all too well, Steinbeck exposes the personal vulnerability behind the impersonal facade. Though he orchestrates powerful emotions in ordinary men, Mac rejects them when they show up in himself. "I'm no good. The Party ought to get rid of me. I lose my head." By his inhuman definition, his pupil is now a better Communist than he is, more daring, more selfless, more fanatical. He is not only frightened for Jim but frightened at the kind of man he has become. He hears his own ideas emerge from Jim's mouth with the icy intensity of total commitment. "You're getting beyond me, Jim. I'm getting scared of you." His protective fears for his apt pupil get in his way, for now he has something he is not prepared to lose.

Jim, for his part, becomes as impervious to argument as he is to fear, and even takes on himself their dead comrade's impulse to martyrdom. He *wants* to be used. Though wounded, he refuses to hang back. Just before he is killed, we are told, "His face was transfigured. A furious light of energy seemed to shine from it." Mac does finally use him, but not in the way he hoped to do. The book develops its fictional logic apart from any ideas of "group-man." An older ethic of personal loyalty and individual emotions undercuts the new concept of man as a collective entity. Steinbeck was clearly fascinated by how a small number of Communists could be the yeast for a large body of powerless, unorganized workers. But he almost leaves out the feelings that would make this effort human rather than dehumanizing. This is where his own relation to the struggle would evolve, and where *Of Mice and Men*, the *News* articles, and especially *The Grapes of Wrath* would mark a departure from *In Dubious Battle*, which is finally a catechism on Communist tactics that gives short shrift to the workers themselves. Steinbeck sees callousness and condescension in the way Mac and Jim approach these benighted men, treating them as an unleavened mass ready to rise, needing only be hurt, angered, and radicalized. Yet, to a degree, his novel treats them the same way, as disposable cannon-fodder.

Their flaws do not mean that Mac and Jim are unrepresentative. Like many of Steinbeck's characters, they are *too* representative. Steinbeck had a good eye for types, but it could lead him astray. Mac is less a person than the embodiment of Steinbeck's observations about Communist tactics and psychology. His view is a complex one but it is precisely that—a point of view. Behind the fictional trappings of *In Dubious Battle* lay a shrewd essay on an urgent subject: How were men to live when, even in the midst of natural plenty, they were oppressed by arbitrary economic power? How were they to survive when their most ardent defenders cared for them less as people than as bearers of the revolutionary cause, mere embryos of a better world? As the "dubious" ending of the novel shows, the migrant workers of the Depression years were caught between a rock and a hard place.

*   *   *

The story of Steinbeck's evolving response to the Depression can be seen in his shifting viewpoint in the years between this novel and the final version of *The Grapes of Wrath*. He went from seeing the migrant workers from the outside as social victims, objects of pity or exploitation, to identifying with them and seeing the world through their eyes. This began in a small way in the spring and summer of 1936 as he worked on *Of Mice and Men*. The book, as everyone knows, is about the hopes and dreams of one of the oddest couples in American literature, the canny George, the caregiver, who thinks he wants to be off on his own, free of responsibility, and Lennie, the lumbering giant, whose thwarted tenderness and dangerous strength are always at risk of crushing whatever he touches, whether mice and pups, or men and women. Some readers have always found these characters to be too elemental, yet they reflect the primal needs that Steinbeck discovered in himself—a longing for animal warmth, the feeling of security, and the reassuring touch of other living creatures. Steinbeck was no doubt inspired by Faulkner's Benjy in *The Sound and the Fury* to create a character who embodies the least common denominator in human longings, a baffled need for simple affection, the sense of having a place in the world. The strange relationship of George and Lennie, which echoes the bond between Huck and Jim, is built on a dream of independence that others around them soon come to share, from the crippled old Candy, who has been hurt on the job and fears that when he "can't swamp out no bunk houses they'll put [him] on the county," to the bowed and embittered black man Crooks, who has always been treated as a pariah. By sticking together and dreaming of their own little homestead, Lennie and George offer a glimmer of solidarity and hope to lonely men who have long been scorned as human driftwood. Everyone comments on how unusual it is for two men—especially these men—to be traveling together, tied to each other, and George ritually laments about how free and easy his life would be if he were on his own. But caring for Lennie, getting Lennie out of trouble, nurturing a pipe dream of independence that is really Lennie's, and finally saving Lennie by taking his life—these are the only things that give *his* life some purpose. In a sense, George and Lennie pick up where Mac and Jim left off, with another bond that culminates in rupture, sacrifice, and loss.

The symbolism of the novel is far too schematic. George and Lennie stand for mind and body, thought and feeling, calculation and visceral need. The accidental deaths of Lennie's pet mice and pup, crushed in his tender, loving grip, foreshadow the ultimate death of Curley's wife. When Candy's old dog must be put out of his misery, the wrenching loss prefigures what the old man fears for himself, and what George will have to do for Lennie. In the fateful world of *Of Mice and Men*, every man must kill the thing he loves, the thing he cares for most. Steinbeck, like a latter-day Thomas Hardy, put his thumb on the scales to make sure that his characters' hopes were thwarted, but he also tried hard to individualize them and see the world plainly from their point of view. As he worked on the book, he wanted his people to "act with all the unexpectedness of real people," and he worried that "building too carefully for an event" would be "doing that old human trick of reducing everything to its simplest design," which proved to be the real weakness of the novel. He reminded himself that "the designs of lives are not so simple." This admission is a far cry from what he felt when he was writing short stories, chafing at the exigency of making his characters seem like real human beings.

The shift in Steinbeck's angle of vision took hold later that year, when he began visiting squatters' camps for his articles on "The Harvest Gypsies" for the *San Francisco News*. Between August 1936, when he did this research, and February and March 1938, when he witnessed the flooding and starvation in Visalia shortly before writing *The Grapes of Wrath*, Steinbeck not only went down into the trenches, as other committed thirties writers did, but grew horrified and helplessly indignant at the migrants' living conditions, which he described with awful vividness in the second of his *News* articles and in his letters. In the *News* article, one of the most effective pieces of Depression journalism, he focuses on the inexorable disintegration of three families in one of the squatters' camps. In his letters of February and March 1938, Steinbeck describes the awful flooding and starvation in the interior valleys, the lack of medical care and sanitary facilities, the government inaction, the hostility of the surrounding towns, and the overwhelming need he feels to publicize these conditions. "I must go to Visalia. Four thousand families, drowned out of their tents are really starving to death. . . . The death of children by starvation in our valleys is simply staggering" (*A Life in Letters* 159). When he goes there he finds it even worse than he expected: "A short trip into the fields where the water is a foot deep in the tents and the children are up on the beds and there is no food and no fire, and the county has taken off all the nurses because 'the problem is so great that we can't do anything about it.' So they do nothing" (161).

If they would do nothing, perhaps he could. "The newspapers won't touch the stuff but they will under my byline," he wrote (159). "I want to put a tag of shame on the greedy bastards who are responsible for this" (162). Under this pressure to do something, Steinbeck shifted from observer to advocate, from would-be scientist theorizing about "group-man" to angry reformer exposing the system's abuses, but above all from seeing the migrants as mistreated objects to seeing them as people trying to preserve their dignity as they struggled to survive. *The Grapes of Wrath* was not simply a new take on the same material; it was a different kind of novel, with all the strengths and flaws that came along with Steinbeck's emotional identification with the migrants' plight.

Despite the accusations of those who derided him as a dangerous radical, John Steinbeck was never a Communist—his politics were those of a New Deal Democrat. He went to Visalia at the urging of the Resettlement Administration, which wanted him to publicize what was happening there.

Even his research for *The Grapes of Wrath* was virtually sponsored by a lower-level New Deal administrator, Tom Collins, and the accuracy of his novel was later defended by Eleanor Roosevelt herself. But he grew fascinated by the same social issues that engaged the Communists. His turn from the union organizers of *In Dubious Battle* to the saga of one migrant family paralleled the party's turn toward the sentimental populism of the Popular Front, which cultivated themes of patriotism and common values and stressed its roots in American democratic traditions. In his *News* articles, Steinbeck tried to show that the migrants were not aliens but neighbors, white people just like themselves, not a plague of locusts who had simply descended upon them. "They are not migrants by nature," he said. "They are gypsies by force of circumstance." Unlike the foreign laborers of the past, going back to the Chinese who had built the railroads, these people were Americans who would not be cowed or sent away and could not be forced into a subhuman standard of living. "It should be understood that with this new race the old methods of repression, of starvation wages, of jailing, beating, and intimidation are not going to work; these are American people."

Steinbeck is appealing to his readers' moral sympathy and human kinship but also to their Americanism, a powerful motif in a period when all social protest was labeled Communist and all Communists were branded foreign agitators. Beginning with the book's title out of "The Battle Hymn of the Republic" and its use of dialect, *The Grapes of Wrath* would try to give a native air to the plight of the migrant workers, for Steinbeck sees their cause as quintessentially American yet apocalyptic in its urgency. "The Battle Hymn is American and intensely so," he wrote to his editor (174). He saw the grapes as an image of the Edenic plenty of America, a land controlled by a small plutocracy while the people starved, yet also an emblem of biblical vengeance coming to fruition as surely as nature itself.

The Grapes of Wrath begins as the story of an eviction, continues with the account of a journey, the difficult passage of a family from their old world to a new one, and concludes with the disillusioning calamities that beset them after they have reached this promised land. Steinbeck underlines the typicality of the family's fate by interspersing brief, poetic chapters of general history and radical rhetoric, as Dos Passos had interwoven newsreels, historical summaries, and capsule biographies of famous Americans into the narrative pattern of *U.S.A.* Steinbeck's novel is full of resonant literary echoes. From the proletarian novel, for example, Steinbeck borrowed protagonists—especially Tom Joad and Preacher Casy, who come gradually to understand the deep-rooted causes of their misery and oppression; in the parlance of a later era, they get their consciousness raised.

The Communists had their own version of the final conflict, which Steinbeck occasionally echoes in the weaker interchapters of the novel. His strength is not in general ideas but in concrete, visceral evocation of things as they are: the facts of the harvest, the camps, the rotting fruit, the dying children, the listless parents, all of which he saw with his own eyes. For all his attempts at homespun philosophizing, his efforts to write an epic saga in biblical, folksy, at times dithyrambic prose, Steinbeck is basically a sensuous, immediate, and visceral writer. Where much of proletarian fiction was willed and theoretical, he has a gift not only for direct storytelling but for absorbing data and breaking it down into something simple and direct. He has no rival in showing how things were done, how they happened. Nothing is more effective in *The Grapes of Wrath* than the nuts and bolts of slaughtering a pig, getting on the road, preparing a meager meal, repairing a broken-down car. Steinbeck's letters and journal show how obsessed he became with the human wreckage he found in the camps, and he was determined to write a novel that would do full justice to their plight. Yet he had no easy explanations or solutions. As with so many thirties naturalists, his initial impulse was simply to tell us what he *saw*. The roots of this writing are journalistic, its effects cinematic. Yet Steinbeck also achieves genuine power by giving the book a large shape and sweep and locating its emotional center in two feisty, difficult characters, a mother and her eldest son, who show an indomitable will to survive and keep the family together. Much of Steinbeck's earlier work had dealt with male relationships (Mac and Jim, Lennie and George), with women (like Curley's wife) as an intrusive, even threatening presence—but the nurturing role of Ma Joad conveys the author's emotional connection to this material. She combines toughness, endurance, and maternal empathy. This awesome female determination in terrible times resonated with Depression audiences, much as it did in *Gone with the Wind*. It would prove to be a key to the book's popular success, which far exceeded the reach of other proletarian fiction.

Steinbeck had always understood the limited appeal of the kind of ideological novel he had written in *In Dubious Battle*. This new work begins in the hard-boiled world of the thirties road novel, with a truculent Tom hitchhiking home after a stint in prison for killing a man. But it turns out there is no "home" for him to come to—this is a rural society in disintegration. In a brilliant stroke, the author transforms the individual drifter of thirties fact and legend into a migrating family that reflects that disintegration. Steinbeck turns the hard-bitten loner into a tenacious upholder of family solidarity, showing how middle-class values themselves are threatened by corporate greed, selfishness, and economic cruelty. To the respectable people they meet along the way, the Okies are simply outsiders, dirty and uncivilized. ("Them goddamn Okies got no sense and no feeling," says one bystander. "They ain't human. A human being wouldn't live like they do.") But Steinbeck would convince them that these are good country people like yourselves, white Americans. And they are families, not lone derelicts or alien outsiders. He harnesses this to a powerful myth, that of the biblical trek, the crossing of the desert in search of the promised land, the westering journey that he had already explored in his story "The Leader of the People," with its reminder of the covered wagons of pioneer days. This mythic resonance helps explain why the book became one of the few proletarian novels to survive its period. Moreover, the great movie adaptation by scenarist Nunnally Johnson, cinematographer Gregg Toland, and director John Ford lent a physical actuality and immediacy to the characters that the novel could not fully provide. Thanks to the perfect casting of Henry Fonda, Jane Darwell, and a great ensemble of character actors, the Joads come through not only as a "fambly" but as sharply etched individuals. Even the vaporous, folksy philosophy of ex-preacher Casy—who too often tells us, in fake-sounding, down-home terms, precisely what to think—is solidly anchored to the long, lean face, cadaverous limbs, and sonorous voice of John Carradine, to the point that it is impossible for audiences to reread the book without seeing and hearing these performers.

Yet Steinbeck's overt purpose, like that of Dos Passos in *U.S.A.*, is to convince us—and his characters—that the individual, even the individual family, scarcely matters any longer. The new concentrations of economic power have made the old yeoman independence a thing of the past. Those who would not be able to adapt, who are too old and too set in their ways, like Grampa and Granma, die on the road, unable to enter the new land. Even Ma and Tom, who are the strongest and most determined, who never lose heart as others do, are at best able to hold some of the family together. They learn that unless they throw in their lot with others—the Wilsons early on, the Wainwrights later, the strikers whose jobs they unknowingly take— they are helpless against the large growers and their minions, the police and the vigilantes who enforce their power. The natural community of outsiders in a book like *Tortilla Flat* gives way to a self-conscious community of the insulted and injured, aware of their common condition—the mass of people whom modern society has rendered powerless.

That we should remember the Joads so well, that their story continues to summarize the Depression for many of us, is a sign that Steinbeck was divided against himself, for in some ways the hero of the book is not a family but an abstraction, the People. For all his literary echoes and political theories, Steinbeck prided himself on working close to the social horror that so troubled him. "I'm trying to write history while it is happening and I don't want to be wrong" (162). Like that of many other writers moved by the social crisis of the thirties, he was trying to catch history on the wing, to humanize it into a narrative everyone could grasp and feel. Though it had already been announced for publication, he destroyed a more satiric,

polemical version of the novel because, apparently, it mocked the growers
and vigilantes without doing justice to the humanity of the victims. "My
father would have called it a smart-alec book," he wrote. "It was full of
tricks to make people ridiculous." Despite his pessimism and fatalism about
migrants like the Joads, who seemed to have little power to shape their own
destiny, Steinbeck could not resist giving their grim story a heavy dose of
populist uplift, in lines like the ones Nunnally Johnson would pull from
the middle of the novel and shape into the conclusion of the movie: "Why,
Tom," says Ma, "—us people will go on livin' when all them people is gone.
Why, Tom, we're the people that live. They ain't gonna wipe us out. Why,
we're the people—we go on." This is another difference between *The Grapes
of Wrath* and the proletarian fiction that preceded it. Though Steinbeck was
far from being a Communist or fellow traveler, *In Dubious Battle* was an
offshoot of the party's so-called Third Period, emphasizing the strike as a
radical means of promoting class conflict, portraying the workers as passive
vessels directed by a vanguard leadership and its tactics. *The Grapes of Wrath*,
by contrast, is akin to the post-1935 Popular Front, with its romance of the
People, a novel in which the Communists are barely mentioned except as
all-purpose bogeymen of the owners and their lackeys. In a famous passage,
Tom learns that "a red is any son-of-a-bitch that wants thirty cents an hour
when we're payin' twenty-five!"—which means, "we're all reds." Earlier, we
had seen Tom refer to himself jokingly as "bolshevisky," as he proceeded
with Casy to reinvent radicalism in all-American terms. When Tom figures
out that if the pickers don't pick the peaches the fruit will rot, Steinbeck is
offering a lesson in collective action and the power of the people. "Well,
you figgered out somepin, didn' you," a young man tells him. "Come right
outa your own head," he says—not from any Red troublemaker. The novel
is full of didactic scenes like this one, where Tom learns something so that
Steinbeck can teach *us* something. But no one ever really talked that way.
The underpinnings of Steinbeck's morality play peep through, even as he gets
his information—and indignation—across.

Steinbeck usually rounds off his scenes of muckraking exposure by
illustrating the potential for group solidarity. When Ma Joad, with her small
pittance but unshakeable pride, is buying groceries at the company store run
by the Hooper Ranch, we see how a man much like herself must glumly
enforce the company's inflated prices. They come to loggerheads when she is
a dime short and cannot buy some sugar for Tom's coffee, though the family
will shortly be earning enough money to pay for it. Caught between Ma's
simple humanity and his own fear of losing his job for extending credit, the
clerk grows more and more uncomfortable. Finally, breaking through to his
own underlying kinship with her, he takes a dime from his own pocket and
drops it in the cash register.

The scene is too pat and contrived, though it deftly transposes the book's key theme into a small encounter. But Steinbeck, with his didactic purpose, is unable to leave well enough alone. As Ma is leaving, she turns and adds, "I'm learnin' one thing good. . . . Learnin' it all a time, ever' day. If you're in trouble or hurt or need—go to poor people. They're the only ones that'll help—the only ones." What Ma says is not far from the truth, but by hitting us over the head with it, Steinbeck weakens the scene and damages its credibility as fiction. His anger gives the book unusual power, and he shows a real feeling for these people's lives, for the touch and feel of their experience. But he cannot resist preaching at us, driving a point home, sentimentalizing his material. Steinbeck was a gifted mimic of country dialect, but his way of putting his own ideas in the mouths of simple characters can sound phony and staged. His sympathy extends less to the people he creates than to their social prototypes, the *real* suffering Joads he had actually seen in the camps and written about in his articles.

The folksy and sentimental touches in *The Grapes of Wrath* betray its Popular Front ambience. They link the novel to the muscular regional paintings of Thomas Hart Benton, who soon illustrated the novel; to the songs of Woody Guthrie, who turned the whole story into a seventeen-stanza ballad; to the splendid folk material in Virgil Thomson's scores for Lorentz's films; to the thirties ballets of Aaron Copland and Martha Graham, and even to that coming blockbuster, *Oklahoma*, with its celebrated Agnes de Mille choreography. Yet none of these works, except the Lorentz films, matched the darker side of Steinbeck's novel, culminating in the disintegration of the family and the final scene in the Visalia-like flood.

Nunnally Johnson and John Ford produced an adaptation that was not only exceptionally faithful for its time but also unusually bold for Hollywood in its treatment of a controversial issue. Their loyalty to this project, however, did not prevent them from toning down the explicit sexual, religious, and political dimensions of the novel. Though Steinbeck himself was wracked with guilt over an affair that threatened his first marriage, in his novels he presents men as horny, randy creatures—lusty animals bursting with natural vitality. Steinbeck worked hard to forestall censorship of these aspects of the novel, especially the frank language, which ultimately led to its being condemned for obscenity by those who objected, more accurately, to its social views. Virtually none of the novel's darker side survives in the movie. Steinbeck's naturalism also fuels the book's religious satire, beginning with Preacher Casy, who is estranged from his calling in part because he cannot condemn or restrain his spontaneous sexual appetite. His conflict eventually leads him to a religion of humanity, a revolutionary radicalism that combines Emerson's Oversoul with Marx's theory of Surplus Value. Very little of this antireligious feeling gets into the movie either.

In his 1957 book *Novels into Film*, George Bluestone showed how the muckraking side of the novel is softened in the film, starting with the ingenious transformation of the interchapters into smooth visual montages—a powerful rhythm of events without much explanation. This way of visualizing the epic dimensions of the novel extends to numerous lines of dialogue in which the plight of the families becomes more vague in origin yet more visceral in impact. As Bluestone summarizes it, "If the religious satire is absent and the politics muted, the love of land, family and human dignity are consistently translated into effective cinematic images." Though they speak for Steinbeck, these deeply conveyed feelings for the land and the family belong even more to the film work of John Ford. The director never claimed the film as one of his favorite works, and even insisted to Bluestone that "I never read the book," yet it contains haunting Fordian touches only dimly suggested by the novel. A few sentences in the novel that describe Ma burning her keepsakes become a wordless scene of inestimable power, evoking Ma first as a younger woman, now as a woman staunchly but poignantly taking leave of the past. The Saturday night dance at the sanitary camp becomes the occasion for another privileged moment, as Tom dances with Ma to the tune of the "The Red River Valley"—a scene of intense communal and personal warmth that is not at all typical of Steinbeck, but was reprised brilliantly by Fonda and Ford after the war in the church dedication dance of *My Darling Clementine*. It's as if Ford could lay bare the emotional core of *The Grapes of Wrath* by borrowing a page from *Sons and Lovers*. The novel is about a social migration; the film is about a mother and son.

By reversing the order of two episodes, and dispensing with Steinbeck's garish (and perhaps unfilmable) symbolic conclusion, Johnson and Ford subtly altered the deeply pessimistic outlook of the novel. By placing the scenes at the sanitary camp *after* the miserable strikebreaking episode at the private ranch, the film in one stroke projects the New Deal, along with the communal democracy of the migrants themselves, as the effective solution to the migrants' problems. This optimism is enhanced by Ma's populist rhetoric, adapted from what she said to Tom earlier in the novel. ("We're the people that live. They can't wipe us out—they can't lick us. We'll go on forever, Pa, 'cause we're the people.") Steinbeck's somber ending, on the other hand, is one of those spectacularly expressionist touches that we often find in supposedly naturalistic novels, as Erich von Stroheim understood when he turned Norris's *McTeague* into *Greed*. Having lost her own baby from shock and malnutrition, Rose of Sharon gives her breast to a starving man, who in turn had stopped eating so his own boy could live. Both are taking refuge from the flood in someone else's barn, where they enact this small, improbable lesson in community and mutual aid which the novel has been preaching from the very start. What Rose of Sharon does is an act of desperation, at the biological bedrock of nature and nurture, far from the reassuring populist platitudes of the movie's ending.

Finally, however, the novel and film have come down to us together as an almost seamless composite of words and images, fictional characters and performances. We may be tempted to turn back to Steinbeck's earlier fiction, as we are drawn, say, to the lively, unpretentious films that Frank Capra churned out before he too began preaching a populist social gospel. In the end, however, Steinbeck's ambitious social novels fulfill the agrarian pastoral dreams of his earlier books by setting them against the awesome conditions of the Depression, which gave him the kind of subject a writer finds only once in a lifetime. Steinbeck's biblical myth of passage, his matriarchal construction of the family as a defense against disintegration, the moral indignation that took the place of his scientific naturalism, the advocacy that shattered his detachment, the sense of individual life that competed with his vision of community—all these represent a much fuller reaction to a social and economic crisis that he could not avoid or ignore, and that we can't ever forget because of how he made us see it. That "moral vision of the thirties" has left its abiding mark.

Works Cited

Quotations from Steinbeck's letters, indicated by page number, are from John Steinbeck, *A Life in Letters*, ed. Elaine Steinbeck and Robert Wallsten (New York: Viking, 1975). Citations from Steinbeck's journals are from Steinbeck, *Working Days*, ed. Robert DeMott (New York: Viking, 1989). Quotations from Steinbeck's *San Francisco News* articles on the "Harvest Gypsies" are from Steinbeck's pamphlet, *"Their Blood Is Strong"* (San Francisco: Simon J. Lubin Society of California, 1938), once difficult to find but now included in the Library of America edition of Steinbeck's novels. Quotations from André Gide's journals are from the fourth volume of *The Journals of André Gide*, trans. Justin O'Brien (New York: Knopf, 1951). The superb, comprehensive biography by Jackson J. Benson is *The True Adventures of John Steinbeck, Writer* (New York: Viking, 1984). The film adaptation of *The Grapes of Wrath* has been carefully studied by George Bluestone, *Novels into Film* (Berkeley: University of California Press, [1957] 1968). Steinbeck's novels are quoted from the following editions: *In Dubious Battle* (New York: Penquin, 1979); *Of Mice and Men* (New York: Bantam, 1975); *The Grapes of Wrath* (New York: Viking, 1958).

Chronology

1902	John Ernst Steinbeck born on February 27, in Salinas, California to John Ernst II and Olive Hamilton Steinbeck.
1919	Graduates from Salinas High School.
1920–25	Attends Stanford and works as laborer intermittently. Publishes first short stories in *The Stanford Spectator*.
1925	Drops out of Stanford and goes to New York. Works as construction laborer and reports for the *American* newspaper.
1926	Returns to California, writes stories and novels.
1929	His first novel, *Cup of Gold*, published.
1930	Marries Carol Henning.
1932	*The Pastures of Heaven*, a novel, published. Moves to Los Angeles.
1933	*To a God Unknown*, a novel, published. Returns to Monterey. *The Red Pony* appears in two parts in *North American Review*.
1934	His mother dies.
1935	*Tortilla Flat* is published. His father dies.
1936	*In Dubious Battle*, a novel, published. Travels to Mexico.
1937	*Of Mice and Men* is published, chosen for Book-of-the-Month club. Travels to Europe and later from Oklahoma to California with migrants.

1938	*Their Blood Is Strong*, nonfiction, is published. A collection of short stories, *The Long Valley*, is published.
1939	*The Grapes of Wrath* is published. Elected to the National Institute of Arts and Letters.
1940	*The Grapes of Wrath* wins the Pulitzer Prize. *The Forgotten Village*, a documentary, is produced. Goes on research trip with Edward Ricketts to the Sea of Cortez.
1941	*Sea of Cortez* published with Edward Ricketts.
1942	*The Moon is Down* published. Steinbeck and Carol Henning divorce. Writes the script *Bombs Away* for the U.S. Air Force.
1943	Moves to New York City, marries Gwendolyn Conger. In Europe covers the war as correspondent for the *New York Herald Tribune*.
1944	Writes script for Alfred Hitchcock's *Lifeboat*. A son, Thom, is born.
1945	*Cannery Row*, a novel, is published. *The Red Pony* published in four parts.
1946	A second son, John IV, is born.
1947	*The Wayward Bus*, a novel, is published. *The Pearl*, a novella, is published. Travels in Russia with photographer Robert Capa.
1948	*A Russian Journal*, an account of his 1947 tour of Russia, is published. Steinbeck and Gwendolyn Conger divorce.
1950	*Burning Bright*, a novella, is published. Marries Elaine Anderson Scott. Writes script for *Viva Zapata!*
1951	*The Log from the Sea of Cortez*, the narrative part of *Sea of Cortez*, is published.
1952	*East of Eden* published.
1954	*Sweet Thursday*, a novel, published (a sequel to *Cannery Row*).
1957	*The Short Reign of Pippen IV*, a novel, is published.
1958	*Once There Was a War*, a collection of his wartime dispatches, is published.
1960	Steinbeck takes a three-month tour of America with his dog, Charley.
1961	*The Winter of Our Discontent*, his twelfth and final novel, published.

1962   *Travels with Charley*, the journal of his 1960 tour, published. Awarded the Nobel Prize for Literature.

1964   Awarded the United States Medal of Freedom and a Press Medal of Freedom.

1966   *American and Americans*, reflections on contemporary America, published.

1966–67   Reports from Vietnam for *Newsday*.

1968   Dies of severe heart attack in New York City on December 20.

Contributors

HAROLD BLOOM is Sterling Professor of the Humanities at Yale University. He is the author of 30 books, including *Shelley's Mythmaking, The Visionary Company, Blake's Apocalypse, Yeats, A Map of Misreading, Kabbalah and Criticism, Agon: Toward a Theory of Revisionism, The American Religion, The Western Canon,* and *Omens of Millennium: The Gnosis of Angels, Dreams, and Resurrection. The Anxiety of Influence* sets forth Professor Bloom's provocative theory of the literary relationships between the great writers and their predecessors. His most recent books include *Shakespeare: The Invention of the Human,* a 1998 National Book Award finalist, *How to Read and Why, Genius: A Mosaic of One Hundred Exemplary Creative Minds, Hamlet: Poem Unlimited, Where Shall Wisdom Be Found?,* and *Jesus and Yahweh: The Names Divine.* In 1999, Professor Bloom received the prestigious American Academy of Arts and Letters Gold Medal for Criticism. He has also received the International Prize of Catalonia, the Alfonso Reyes Prize of Mexico, and the Hans Christian Andersen Bicentennial Prize of Denmark.

EDWARD E. WALDRON is the author of *Walter White and the Harlem Renaissance.*

LOUIS OWENS was professor of English and Native American Studies and director of creative writing at the University of California, Davis at the time of his death in July, 2002. Louis was the author *The Grapes of Wrath: Trouble in the Promised Land* and *John Steinbeck's Re-Vision of America.* He was also a novelist and wrote the acclaimed *Other Destines: Understanding the American Indian Novel.*

HOWARD LEVANT is the author of *The Novels of John Steinbeck: A Critical Study.*

NELLIE Y. MCKAY, professor of Afro-American studies at the University of Wisconsin, died in 2006 of colon cancer. She was the author of *Jean Toomer, The Artist: A Study of His Literary Life and Work*; editor of *Critical Essays on Toni Morrison*; and co-editor of the *Norton Critical Edition of Harriet Jacobs's Incidents in the Life of a Slave Girl*, among other books. Her most important literary contribution was her co-editorship (with Henry Louis Gates, Jr.) of the *Norton Anthology of African-American Literature.*

JAY PARINI teaches at Middlebury College. He is the author of many books, including *Robert Frost: A Life; John Steinbeck;* and *One Matchless Time: A Life of William Faulkner.*

ROBERT DEMOTT is Edwin and Ruth Kennedy Distinguished Professor at Ohio University. He is the author of *Steinbeck's Typewriter, Steinbeck's Reading, After The Grapes of Wrath* (co-edited), *and Dave Smith: A Literary Archive.* He is editor, with Elaine Steinbeck as special consultant, of the Library of America's three-volume Steinbeck project.

CLIFFORD ERIC GLADSTEIN is the President of Gladstein, Neandross & Associates, a Santa Monica, California–based environmental consulting firm.

MIMI REISEL GLADSTEIN is a professor of English, Theatre Arts, and Women's Studies at the University of Texas at El Paso. She is the author of the *Indestructible Woman in Faulkner, Hemingway, and Steinbeck*, and has contributed numerous articles to scholarly anthologies and journals.

MARILYN CHANDLER MCENTYRE is a professor at Westmont College and the author of three volumes of poetry.

DAVID WYATT is the editor of *New Essays on The Grapes of Wrath.*

MORRIS DICKSTEIN teaches at the City University of New York (CUNY) Graduate Center. He is the author of several books on literature, including *The Mirror in the Roadway: Literature and the Real World.*

Bibliography

BOOKS AND ARTICLES

Astro, Richard. *John Steinbeck and Edward F. Ricketts: The Shaping of a Novelist.* Minneapolis: University of Minnesota Press, 1973.

Beegel, Susan F., Susan Shillinglaw and Wesley N. Tiffney, Jr. *Steinbeck and the Environment: Interdisciplinary Approaches.* Tuscaloosa: University of Alabama Press, 1997.

Benson, Jackson T. *The Short Novels of John Steinbeck: Critical Essays with a Checklist to Steinbeck Criticism.* Durham: Duke University Press, 1990

Crockett, H. Kelly. "The Bible and *The Grapes of Wrath*." *College English* 24 (1962): 193-99.

Davis, Robert Murray, ed. *Steinbeck: A Collection of Critical Essays.* Englewood Cliffs, NJ: Prentice-Hall, 1972.

DeMott, Robert, ed. *Working Days: The Journals of The Grapes of Wrath.* New York: Viking, 1989.

———. *Steinbeck's Typewriter: Essays on His Art.* Troy, NY: Whitson Publishing Co., 1996.

Ditsky, John, ed. *Critical Essays on Steinbeck's The Grapes of Wrath.* Boston: G.K. Hall & Co., 1989.

———. *John Steinbeck and the Critics.* Rochester, NY: Camden House, 2000.

French, Warren, ed. *A Companion to The Grapes of Wrath.* New York: Penguin, 1989.

167

———. *John Steinbeck*. Boston: Twayne, 1975.

———. *John Steinbeck's Fiction Revisited*. New York: Twayne, 1994.

Hadella, Charlotte. *Of Mice and Men: A Kinship of Powerlessness*. NY: Twayne Publishers, 1995.

Hayashi, Tetsumaro, ed. *John Steinbeck: The Years of Greatness, 1936-1939*. Tuscaloosa: University of Alabama Press, 1993.

———, ed. *A New Study Guide to Steinbeck's Major Works, With Critical Explications*. Metuchen, NJ: Scarecrow, 1993.

Heavlin, Barbara. "Judge, Observer, Prophet: The American Cain and Steinbeck's Shifting Perspective." *South Dakota Review* 34, no. 2 (Summer 1996): 92-206

———., ed. *The Critical Response to John Steinbeck's The Grapes of Wrath*. Westport, CT: Greenwood Press, 2000.

Levant, Howard. *The Novels of John Steinbeck: A Critical Study*. Columbia: University of Missouri Press, 1974.

Lisca, Peter. *John Steinbeck, Nature and Myth*. New York: Crowell, 1978.

———. *The Wide World of John Steinbeck*. New Brunswick, NJ: Rutgers University Press, 1958.

Motley, Warren. "From Patriarchy to Matriarchy: Ma Joad's Role in *The Grapes of Wrath*." *American Literature* 54, no.3 (1982): 397-412.

Noble, Donald R., ed. *The Steinbeck Questions: New Essays in Criticism*. Troy, NY: Whitson, 1993.

Owens, Louis. *The Grapes of Wrath: Trouble in the Promised Land*. Boston: Twayne, 1989.

———. *John Steinbeck's Re-Vision of America*. Athens: University of Georgia Press, 1985.

Parini, Jay. *John Steinbeck: A Biography*. New York: Henry Holt, 1995.

Railsback, Brian E. *Parallel Expeditions; Charles Darwin and the Art of John Steinbeck*. Moscow: University of Idaho Press, 1995.

Shillinglaw, Susan and Kevin Hearle, eds. *Rereading John Steinbeck*. Tuscaloosa, AL: University of Alabama, 2002.

Simmonds, Roy. *John Steinbeck: The War Years, 1939-1945*. Lewisburg, PA: Bucknell University Press, 1996.

Timmerman, John. *John Steinbeck's Fiction: The Aesthetics of the Road Taken*. Norman and London: University of Oklahoma Press, 1986.

Tuttleton, James, W. "Steinbeck Remembered." *The New Criterion*. March 1995, 13:7, 22-28.

Wyatt, David, ed. *New Essays on The Grapes of Wrath*. Cambridge: Cambridge University Press, 1990.

Websites

Today in Literature
John Steinbeck
   http://www.todayinliterature.com/biography/john.steinbeck.asp

NPR
Grapes of Wrath
   http://www.npr.org/programs/morning/features/patc/grapesofwrath/

Wikipedia
John Steinbeck
   http://en.wikipedia.org/wiki/Steinbeck

PAL: Perspectives in American Literature—
   A Research and Reference Guide
John Steinbeck
   http://www.csustan.edu/english/reuben/pal/chap7/steinbeck.html

Acknowledgments

Edward E. Waldron, "*The Pearl* and *The Old Man and the Sea*: A Comparative Analysis," *Steinbeck Quarterly,* 1 (Summer-Fall 1980). Used by permission.

Louis Owens, "*Of Mice and Men*: The Dream of Commitment." Reprinted by permission of Mrs. Louis Owens.

Howard Levant, "John Steinbeck's *The Red Pony:* A Study in Narrative Technique," *The Short Novels of John Steinbeck,* Durham, NC: Duke University Press, 1990. Reprinted from the *Journal of Narrative Technique.*

"'Happy[?]-Wife-and-Motherdom': The Portrayal of Ma Joad in John Steinbeck's *The Grapes of Wrath,*" *New Essays on The Grapes of Wrath,* ed. By David Wyatt, 1990, Cambridge University Press. Reprinted with the permission of Cambridge University Press.

Jay Parini, "The Front Line of Poverty," *John Steinbeck: A Biography.* New York: Henry Holt and Co., 1995.

Robert DeMott, "'Working at the Impossible': The Presence of *Moby-Dick* in *East of Eden,*" *Steinbeck's Typewriter: Essays on His Art.* Troy, NY: Whitston, 1996.

Clifford Eric Gladstein and Mimi Reisel Gladstein, "Revisiting the *Sea of Cortez* with a 'Green' Perspective," *Steinbeck and the Environment,* ed. Susan

F. Beegel, et al., University of Alabama Press, 1997. Used by permission of The University of Alabama Press.

Marilyn Chandler McEntyre, "Natural Wisdom: Steinbeck's Men of Nature as Prophets and Peacemakers," *Steinbeck and the Environment,* ed. Susan F. Beegel, et al., University of Alabama Press, 1997. Used by permission of The University of Alabama Press.

David Wyatt, "Steinbeck's Light." *The Southern Review,* spring 2002, vol. 38, no. 2. Reprinted by permission of David Wyatt.

Morris Dickstein, "Steinbeck and the Great Depression," *The South Atlantic Quarterly,* 103:1, Winter 2004. Used by permission of the author.

Every effort has been made to contact the owners of copyrighted material and secure copyright permission. Articles appearing in this volume generally appear much as they did in their original publication with few or no editorial changes. In some cases, foreign language text has been removed from the original essay. Those interested in locating the original source will find information in the bibliography and acknowledgments sections of this volume.

Index